# LIBRARY MANUALS

Volume 9

# MANUAL OF BOOK CLASSIFICATION AND DISPLAY

# MANUAL OF BOOK CLASSIFICATION AND DISPLAY
## For Public Libraries

ERNEST A. SAVAGE

LONDON AND NEW YORK

First published in 1946 by George Allen & Unwin Ltd

This edition first published in 2022
by Routledge
4 Park Square, Milton Park, Abingdon, Oxon OX14 4RN

and by Routledge
605 Third Avenue, New York, NY 10017

*Routledge is an imprint of the Taylor & Francis Group, an informa business*

Copyright © 1946 by Taylor & Francis.

All rights reserved. No part of this book may be reprinted or reproduced or utilised in any form or by any electronic, mechanical, or other means, now known or hereafter invented, including photocopying and recording, or in any information storage or retrieval system, without permission in writing from the publishers.

*Trademark notice*: Product or corporate names may be trademarks or registered trademarks, and are used only for identification and explanation without intent to infringe.

*British Library Cataloguing in Publication Data*
A catalogue record for this book is available from the British Library

ISBN: 978-1-03-213109-2 (Set)
ISBN: 978-1-00-322771-7 (Set) (ebk)
ISBN: 978-1-03-213173-3 (Volume 9) (hbk)
ISBN: 978-1-03-213174-0 (Volume 9) (pbk)
ISBN: 978-1-00-322799-1 (Volume 9) (ebk)

DOI: 10.4324/9781003227991

**Publisher's Note**
The publisher has gone to great lengths to ensure the quality of this reprint but points out that some imperfections in the original copies may be apparent.

**Disclaimer**
The publisher has made every effort to trace copyright holders and would welcome correspondence from those they have been unable to trace.

# MANUAL OF BOOK CLASSIFICATION AND DISPLAY
## FOR PUBLIC LIBRARIES

*by*

ERNEST A. SAVAGE
LL.D., Edin.
SOMETIME LIBRARIAN EDINBURGH PUBLIC LIBRARIES
PAST-PRESIDENT OF THE LIBRARY ASSOCIATION

LONDON
GEORGE ALLEN & UNWIN LTD
AND THE LIBRARY ASSOCIATION
1946

FIRST PUBLISHED IN 1946

*All rights reserved*
PRINTED IN GREAT BRITAIN
*in 11-Point Old Face Type*
BY UNWIN BROTHERS LIMITED
WOKING

# GENERAL INTRODUCTION TO THE SERIES

THE publication of a systematic series of authoritative Manuals of Library Work, which shall survey Library polity and practice in their latest aspects, is a requirement of which administrators, librarians and students have long been conscious, and is much overdue.

The Library Act of 1919 marked the end of one long epoch and the beginning of a new. The removal of the rate limit paved the way for remarkable extensions and innovations, both in buildings and service. The great work of the Carnegie Trustees in fostering the development of urban Public Libraries has been largely diverted into fresh channels, and County Library Systems now cover the country from Land's End to John o' Groats. The public demand for, and the appreciation of, Libraries have increased enormously. The evolution of Commercial and Technical Libraries and the development of Business and Works Libraries would amply suffice to indicate this progress, but, during the last decade or so, the entire field of Library service has been subjected to review and experiment, and little, in administration or routine, remains unchanged.

It will, therefore, be obvious that old textbooks on practice can no longer serve, and there is a need for new manuals, written by persons of experience and authority, and treating of the new conditions in a full and practical manner. These Manuals are designed to fill the void, and the fact that they are issued by Messrs. George Allen and Unwin Ltd., in conjunction with the Library Association, should afford adequate proof of the qualifications of the authors to treat of the subjects upon which they will write.

The volumes will be supplied with bibliographical references throughout, and will be illustrated when necessary. No effort will be spared to make the series an essential tool for all those who are engaged in Library work, or who intend to embrace Librarianship as a profession.

WILLIAM E. DOUBLEDAY
*General Editor*

# PREFACE

I owe thanks to the following helpers:

Mr. T. S. Carruthers, one of my former assistants, has skilfully prepared many posters or placards for the Edinburgh Libraries. A few examples of his work are in this book, but black and white reproductions give but a poor idea of his rich and delicate art in colour.

Mr. Carl Roden, Librarian of the Chicago Public Libraries, kindly allows me to reproduce three photographs of display, two of which are designs by Miss Mathilde Kelly for the Hild Regional Branch Library, Chicago. Miss Kelly's work is admired by librarians throughout the U.S.A. Mr. Roden sent me eight photographs, and it was not easy to choose three from them.

Mr. W. H. Smettem, Librarian of the Scarborough Public Library, kindly gives me permission to use two photographs, one of which is reproduced. The Scarborough windows are much admired.

Mr. C. S. Minto, Deputy-librarian of Edinburgh, and my son, Mr. Frank B. Savage, took some of the excellent photographs in this book. Mr. Minto, I should add, is adept at reproducing pictures for placard display.

I am grateful to the Editor, Mr. Doubleday, for advice and judicious oversight.

A manual should be an argument and a discussion rather than a digest of inveterate practice; a statement explaining much in this book.

ERNEST A. SAVAGE

*June 30, 1946*

# CONTENTS

| | | |
|---|---|---|
| | General Introduction to the Series | 5 |
| | Preface | 6 |
| | Introduction | 9 |

## A
## DISPLAY BY FORMAL CLASSIFICATION

CHAPTER                                                                            PAGE

| | | |
|---|---|---|
| I | Function of Classification in Revealing Knowledge in Books | 13 |
| II | Function of Classification in Displaying Books | 32 |
| III | Practice of Classification: Relations with Cataloguing and Display, Preparatory Reading and Schemes | 53 |
| IV | Practice of Classification: Rules and Codes | 73 |

## B
## DISPLAY FOR PARTICULAR PURPOSES

| | | |
|---|---|---|
| V | The Home Reading Library as an Exhibition of Books | 90 |
| VI | General Reference Libraries | 115 |
| VII | Special Libraries | 133 |
| VIII | Entrance, Corridor and Window Displays | 150 |

## C
## DISPLAY BY SELECTIVE PROCESSES

| | | |
|---|---|---|
| IX | Classification and Display in Relation to Bookstock | 170 |
| X | Home Reading Books in Retirement | 184 |
| XI | Rotation of Stock | 196 |

## D
## PRACTICAL DISPLAY

| | | |
|---|---|---|
| XII | Organization, Methods and Materials | 210 |
| | Index | 232 |

## LIST OF ILLUSTRATIONS

|   |   | FACING PAGE |
|---|---|---|
| 1 | Display Window, Woodlawn Branch, Chicago Public Library | 48 |
| 2 | Display Slope and Reading Table, Morningside Branch, Edinburgh | 49 |
| 3 | Exhibition Booth by Mathilde Kelly, Hild Regional Branch, Chicago Public Library | 64 |
| 4 | Shelf Placard | 65 |
| 5 | Illuminated Double-Sided Book Showcase, Fountainbridge Branch, Edinburgh | 96 |
| 6 | Wall Display Slopes for Books, Trade Catalogues, and Pamphlets | 97 |
| 7 | Art Department Placard by T. S. Carruthers | 112 |
| 8 | Music Department Placard by T. S. Carruthers | 113 |
| 9 | Technical and Commercial Department Placards by T. S. Carruthers | 144 |
| 10 | Fountainbridge Branch, Edinburgh, with visible interior | 145 |
| 11 | Illuminated Show Window on Stair, Scarborough Public Library | 160 |
| 12 | Window Display by Mathilde Kelly, Hild Regional Branch, Chicago Public Library | 161 |
| 13 | Book Cradle and Illuminated Showcase for Series, Leith Branch, Edinburgh | 192 |
| 14 | Rolling Bookcases, Fountainbridge Branch, Edinburgh | 193 |
| 15 | Reading-Biography Placard by T. S. Carruthers | 208 |
| 16 | Ensign Poster, Edinburgh Public Library, by Miss W. Forgan | 209 |

# INTRODUCTION

AFTER choosing the books for a public library, the librarian organizes them for use, tries to make them productive. The methods he adopts —classing, cataloguing, indexing, personal guidance, display and publicity—are directed to one end, the making known of books and their contents. If he and his assistants—classers, cataloguers, indexers, shopwalkers, displayers and drummers—do not think of these methods as parts of one expressive function, they fail to understand the true unity of librarianship, and will labour independently, even in one service, in windowless cells of their own. What difference in aim has the librarian who prints a list of books recommended as the best on a subject, and he who exhibits them in a bookcase apart, or in a showcase? Virtually none. Both make books known, both heighten the effect of classing; though the librarian who prepares a list on a subject may not approve grouping of books by subject.

As the whole art of librarianship, after the library is formed, lies in making books known, I should have preferred to write about all these methods together, in their relation to each other and to their common function. This *Manual*, however, belongs to a series in which some methods have been described already. I am therefore restricted to display (1) by Classing and (2) by Selection and Segregation. Let it be plain that by classing I mean the co-ordinated subject grouping of bibliographical material. The Library of Congress scheme, begun about 1898, was the earliest, I believe, to be founded on something like an analytic and volumetric survey of bibliography. Mr. E. Wyndham Hulme, one-time librarian of the Patent Office, London, was the first, as far as I know, to teach that a classed library would be like a boy in father's clothes unless it was founded on literary warrant, and co-ordinated for particular communities of readers. To the makers of the Congressional tables and to Mr. Hulme this *Manual* owes much.

A classed library is an exhibition. I decline to look upon it as anything else. And why? Because nowhere have I seen a library, however voluminous, which gave me an atomic hint that a philosophical or scientific chart of man's knowledge was embodied in it, that "the order of ideas, history or evolution" (whatever that may mean) was followed "in its form". A scheme based on a tabulation of knowledge prevents any library to which it is applied from being a revelatory exhibition. Record is the only warrant, bibliography the firmest ground. When the gods want to destroy classifiers they first set them to play somersaults with Bacon.

A classed array of books in one unbroken order from beginning to end generally has a "flatness" which no imaginative curator would tolerate in a museum, no cunning bookseller in a shop. Thinking of the array as an exhibition, I believe that this flatness must be excavated and upheaved; and therefore that every method of making books known, of revealing the knowledge in them, is legitimate and indeed thrust upon us. The librarian who would serve his readers well looks upon classing not only as good in itself, but as a requisite foundation for display. He throws some of his books continuously, and nearly all of them at one time or another, into prominence by exhibiting them in showcases, or advertising them in corridor, entrance or front windows. He diversifies his library, warms and lights it up in and out, displays books which will be more adequately used when readers know about them, and keeps his library from becoming stale by such selective processes as accumulating reserves and rotating stock.

The key part of this book is Chapter IX, Classification and Display in relation to Bookstock. If the conditions laid down there are not fulfilled we need not waste time in classing and display: the mill without water stands.

A note on terminology. I use the word *classifying* to denote the process of naming and defining classes and of co-ordinating them in tables by a *classifier*, and the word *classing* to denote the job of allocating books by a *classer* who writes class marks upon them. The distinction between the two sets of terms is convenient, as our lax way of writing *classification, classify, classifier* instead of *class, classing* and *classer* leads examiners (and at times even the less intelligent students) to forget the difference between class making and class marking. Again, frequently I use the words *group* and *grouping*, instead of *class* and

## INTRODUCTION

*classing*, expressly to weaken the prevalent idea that our kind of classing is in any way scientific or exact, when in truth it is but a valuable artifice.

Throughout I have used the term *placard* to denote *poster*, *placard* or *showcard*.

Some space has been saved by the use of the following abbreviations: DC for Dewey Decimal Classification; UDC for Universal Decimal Classification; LC for Library of Congress Classification; and SC for Subject Classification.

## A. DISPLAY BY FORMAL CLASSIFICATION

CHAPTER I

### 1. THE FUNCTION OF CLASSIFICATION IN REVEALING KNOWLEDGE IN BOOKS

I

NEARLY forty years ago the late James Duff Brown and Mr. L. Stanley Jast opened their campaign for classed libraries. They chose as their model the Decimal Classification (DC) of Melvil Dewey. Good advocates, they refrained from openly recognizing faults in the child of their adoption, and fighting and hitting hard, they made sure that their opponents would be in no mind to be saved from the grip of conservatism. Aroused roughly from official slumber, and prevented, even in those ruder days, by the courtesy of public debate from telling Brown and Jast exactly what they thought about them, these opponents were goaded to unearth Dewey's faults, and laboured so hard that none was left unrevealed and unadvertised: students wishing to appear clever in picking the DC to bits in exam papers should read the accounts of these early controversies rather than textbook pemmican. Here I content myself with noting that DC, being so thoroughly ill-contrived, was bound sooner or later to meet with general approval. And so it turned out. Advocates, because they could do naught else, and opponents, because they could find nothing better, adopted it, and cock-a-doodled loudly about progress in their annual fables. In due time all librarians craving modernity or better jobs arranged their libraries in class order. Local authorities, eager to be thought progressive, even advertised for Deweyite librarians and assistants, as Victorian gentry advertised for teetotal and good Anglican coachmen in the heyday of the Oxford movement and Emma Jane Worboise. Librarians, cantankerous by nature, did not embrace the whole gospel. No; tribute had to be paid to self-esteem. Some of them altered the schedules to demonstrate originality. Others were afraid to employ more than three digits of the notation. Even that red-hot advocate Mr. Jast (before he and Brown had burned their boats at Belfast in 1894) kept to three digits in the Peterborough, the first general DC catalogue printed in this country. (The didactic habit which made the anti-Deweyites bristle angrily is well-illustrated in this *Catalogue*, the direction to users being: "Hold this book in the right hand and turn with the left." It's not quite certain what has to be turned!). The second general printed DC catalogue in this country was compiled by the librarian of Watford Public Library, the late John Woolman, a gentler spirit with a stouter heart, for he plunged into the full DC. Few printed class catalogues followed those of Peterborough and Watford. The advocates of classing and open shelves—the tin-trumpeters in the march of progress in the late nineties and early nineteen hundreds—out to win adherents at all costs, broadcast the wicked heresy that card catalogues were good enough for readers admitted to choose books at the shelves. Brown proved far less loyal to DC than his brother-in-arms, for he became an incurable inventor, concocting first the modest *Adjustable*, and much later the *Subject Classification* (SC). Mr. Jast, however, never seemed likely to desert his Dewey. Not until 1927 did a sign appear that his faith was a little shaken; then he wrote: "In large reference libraries either the Decimal or Library of Congress Scheme is recommended", while he goes on to suggest that "the most admirable features" of LC "can be adopted without difficulty to the Decimal notation"; a statement no doubt true, and a practice quite unobjectionable if we don't mind class marks a mile and a fathom long. Mr. Jast is commonly less unpractical and more downright, but he was writing in a government report (that of the Departmental Committee on Public Libraries) in which a fence is a favourite perch, even for thinkers of revolutionary temper.

During these forty years what ground has been won? It is generally accepted that the classing of books is beneficial and profitable, and common-sense ideas of its nature and purpose are now more prevalent. Classification has become, in practical aim, a good servant instead of an oracular and a cabalistic master. Except among a few diehards it is now an ordinary business method, rather than an object lesson in applied logic.

## II

Mr. Wyndham Hulme (a librarian whose pioneer labours in several fields have never been fully recognized) was the first to change our approach to *book* classification. His articles, though incomplete, contain the best that has been thought and written on the subject. A practical librarian with ideals, a bibliographer of high standing, administering with zeal and originality the most valuable technical library in London, he looked at classification bibliographically, and stripped from it the weeds and barnacles impeding progress. He distinguished between making a classification of knowledge and grouping the books of authors who chose an order of their own in presenting information and arguments. He indicated (what should have been clear even to the blindest) that dichotomy or bifurcate division was inapplicable to books, which therefore could not be classed, in the logical meaning of that word. He yielded to Solomon and Solon the joy and labour of tabulating all knowledge, and preferred, like a good man of business, to group his papers in manageable order; papers which, by the way, he knew thoroughly.

Mr. Hulme began by quoting Dr. E. C. Richardson, the American writer, who had said: "The closer a classification can get to the true order of the sciences and the closer it can keep to it, the better the system will be and the longer it will last" (Richardson, p. 69; *L.A.R.*, V. 13: 354). After recording his disagreement with Dr. Richardson, Mr. Hulme continued: "If the sequence of classes . . . is to be determined mainly by that of the true order of the sciences, it must be for the reason that the functions of the two orders are identical, or at any rate, closely allied; for we have started from the axiom that function and order are intimately connected. But this is a proposition which no one attempts to defend. Philosophical classification aims at teaching the essential relations between classes of things: while book classification, according to Dr. Richardson, is 'the having the most-used books together (i.e. the books most used *together*) in the classes in which they are used together' (Richardson, p. 55). The functions of the two orders, therefore, are essentially distinct, and this being so there will be a strong prima facie case for believing that the orders of the two systems will also be divergent." One comment here. Both Mr. Hulme and Dr. Richardson take for granted the fact that "a true order of the sciences" is known. Every attempted order is hypothetical. Nevertheless Mr. Hulme's meaning is clear.

He went on: "Hitherto the definition of book classification has not been accurately formulated. The confusion of its type with that of philosophical classification has not only obscured its real nature but has materially hindered the formation of sound canons of construction and criticism. Hence systems abound, while as yet no sound theory of construction has been formulated. Until this has been done no consistent teaching of the subject is possible and the advent of any scheme of universal classification indefinitely deferred" (*L.A.R.*, V. 13: 355). Two comments on this passage. I would emphasize that to confuse book with logical classification has ill effects on progress in the arts of grouping books to reveal knowledge, and of forcefully introducing them to the public, let alone in the art of teaching to those practical ends. On the other hand I cannot imagine the advent of a scheme of universal classification, if by that Mr. Hulme means one that is everywhere welcome.

Mr. Hulme then defined: "Book classification", he said, "is a mechanical time-saving operation for the discovery of knowledge in literature. Books are our theme: and the discovery of knowledge in books by the shortest route our aim and object." This point of view, as I remember, had never been taken up by me before, though I had some dim recollection of a similar definition, the clue in which I had failed to note. Searching, I found it in Mill's *Logic*, which I had read in those far off days when Mill *On Liberty*—"boundless babblement!"—was an oracle to young radicals in debating societies. Classification, wrote Mill, "is a contrivance for the best possible ordering of the ideas of objects in our minds; for causing the ideas to accompany or succeed one another in such a way as shall give us *the greatest command over our knowledge already acquired and lead, most directly to the acquisition of more*". (My italics; Mill, *System of Logic*,

8th ed., IV. VII.) Whether Mr. Hulme had this passage in mind or not is immaterial (except that his definition, if arrived at independently, is thereby strengthened) but clearly the principal difference between the one definition and the other is that Mill is thinking of ideas in our minds, and Mr. Hulme of ideas as incorporated in books: the *raison d'être* of classification is the same. (Mr. Hulme does refer to Mill's *Logic* on p. 445, *L.A.R.*, V. 13.)

Another illuminating passage in the *Logic* upholds the opinion that Mr. Hulme, in defining his principles, was a follower of Mill: "The end of classification, as an instrument for the investigation of nature, is . . . to make us think of those objects together which have the greatest number of important common properties, and which, therefore, we have oftenest occasion, in the course of our inductions, for taking into joint consideration. Our ideas of objects are thus brought into the order most conducive to the successful prosecution of inductive inquiries generally. But when the purpose is to facilitate some particular inductive inquiry more is required. To be instrumental to that purpose, the classification must bring those objects together, the simultaneous contemplation of which is likely to throw most light upon the particular subject" (*op. cit.*, IV. VIII). I need not point out how apposite this quotation is to the subject of book grouping, or for that matter to any cognate operation, such as the arrangement of material by an author, an advocate, a preacher, or by a museum curator.

Jevons said truly enough that the classing of books "by subjects would be an exceedingly useful method if it were practicable, but experience, or indeed a little reflection, shows it to be a logical absurdity". Mr. Hulme countered this statement prudently, not by vainly denying it, but by demonstrating that while, in logic, the subject classing of books is an absurdity, subject grouping of books based upon a survey and measurement of bibliography, and co-ordinated for the benefit of students and readers, was not only possible, but was an art of nearly inestimable value to them and to the librarian. The division of all sections of literature, wrote Mr. Hulme, "is determined mainly upon formal and non-philosophic lines. Books, in short, are concrete aggregates of facts selected from the common stock of knowledge, and are produced under the laws of supply and demand to meet the wants of the various bodies of the community. The result is a welter of cross-classifications and of overlapping areas of definition, for the reception of which the framework of philosophic classification is quite insufficient". The framework is not only insufficient, but wrongly-built to receive the intractable material in books. I add that year by year cross-classifications are more intricate, and areas of definition more encroaching, as knowledge accumulates.

"Hence," continues Mr. Hulme, "we must turn to our second alternative which bases definition upon a purely literary warrant. According to this principle definition [of headings] is merely the result of an accurate survey and measurement of classes in literature. A class heading is warranted only when a literature in book form has been shown to exist, and the test of the validity of a heading is the degree of accuracy with which it describes the area of subject-matter common to the class. Definition, therefore, may be described as the plotting of areas pre-existing in literature. To this literary warrant a quantitative value can be assigned so soon as the bibliography of a subject has been definitely compiled. The real classifier of literature is the book-wright, the so-called book-classifier is merely the recorder. Hence there is a definite limit to the extension of book classification in respect of the literature of a given period; for the extension of a classification is merely a reflex of the degree in the specialization of literature."

"This theory, however, of definition [of headings] stands in need of some qualification; for the blind adherence in practice to the principle laid down would unquestionably lead to confusion. For instance, if every area represented in literature were to be transferred automatically to the Headings List there would be a bewildering number of headings of imperceptibly differing areas, together with others combining fanciful and evidently inappropriate associations of unrelated subject-matter. We must, therefore, arm our classifier with certain limited discretionary powers:

(*a*) To amalgamate under a common definition works of slightly differing areas.

(*b*) To register by duplicate or plural entry works containing subject-matter, the association of which in books is shown, as a result of survey, to be infrequent, accidental or purely fanciful.

The admission of these qualifications, however, does not materially affect the function of definition, the warrant for which is essentially literary and quantitative—the strength of the warrant varying with the number of works conforming to the type of each class definition" (*L.A.R.*, V. 13: 446–7).

I make no apology for the length of this quotation, the wisdom and significance of which are illuminating. But students of acute intelligence have asked two questions, which I will try to answer.

"Assuming that definition of headings is based upon literary warrant, how is an 'accurate survey and measurement of classes in literature' to be made?"

In a large or a special library the labour is not heavy. Imagine that our collection of ten thousand volumes is highly specific: on Shakspere, for example. First draft a trial scheme. Then into each book put a slip bearing the first part of the mark. Next arrange the books in order of the marking. After counting the books in all the groups so formed, revise the tentative scheme until it is nearly in its final state. Lastly, class the books on the revise, trimming and shaping it as we proceed. This job done carefully, our classification may be regarded as approved, only minor adjustments being required from time to time. Thus well-founded on a survey of the material to be arranged, our scheme, is far more comprehensive, more made-to-measure than any hypothetical framework scheme. This is the right procedure in making a classification. Note, however, that when we apply an existing scheme to an unco-ordinated collection, it is better first to rough-class the books so that we can finally mark them in groups, homogeneous subject-matter being easier to class distinctively. Another hint: accessions must be marked as isolated units, but when we are doubtful about our classing of any book take it to the place where it will stand on the shelves, and if it does not look at home among its companions, seek another heading. Trial co-ordination is a guide to fine co-ordination.

Another question. Mr. Hulme states: "If every area represented in literature were to be transferred automatically to the Headings List there would be a bewildering number of headings", and so on. But if we are to amalgamate under a common definition works of slightly differing areas are we not limiting classification, the ultimate aim of which is to differentiate one book from all others?

This question is more difficult, and cannot be answered without making a rather unreal distinction between class and work marks. The class mark for a History of Architecture in France is 720 (Architecture) 9 (History) and 44 (France); the work mark R26 is the Cutter number representing the author's name; the whole being 720.944 R26. In fact, however, the class mark is extended by the work mark, which, if carried far enough, isolates a book from its companions on the same topic. Suppose that the author writes two books on the above subject: then, if we wish to be precise, or to use marks as charging numbers, we may distinguish them by Biscoe numbers for publication dates:

720.944 R26 P8 where P8 = published in 1898
720.944 R26 Q6 where Q6 = published in 1906

Any class or group which contains books markedly dissimilar in treatment of allied subject-matter, or looking at the same subject from quite different points of view, should be divided into smaller groups, otherwise the aim of classing to reveal knowledge partly fails. If an ideal arrangement of books were possible, each book would stand alone, isolated and differentiated from its neighbours. Many books classed by UDC receive marks which, in effect, are shorthand descriptions of contents, scope, language, period, form and so on. Indeed, but for the faults inherited from the parent DC, this scheme would be a most effective instrument for distinguishing a book from its companions. Mr. Hulme's recommendation to amalgamate slightly differing areas of record instead of fitting them with headings is prudent, but I would emphasize the word "slightly", because the need of co-ordination in small groups carefully named is to-day more generally accepted than when he wrote thirty years ago, particularly in large general and special libraries.

It is but the plain truth to say that these masterly articles by Mr.

Hulme blew out of existence almost all that one librarian had then read about book classification, and nothing has been written later of equal value upon theory and practice, apart from the later volumes of the LC, which are as near perfection as any that I can imagine. I hoped that he would expand and reproduce the articles in book form. To my great regret, however, students looking for a rational commentary upon the practical arrangement of books by subject-matter must turn to the *Library Association Record* where his work is half-buried, but, having read it, they will surely be convinced, as I was, that bibliography is the firm foundation of book classification. However, Mr. Hulme's ideas are now accepted nearly everywhere outside examination rooms, mainly because the classification makers of the Library of Congress had been thinking along the same lines.

## III

Before I leave this part of my subject let me refer to the classification of the Patent Office Library, in which Mr. Hulme's theory became practice. The scheme was compiled mainly by his deputy, the late Henry Vaux Hopwood, in his time one of the ablest and most energetic librarians and bibliographers in the country (*L.A.R.*, V. 22: 27, 1920, obituary notice). Hopwood contributed valuable articles to library literature, the chief being *Reference Shelf-Placing: Ideal and Practical* (*L.A.R.*, V. 6: 241–60, discussion, 309–12, 1904) and his exposition of the UDC in *Dewey Expanded* (*L.A.R.*, V. 9: 307–22, 1907). His untimely death in 1919 deprived us of the services of an acute thinker and zealous worker who might have thrown a brilliant light on book arrangement and display.

Though Hopwood was mainly responsible for compiling the Patent Office classification, the principles underlying it were Mr. Hulme's. The tables may be studied in the parts appended to the P.O. Subject Lists. A short example is added to one of Mr. Hulme's articles (*L.A.R.*, V. 14: 41–2) as an illustration of co-ordinated headings. Having affirmed that book classification can answer its purpose only when founded on a survey and measurement of literature, and that headings must likewise be defined on literary warrant, he extends the argument to co-ordination: "Class definitions", he writes, "we have learned to regard as definitions of specific areas of literary matter. Hence classes allied by the possession of common subject-matter must stand in one of two relationships to one another. Either one area is included in the other; or, the two areas intersect one another at given points and thus enclose a common space. . . . In the first-mentioned case, then, we have a relationship akin to that of genus and species—using the terms in their non-logical and popular sense. . . . Again, a specific class in literature is not, as in logic, confined to the membership of a single generic class. It may be and generally is a strand common to the fabric of many classes. Hence we must recognize at the outset that co-ordination by a selected property means distribution in respect of the remainder." A scrutiny of the P.O. classification for the Textile Industries indicates the application of these principles clearly to anybody knowing the bibliography. As literary warrant determines the headings so it determines their relations to each other, the books of the highest degree of homogeneity in subject-matter standing in the closest relation. But when a specific area of record is not confined to a generic area the question of co-ordination or distribution must be decided as may be most convenient for the readers of the particular library. Mr. Hulme illustrates further subdivision when division by characteristic subject-matter is exhausted: "While co-ordination by the attribute of common subject-matter takes precedence over all other principles"—a most important rule, never to be overlooked without confusion—"it is not necessarily the only one to be employed. For instance, where the generic heading is a comprehensive one, embracing a great number of specific sub-classes, the latter, while preserving their relation to the generic heading, can generally be plotted in some rational order—philosophical, philological, chronological or what not. Thus in place of:

   Mineral Industries—
      (specific classes arranged alphabetically)
      Alum
      Asbestos, etc

we may substitute

>Mineral Industries—
>  (saline)
>Alum
>Borax
>Salt, etc.
>  (earthy)
>Asbestos
>Gypsum, etc.
>  (Silicate)
>Precious stones
>Talc, etc.

... The latter arrangement has several advantages. It brings together classes possessing real affinities, facilitates the grouping of references, and generally enhances the utility of a classification without detracting from its value as an instrument of research." Mr. Hulme's second example fails to illustrate an unassailable argument. True, it greatly adds to the analytic value of the index to the classification, but it does so, not because division by subject has failed, but because it is continued, for the Saline, Earthy and Silicate Minerals form subject groups, each of which may be indexed as a group under its name. It is not an illustration of rational order when classing by subject is no longer practicable. Our principle of division being subject-matter, any other characteristic must be accidental in relation to subject, and therefore the principle of an arbitrary order. For example, a book on the Vibration of Sound is marked GG 20 in the Patent Office classification. No further division by subject is possible. The next order may be by date of publication, by author or by language, all orders which help to differentiate one book from another, but quite arbitrary in operation. It is important to remember that the only rational order is determined by the chief principle of division, whatever that principle may be.

No critical study of Mr. Hulme's article weakens my opinion that he is most luminous on the subject of co-ordination: to illustrate it on his theory he ends his articles with an outline of the sciences of Geology and Chemistry, together with the applied literature lying between the two; and as we study it we cannot help regretting that other classification makers have preferred to be governed by some imaginary "true order of the sciences" rather than, *a posteriori*, by bibliographical warrant.

## IV

The attentive reader of this book will mark that nowhere in it do I contrast book classification with scientific or exact classification. My distinction is invariably between book and logical classification; book classification being the artificial ordering of like books in groups ranged by degrees of likeness; logical classification the dichotomous progression of the well-known Tree of Porphyry. The perfect logical method, Jevons tells us, divides "each genus into two species and not more than two, so that one species possesses a particular quality and the other does not". That and that only is exact classification. My argument in this section is that no classification, not even the scientific, is free from artificiality and overlapping definitions; all may be constructed by logical processes, and yet not strictly conform with logic. Therefore such a highly revelatory method as book classification ought not to be damned because it too, while built up by logical processes, has its artificialities and overlapping definitions. The exam candidate should be required to explain not the difference between a classification of books and one of knowledge, or between book and scientific classification, but the *likeness* between them, and the difference between all of them and logical classification.

Mr. Walter Shepherd, in *Science Marches On* (Harrap, 1939), pp. 269–70, has some prudent words on this subject:

"There is a strong element of artificiality in any hard-and-fast sort of classification of living things," he writes. . . . "All depends on the size of the category; speaking generally, broad divisions, when reasonable, are allowed without much bother, so long as it is understood that they *are* broad, and not clear-cut and sharp. So long as the dividing is done with fuzzy bands working approximations are easily found, but it is when we try to divide by *lines* that we find that no such lines really occur in nature, and that if we want them—as we always do—we have to *invent* them. Thus *no* actual division between the living and the non-living has ever been discovered, and no such division probably exists. Classifications impose a definiteness on nature which has no counterpart in the real world."

This subject is discussed even more cogently in the essay *On the Aims and Instruments of Scientific Thought*, by W. K. Clifford, in *Lectures and Essays*, V. 1: 159–60 (1901):

"But more serious consequences arose when these conceptions derived from Physics were carried over into the field of Biology. Sharp lines of division were made between kingdoms and classes and orders; an animal was described as a miracle to the vegetable world; specific differences which are practically permanent within the range of history were regarded as permanent through all time; a sharp line was drawn between organic and inorganic matter. Further investigation, however, has shown that accuracy had been prematurely attributed to the science, and has filled up all the gulfs and gaps that hasty observers had invented. The animal and vegetable kingdoms have a debatable ground between them, occupied by beings that have the characters of both and yet belong distinctly to neither. Classes and orders shade into one another all along their common boundary. Specific differences turn out to be the work of time. The line dividing organic matter from inorganic, if drawn to-day, must be moved to-morrow to another place; and the chemist will tell you that the distinction has now no place in his science except in a technical sense for the convenience of studying carbon compounds by themselves. In Geology the same tendency gave birth to the doctrine of distinct periods, marked out by the character of the strata deposited in them all over the sea; a doctrine than which, perhaps, no ancient cosmogony has been further from the truth, or done more harm to the progress of science. Refuted many years ago by Mr. Herbert Spencer, it has now fairly yielded to an attack from all sides at once, and may be left in peace."

Some book classifiers are to blame for recent criticism of their methods, because they have endeavoured to tabulate the universe rather than books. A tabulation of the universe and everything in it could only be drafted were all our knowledge complete and final, and only books written *after* that climax of the improbable would fit into the tables! J. A. R. Newlands discovered that "when the chemical elements were arranged in order of atomic weight certain important physical characteristics were repeated in every eighth element". This Law of Octaves was developed into the Periodic System, the *known* chemical elements being arranged in a table by Mendeléef, who foretold, accurately as it proved later, that elements then unknown, but possessing certain properties, would occupy the blanks in the table. But apart from the sciences which depend on number or mathematics it rarely happens that we can guess the unknown by any synthesis of the known. While therefore book classification is no more than an artificial grouping and co-ordination of extant books, every other kind of classifying, save the purely logical, is equally man-made, artificial, and therefore inexact, because it is founded only on *known* things, and in every branch of knowledge many things are unknown and cannot be provided for.

Were scientific classification exact it would be changeless. As it is not and cannot be changeless until all is known, it is in no better trim than book classifying, so often damned as a logical absurdity. The Indian scientist, Sir Jagadis Bose "has suggested that *nothing* which exists can be really inanimate. Even in a stone, he says, life is present, though not demonstrative. Modern authoritative science, at any rate in Europe, does not go with him as far as that" (Shepherd, *op. cit.*, p. 148). But imagine that he were right? Then what an upheaval in biological classification! As it is brother scientists have been compelled to admit that he has proved certain plants to have something like intelligence.

However, we need no epoch making discovery of the origin of the universe, of life, of electricity, to demonstrate the fluidity of scientific classification. Analysis of the orders and genera of Insects and Birds tells us that the characteristics chosen are neither consistent nor exclusive. That different classifications of birds have been formulated from time to time proves the need of changes and developments with the growth of knowledge, as we should expect. However intensive the classifying, alterations in detail must occur. Yet the classifications are none the less convenient. If ornithological students did not group the birds which are alike morphologically, physiologically or phylogenetically, they would fail to gain the additional knowledge which is revealed when they sum up any affinities that may be discovered.

Though our knowledge of plant life is abundant it is far from being complete, and therefore classification is not yet final. Three simple examples from the natural history of plants will be enough to demonstrate that their classification is no more made up of mutually exclusive and regularly modulating headings than is book classification.

In the Crytogamia the fungi, unlike all other orders, have no chlorophyll, and therefore do not create life out of inorganic matter; no true plants, they live upon other plants as parasites, or upon decaying leaves or roots as saprophytes. Between the fungi and the Pteridophyta, both cryptogamic, the difference is greater than that between the Pteridophyta (Fern group) and the Phanerogamia, the Pteridophyta with their roots, stems, leaves and vascular bundles modulating, as it were, into the Phanerogamia. Indeed the relation between the Pteridophyta and the Gymnospermae (Phanerogamia) is closer than between the Gymnospermae and the Angiospermae. The further study of fossil botany has brought to light a class of Pteridospermae (seed-bearing ferns) which has gone far to bridge the gap between the Pteridophyta (Fern group of spore plants) and the Gymnospermae (seed plants).[1]

Again, note an interrelation between two classes of the Cryptogamia, the Bryophyta and the Pteridophyta. The spores of ferns (Pteridophyta) do not grow into new ferns right away, but into tiny leaf plants very like liverworts and mosses (Bryophyta), fructifying in the same way as they, and in time producing new ferns: an alternation of generations which reminds us of cross-classification in the subject-matter of books.

A last example, this time something analogous to composite subject-matter. The lichen is a symbiotic organism consisting of a single-celled alga (seaweed) living in a very tiny pool of salt water in a fungus; so a specimen from each of two sub-classes of the Thallophyta, the fungi and algae are intimate companions in one organism, partly fungi and partly true plant.

What I have said above is borne out by the past and present state of plant classification. I need not trace the history of this classification

---

[1] This fact reminds me that fossils, at one time almost wholly within the department of the geologist, are now primarily the concern of the botanist and the zoologist; and whereas in DC Palaeobotany and Palaeozoology are allocated to Geology, in SC they are allocated to Botany and Zoology.

from Linnaeus, through Bernard and Antoine de Jussieu, de Candolle, Endlicher, Brongniart, Hofmeister, Bentham and Hooker, Van Tieghem, Engler to Hutchinson. Three systems now occupy most of the field. That in Bentham and Hooker's *Genera Plantarum* (1862–83) was applied to the herbaria at the British Museum and Kew. Engler and Prantl's *Die natürliche Pflanzenfamilien* (1887–1909) has won great favour, particularly in Europe. The latest form is that in Engler-Diels, *Syllabus* (1936). But both these schemes have been assailed, mainly from a phylogenetic standpoint, and Bentham and Hooker's in particular has lost ground because it was conceived under the influence of the old idea of fixity of species. J. Hutchinson, an assistant in the Herbarium at Kew, therefore drew up a third system of the Phanerogamia, based on the *probable* phylogeny of plants, and he published it in *Families of Flowering Plants*, 2 v. (1926–34).[1] On p. 8 of the foregoing work will be found a table summarizing the fundamental differences between the systems of Bentham and Hooker, Engler and Prantl, and Hutchinson, and it is worth studying because it clearly indicates not only the changing character of botanical systematization, but the necessity, in any special botanical library, of classing books, monographs and articles on any order, genus or species, the names of which the authors may have taken from any scheme, old or new.

Let us note how the current library schemes have tried to offer hospitality to the medley.

The SC is based on Engler, on what edition is not stated, but the classing of monographs, particularly on the orders and genera in other plant classifications, would be difficult, for even the scheme incorporated isn't fully indexed, let alone is it concordanced with others. For example the following headings in Engler are not included:

| | |
|---|---|
| Achariaceae | Adiniferidea |
| Achlamydosporeae | Aextoxicaceae |
| Acrasiales | Alangiaceae |
| Actinidiaceae | |

[1] A book for every reference library. The illustrations are among the clearest I know, and the numerous maps showing the distribution of orders and genera are invaluable.

Therefore a large part of Engler is not indexed in SC (1939) though all is in DC (14th ed., 1932).

The UDC, following Engler-Diels, has a special index, serving also as a concordance to the DC, in which it is reprinted immediately after the relative index. The UDC, by the way, begins with Cryptogamia, the DC with Phanerogamia, another indication that classifiers will never agree upon a universal scheme.

The DC tables for plants are based on the 1928 edition of Bentham and Hooker, and under each heading, when necessary, notes give directions for placing the orders and genera of other plant classifiers. For example:

> 583.1147 *Monimiaceae*
> > Changed from 583.928 as most authorities consulted class under Ranales. Classed by J. Hutchinson [*Families of Flowering Plants*, 2v.] under Laurales (see 583.931).
>
> 583.297 *Coriariineae. Coriariaceae. Coriarieae*
> > Class here Coriariales, given by Hutchinson as an order with only one family, Coriariaceae. Changed from 583.298 to bring into affiliation with Sapindales (583.28) under which it is classed by Engler and Gilg.

The plant classification adopted in LC is systematic only in the principal branches of the subject:

> Spermatophyta
> Cryptogamia
> Pteridophyta
> Musci. Mosses
> Hepaticae. Liverworts
> Algae
> Lichens
> Fungi

Then, under each, without further ado, except for some analysis of Fungi, the orders and genera are arranged by alphabetic numbers.

Whether UDC, DC or LC have provided most effectively for the reception of the highly specialized contents of a botanical library I do not know, as I have not had charge of one. But here the answer does not matter. My object is different. From what I have said above two conclusions are plain:

(1) No final classification is possible until all is known about the subject to be classed, and even then only when authorities are agreed about the definition and co-ordination of headings. Plants, though knowledge about them is abundant, have not been classed definitively, and no tabulation of them is more purely logical than that of books; it is man-made, and therefore an artificial ordering of things known, for all that it is based on phylogenetic characteristics. Note the word "probable" in the sub-title of Hutchinson's book. The conclusion is important to us if only as an adequate rebuttal of opponents who underrate book classification and magnify scientific.

(2) If final classification is impossible until all is known about the subject to be classed, and even then only when the authorities are agreed about the definition and co-ordination of headings, and if meantime the literary record is based on different and changing interrelations of subject-matter, it follows that, without taking into account the varying points of view from which authors look at their subjects, no classification of books is of practical value unless founded on bibliography. As in science, we can class only the *known and static record*, the books extant. From present record we try to forecast the nature and development of future record, and provide for it, but this forecast, as experience proves, is by no means always right or adequate, and therefore, as in scientific classification, every book classification must be altered and enlarged, as the need arises, without grudging the labour of re-marking books, if changes require it.

## REFERENCES

1895 BROWN, J. D., and QUINN, J. H. Classification of books for libraries in which readers are allowed access to the shelves. *Library*, V. 7; 75–82.

1895 JAST, L. STANLEY. Classification in public libraries, with special reference to the Dewey decimal system. *Library*, V. 7: 169–178.

1896 JAST, L. STANLEY. The Dewey classification in the reference library, and in an open lending library. *Library*, V. 8: 335–50.

## REVEALING KNOWLEDGE IN BOOKS

1897 JAST, L. STANLEY. The Class list. *Library*, V. 9: 41–4.

1897 BROWN, J. D., and JAST, L. STANLEY. Compilation of class lists. *Library*, V. 9: 45–67.

1897 JAST, L. STANLEY. The Dewey classification and some recent criticism. *Library*, V. 9: 340–45.

*Note.* The above works are now only of historical interest, but are well worth reading.

1900 HULME, E. WYNDHAM. Principles of dictionary subject cataloguing in scientific and technical libraries. *L.A.R.*, V. 2: 571–6, discussion, 668–70.

1901 HULME, E. WYNDHAM. On the construction of the subject catalogue in scientific and technical libraries. *L.A.R.*, V. 3: 507–13, discussion, 486–9.

1902 HULME, E. WYNDHAM. On the co-operative basis for the classification of literature in the subject catalogue. *L.A.R.*, V. 4: 317–26.

1911–12 HULME, E. WYNDHAM. Principles of book classification. *L.A.R.*, V. 13: 354–8, 389–94, 444–9; V. 14: 39–46, 174–81, 216–21.

*Note.* I have quoted only the 1911–12 articles by Mr. Hulme, but his other articles are noted because they indicate the development of his thought upon classification.

CHAPTER II

## 2. THE FUNCTION OF CLASSIFICATION IN DISPLAYING BOOKS

I

THE above title is hardly more than a variant of the title of my first chapter, but it indicates more clearly the drift of my argument towards display, a word to which I give a wider definition than common. Approve the reasoning in the foregoing chapter and it follows

(1) that book classification is book grouping, one of the methods of displaying or exhibiting knowledge in books.

(2) that no catholic, truly dioristic, or exhaustively analytical scheme for grouping books can be drawn up save by competent people who are in a position to survey, subjectively and quantitatively, the literature to be co-ordinated. (See also Hulme, *L.A.R.*, V. 13: 448.)

(3) that the more exactly the class headings define the areas of record they are to embrace, the easier will it be to master the contents of any library analysed and co-ordinated by them: a heading which truly labels a class is a guide to the subject-matter in it.

(4) that as knowledge grows, and as fresh relations between branches of knowledge come to light, many new areas of record must be plotted and accommodated at any point in a scheme; hence the need of flexible tabulation and expansible notation is paramount, any hindrance to including carefully defined headings for new areas, adjacent to related areas, being an obstacle to the discovery or display of knowledge in books.

(5) that if the foundation of a general scheme can be well and truly laid only in a great public library, and that of a special scheme only in a comprehensive special library, uniformity in book classification is a remote end, and is only practicable if we abandon the ideal of grouping books for the convenience of particular groups of readers.

## CLASSIFICATION IN DISPLAY

These statements, if well-founded, are revolutionary: the whole outlook upon classification is transformed. When compiling a scheme we may adopt a "true order of the sciences" (there are varieties to please every fancy) as a framework, but we must modify it to receive and group the areas of record. And when a scheme is compiled we or anybody who applies it must break the order of the schedules as may be plainly advantageous to the readers for whom the books are grouped.

## II

That our classification is but book grouping, one of the methods of displaying or exhibiting knowledge in books, I hope to make clear in chapter V. Here a summary of the argument will do.

If book classification is a time-saving operation for the revealing of knowledge in literature: if books are our theme, and the discovery of knowledge in them by the shortest route our aim and object: then we must (1) group those most alike in subject-matter, (2) label each group plainly, (3) co-ordinate the groups in relation to subject-matter, and (4) guide readers directly to the groups they wish to examine. But it is the *books* we arrange and group, the record in them we exhibit. Only by the absurd practice of cutting books into pieces, or of limiting our collection to pamphlets on highly specific topics, could we fit recorded knowledge into something distantly approaching a logical framework. Plants can transmute non-living matter into living; animals cannot. The wall of a plant cell is usually of cellulose, and that of an animal cell never. But when we ask about a book: Is the subject X and not Y or Z? the answer rarely will be an unqualified Yes or No. George Moore's novel *A Mummer's Wife*, a terrible study of intemperance, is much more than a thesis. Peattie's *Cargoes and Harvests*, a book about spices, quinine, rubber, dyes, tobacco, cotton and other economic plants, is stronger on the commercial than the botanic side, and, as we have only one place for it (unless we buy two copies) the "most useful" for our readers is chosen; we group, not class it. We look at Fairchild, *Exploring for Plants*, from three points of view (1) the human aspect of exploring for (2) economic plants which may be introduced profitably into (3) the agriculture of the United States, and in this country we class and display with economic botany and display with books of travel. Books on air photography, if conjoined with books on aeronautics, will find more readers, yet the subject is photography, all books on which might well be grouped together, and so they offer material for display on two subjects and for classing and display under alternative headings: but we group rather than class.

Let us pass from science to literature, in which we sometimes arrange books first by language, then by form of literature, afterwards by period, and finally by author. But is a German translation of Shaw's plays German or English literature? Clearly the latter. But try an experiment. Put his plays in German with the originals, as logic dictates, and we find they are not often read. Where classing fails the catalogue must lend a hand; it can do so, but clumsily, by grouping all translations into German under a general heading (German language, books in) but few libraries adopt such a heading, and no code prescribes it. Move the plays to the German section and the results are far better: is it common sense or not to break the rule?—don't we reveal Shaw to the German reading public? Indeed, can we apply a rule consistently? Sir James Jeans, *Durch Raum und Zeit*, a translation of *Through Space and Time*, is well-read if classed with the original, because many scientists know German. I have been censured for grouping Florio's Montaigne with sixteenth-century French literature instead of with Elizabethan literature, and my critic was not unreasonable, though I cannot admit he was right. In Elizabethan times Florio revealed Montaigne to his contemporaries; has he ceased to do so to us? Yet is a display of Elizabethan literature complete without Florio? D. F. Canfield, *Corneille and Racine in England*, by rule goes with English literature, the literature affected by these dramatists; but are we so content to arrange Jusserand, *Shakespeare in France*, in French literature? In this country English literature is the more important subject, and we reveal knowledge most effectively by putting both works in that class: in other words we break the rule in the interests of display.

Another point. A book may come to attract few readers or none for its literary part, while the illustrations appeal to artists, or, in an art department, it may be acquired only for its illustrations. Thus *Italian Journeys*, *Tuscan Journeys*, and *Venetian Life* by W. D. Howells, or even *A Little Journey in France* by Henry James, in a general library might be classed, and certainly would be in an art department, under Joseph Pennell, the illustrator. The original or early editions of Kate Greenaway's books arrange either with the art books or with a reference collection of children's books, if one has been formed. Here is an example of an aberrant book of particular charm to the bibliographer. In a general library Charles Butler's *Feminin' Monarchi'* (3rd ed., 1634) would be classed under Bees and Beekeeping; but it is bought by music librarians for its notation of the humming of bees at swarming and for the madrigal in it, and by specialists in philology because it is the first English book in phonetic spelling. Where would the music librarian and the philologist class it?

A classical scholar nearly had apoplexy on discovering the Latin version of Caesar's Gallic *Commentaries* in early French history. It was vain to ask him where he would put an English version, or T. Rice Holmes, *Caesar and the Gallic Wars*. Yet was he wrong? We look at the *Commentaries* from the points of view of three groups of readers: those studying (1) Latin literature, (2) Roman history and (3) French history. We cannot always determine which is the "most useful place," the place most revelatory of knowledge, for even experiment does not always indicate the right decision. Group everything by and about Caesar in Roman history, the only place where he is at home, and depend upon shelf reference blocks, the catalogue and display to guide students of Latin literature and French history students to him. Another example and I have done. Are the many books and pamphlets on local events of the English civil war to be scattered under Oxford, London, Dorset, Devon, Cornwall and other places, or gathered under English history? In a general library or a subject department for English history, aggregation is preferable, but in a topographical library distribution by place will attract more use: so much depends upon point of view.

I might fill a daily newspaper with like examples, but enough have been given to buttress the argument that classing, in the exact meaning of the term, is a logical absurdity when books are concerned. The grouping of books is an art, a rather delightful art, not a science. My aim is to throw off the fetters of pedantry and vain endeavour.

The word "group" then is preferred as being more explicit and truthful than the word "class". And clearly the grouping of books with care to reveal likeness of principal subject-matter, a process demanding small groups, is but a part of the whole business of expounding the contents of books. Cataloguing and indexing are literary methods of exposition or display; book grouping is a mechanical method.

## III

A reader content with the foregoing section must, I think, agree that no catholic, truly dioristic, or exhaustively analytical scheme for grouping books can be drawn up save by competent people who are in a position to survey, subjectively and quantitatively, the literature which has to be co-ordinated. Mere eclecticism is not enough.

To-day the most liberal and omniscient tabulation of book knowledge is the Congressional (LC), published by a library encyclopaedic in range and Alexandrian in volume. The officials of the Brussels Institute of Bibliography, undaunted by the outpourings of the world's press, have nearly succeeded in turning the Procrustean DC into a flexible and expansible tool of documentation. And special librarians, with much material of narrow subject-matter to organize for use, have plotted expansions of DC and of LC more adequately than we jacks-of-all-books could hope to do.

Books are readily grouped by the LC because its tables are hypothetic in origin and empirical in development; the first draft of them was revised, as the classing proceeded, to offer hospitality to the towering quantity of books that had to be accommodated. Books were not rammed into a "true order of the sciences", but insinuated into affined groups in which they, and any published later, would give support to each other: a great library, well-classed on this plan, could adopt the fasces as its symbol with more propriety than the state which Mussolini gummed together with castor oil and blood. The bibliographical foundation of the LC is traceable throughout the schedules. Here is a book difficult to class. But, no. The right place, the heading picked to describe it, is there. Indeed at the time he wrote Mr. Hulme might have considered some of the headings to embrace books which are conjoined infrequently, accidentally or purely on fanciful grounds. At the beginning of the Philosophy class we can arrange books on the relation of philosophy to (1) theology, (2) history, (3) economics, (4) law, (5) political science, (6) literature and (7) science. In most schemes corners for such linked subjects are not to be found, and the want of them is manifest as we group our material. Places are ready for books on sociology in relation to (1) philosophy, (2) psychology, (3) ethics, (4) politics, (5) law, (6) economics, (7) history, (8) anthropology, (9) science, (10) art and (11) literature. And none of these headings is redundant. No classification is good unless related books can be comfortably grouped in it. The marking of these books is generally a simple matter. Where do we put a book on sociology in relation to philosophy? Both "relation" headings are there for our convenience, one in one class, the other in the other. The answer depends upon the point of view of the author. Mr. Hulme's opinion on LC is worth quoting: "Our conclusion is that the Congress schedules are such as will admit of the exact classification of the bulk of the world's literature to date at the lowest possible cost; and that in this respect the class headings of the Congress scheme have reached the theoretical high-water mark of efficiency indicated" in his articles.

The editors of the *Classification Décimale Universelle* revised DC to give it the flexibility demanded by the growth of knowledge, and the infinite variety in the areas of record. And perhaps they have guaranteed for their expansion a longer life than its parent, with a less accommodating notation, can expect. For example, the colon linking together two subject marks, indicates the relation of one to the other. A book on Morality in relation to art is marked 17 : 7 (17 = Ethics, 7 = Art) or 7 : 17 if the book appeals more to artists and art-lovers. The Conditions of labour in the chemical industries is marked 331 : 66 (331 = Conditions of labour, 66 = Chemical technology). UDC is vastly more accommodating than LC in receiving poor relatives! The tables and the notation ought to accommodate an intruder

## MANUAL OF BOOK CLASSIFICATION

where he naturally belongs. Can we limit the tabulation? No more than we can stop the flow of books from the press. And we must find marks for all the headings that throng in. A Procrustean scheme throttles a library as too small a pot binds a plant. Wherever in the tables the editors of the UDC have shaken themselves free from Dewey they have achieved this major aim of offering hospitality to new areas of record.

### IV

The more exactly the class headings define areas of record the easier it is to master the contents of any library analysed and co-ordinated by them; and for these reasons: (1) a heading which truly labels a class is a guide to the subject-matter in it, (2) the subject-index to the library, if intensely analytical (see p. 85), focuses that knowledge, and (3) the librarian, when serving readers, obtains clearer light from a grouping which reflects and strengthens bibliographical knowledge. Let all roads in a library converge, in straight Roman lines, to the point of use. The adept classer puts a book into a group, and the good cataloguer under a subject heading, which most cogently indicate subject-matter; the subject-indexer under the entry which points to the *book* as well as to the group.[1] The aims are identical: to reveal the knowledge in books: and the more fully these aims are achieved the plainer are the librarian's signposts to his goal.

Mr. Hulme's definition: "Book classification is a mechanical time-

---

[1] It is strange how many people fail to understand what a subject-index is. Mr. Desmond MacCarthy, in a review of a book of quotations, writes: "The so necessary index [to the quotations] must not be, strictly speaking, a subject-index, for it is too often impossible to guess under what heading any user of the dictionary will look for what he wants. Suppose I wanted to find

'There was a star danced, and under it was I born'

in a subject-index, I should not know whether to look for it under 'Gaiety: inborn' or 'Astronomy', or other headings. But if I remembered the line at all, the idea of a dancing star would surely have stuck in my mind: 'star' is the reference key-word. It is under 'key-words' that references to the quotations themselves are best arranged" (*Sunday Times*, 21st September, 1941). But if I wanted a quotation to illustrate inborn gaiety would not the heading "Gaiety" lead me to it? And is not "star" a subject as well as a keyword? The one heading, in penetrative indexing, is as necessary as the other.

## CLASSIFICATION IN DISPLAY

saving operation for the discovery of knowledge in literature" contains the clue. Classification is at one and the same time a synthetic and analytic process. A librarian taking charge of a large unclassed reference library depends mainly upon the catalogue for his knowledge of it. No matter whether his catalogue is class or dictionary he will flip over many cards before he begins to know the wealth at his command, and he does not materially strengthen this command however often he walks round the library to look at arrays of inco-ordinated books. Run through a general museum where the objects stand in order of acquisition (if you can find one), and then we have a faint notion of the difficulty of controlling an unclassed library. We assume that a particular book is in a huge national library rather than not, but we cannot take, as it were, an aerial survey of its contents, of the various bibliographical fields, unless the books are classed. When the librarian begins to class subject-matter, he and everybody working with him quickly take a grip of it quite unimaginable to people who have never administered a mass of books analysed and exhibited in co-ordinated groups. A novice with little or no bibliographical training soon acquires much knowledge of great practical benefit to himself and to the readers he serves. An experienced bibliographer, in a general library even of a quarter of a million volumes, at once becomes an accurate critic, noting old editions, obsolete books, and the absence of material in weakly represented subjects. Classification therefore is a map of bibliographical areas, and an index to them; an invaluable time-saving aid in mastering a library and in acquiring encyclopaedic bibliographical knowledge, by a librarian gifted with a retentive memory and an orderly mind. A classed library, in short, is literature and information organized for use in the most direct way; discovering knowledge in books by the shortest route is achieved. If any reader doubts the fact let him study DC tables for American history, or better still the LC tables for PA, Philology, Linguistic, Classical Philology and Classical Literature, PQ French, Italian, Spanish and Portuguese Literatures, and PT German Literature, which give a command over these bibliographical areas to be gained in no other way.

That is the simplest view of this part of my subject. The main classes and divisions are better (or are they?) in one of the "true orders," but as the headings in subdivisions, sections, and subsections run into more detail, become fuller of meaning, never forget that librarians, let alone readers, are not mapping the field of knowledge (a job no philosopher has undertaken to the contentment of any other) but they are thinking of each book as a tool wherein a theme is developed in a manner and order beneficial to a reader looking at it from a particular point of view. Mme. Montessori wrote on *Pedagogical Anthropology* for teachers; others have written, and more will write similar books, which, if classed in education under a broad heading, rather than under one fitted to their measure, are not differentiated with the precision and clarity so illuminating to librarians, and through them to readers. Likewise the classification should provide a corner for books on Medical ethics under Medicine, the most useful place for them: DC has no heading there, 174.2 being preferred, but the UDC and LC have. Examples abound. A book in a group of its own small family is pushed into view; in the crowd of a general division it escapes notice. Not only "give every book the most specific number which will contain it", but provide that number, or choose a notation which will allow it to be provided. (Hitherto classification makers, with a too punctilious regard for the imaginary rights of predecessors, have sought for original notations. A mistake, and I note gladly that Mr. Bliss has not hesitated to follow Cutter in using three letters.) And clearly the more specific the headings, the more accurately they designate bibliographical areas, however limited, the quicker and surer is the guidance offered by the library's own analytical index to the subject grouping. We are apt to think of a mark as only a means of arranging a book in order by subject, author or form, but if practicable it should be also a shorthand indication of its principal theme.

## V

Knowledge grows and fresh relations between branches of knowledge come to light. Many new areas of record must be plotted. The need of flexible tabulation and an expansible notation, whatever classification we apply, is therefore paramount.

LC's extensive notation seems, as far as we can tell, all embracing,

## CLASSIFICATION IN DISPLAY

and yet the tabulation may not be flexible enough as time passes. I think this probability has been foreseen, because the classes printed in late years are comparatively fuller, more exhaustive, than the earlier classes; they have a more elastic property. Congestion is imminent even now, here and there. How difficult it is to forecast the development of record, its extent and direction! No classification maker is to be judged unfavourably because he could not imagine that human beings would live down to Swift's opinion of them as the lowest form of animal life. In 1914–18 they did so by trying to kill each other all over the world. Between D469 and D901 in the 1916 edition of LC a gap was left for General Modern History. In the 1933 supplement to D (History) all the numbers between D501 and D725 are taken for the Great War of 1914–18 and its consequences. Now again we are slaughtering the world over, and seem likely to continue until only the dead are happy. All these stupidities and brutalities must be recorded for our information and guidance in future! But only the numbers D726 to D900 are left for this great war, and all history to the millennium. Here is a simple way out of the impasse: add one digit to the marks between D901[0] and D980[0] for European description and travel, and then we shall have 7,000 or more marks, which at the rate of 250 headings for each, will leave room for twenty more holocausts, a number that should last Europe's incompetent or criminal politicians fully a century, with a little economy and care.

Another example of thronged headings is in DC, where 940.1 to 940.29 cover all European history for fifteen hundred years between 476 and 1914; where 940.3 to 940.47, expanded through 35 pp., are crammed with Great War headings (seven numbers being used in many places, e.g. 940.4393) and where only 940.5 to 940.9 are vacant to plot the record of the new dark ages. Nothing but a drastic recasting of class 9 will give History living room.

As DC for History became longer and more congested, UDC for it became short enough to print the main divisions on one page, and the whole on a few leaves. If our descendants fancy a great war in 1955 the UDC has room for an unlimited number of books about it, written from any and every point of view. But in those classes which have not been relieved, to the same degree as History, by the common subdivisions for form, country, period and so on, the UDC is not indefinitely elastic.

The notation of the UDC has more significance than that of any other scheme: its marks are shorthand descriptions of books. The tabulation is also more flexible. Two examples are given on p. 37; three on p. 132; here are others. In any general library or in a collection on agriculture Grant, *Everyday Life on an Old Highland Farm*, 1767–1782, would be classed 63(41.21) "1769 : 1782"—63 = Agriculture; 41.21 = Inverness; "1769 : 1782" = the period. But were it desirable, as it is in Edinburgh, to inaugurate a subject department for Scotland, then the mark might be (41.21) 63 "1769 : 1782", the country mnemonic coming first, though this ordering would group all the material about Inverness (.21), and distribute that about Scottish agriculture. It may be asked: In a department where all the subject-matter is Scottish why not leave out the mark for country? A reasonable question. In Edinburgh we prefix X to the LC classmarks for books about Scotland and Y to those for books about Edinburgh. So with the UDC we might prefix the letter S, Grant's book being marked S63 "1769 : 1782" (41.21) or better still (.21), an order of symbols which would bring Scottish agriculture together, if we wanted to do so. We could still mark topographically the books best grouped in that way.

Against the following books I note the various marks which may be applied to them:

THE SCOTTISH SOCIALISTS: A GALLERY OF CONTEMPORARY PORTRAITS (1931)

(41) 92 : 335 "1931"—if Scots biography is to be grouped.

(41) 335 "1931"   —if Socialism rather than biography is to be grouped under Scotland.

335 (41) "1931"   —if, in a general library, all the books on Socialism are to stand together.

92 : 335 (41) "1931"—if all biography is to be grouped, an arrangement hardly to be recommended in a general library, though useful if the aim were to collect ephemeral biographical material in a vertical file.

## CLASSIFICATION IN DISPLAY

The last example indicates a development by no means undesirable. The facts of contemporary biography are difficult to find in a hurry, and, time and money permitting, a vertical file of clippings and typed references is as welcome to readers in reference libraries as to sub-editors in newspaper offices; let 92 or B indicate the file, 335 Socialism and (41) Scotland, thus bringing into a handgrip all the biographical data about Scots Socialists.

Strong, *History of Secondary Education in Scotland*, to 1908
   (41) 373 "563 : 1908" —in the Scots collection.
   373 (41) "563 : 1908" —in a general or a sociological collection.

Polson, *Scottish Witchcraft Lore*
   (41) 133.4           —in the Scots collection.
   133.4 (41)         —in a general or a folklore collection.

Scottish Amateur Athletic Association, *Fifty Years of Athletics*, 1883–1933
   (41) 796.8 "1883 : 1933"—in the Scots collection.
   796.8 (41) "1883 : 1933"—in a general or a sports collection.

Mackenzie, *Medieval Castle in Scotland*
   (41) 728.81 "11 : 14" —in the Scots collection.
   728.81 (41) "11 : 14" —in a general, or an architectural collection.

Other examples of UDC elasticity are the several alternative arrangements of music scores. Instead of the illogical "order" by forms, alphabetic order by composer is permitted, though the class marks are cumbrous enough to scare anybody from using them anywhere but in a card catalogue. The fundamental error of ignoring bibliographical areas was notably exemplified by Dewey when he jammed Music into one division, 78 or 780. Music is a voluminous subject, requiring a whole class to itself, and LC does not neglect this tribute to the greatest of the arts.

But the future of UDC was heavily mortgaged when its editors adhered to the awkward dislocations of parent Dewey. With Electric Science in 537 and Electric Engineering in 621.3; Chemistry in 54 and Chemical Technology in 66; Military and naval science in 355 and 359, Customs of War in 399 and Military and Naval Engineering in 623; Building in 69 and Architecture in 72; Bibliography in 01,

## MANUAL OF BOOK CLASSIFICATION

Book Rarities in 09, Early Printing in 09 and Printing in 655; Botany in 58, Agriculture in 63 and Landscape Gardening in 71; with these and other "faultings" not only have DC and UDC no relation to a "true order of the sciences", but, worse still, they have none to the definition and co-ordination of headings by literary warrant. Was it necessary for UDC to follow where DC led? I think not. How regrettable that the UDC editors, having devised an elastic notation, did not thoroughly redistribute the headings, and tabulate them in fairer proportion.

Here I add a word or two on the notation. For a long time I was prejudiced against the long articulated marks: 796.8(41) "1883 : 1933", Athletics in Scotland, 1883–1933, or 512(09)(32), Algebra in ancient Egypt, or 9(44)"17"(001), documents relating to the history of France in the eighteenth century. Later the significance of the notation attracted me, because the ideal classmark for a book is a shorthand description of its principal theme. In the LC mark DA 572 only the letters have meaning, but each part of 9(44)"17"(001) has the same meaning in all places and all conjunctions, a valuable indication of the contents of books, particularly when the marks translate more than the brief titles on the covers of books. Experience in later years with LC taught me that long marks are not objectionable in a card catalogue, and, if divisible clearly, they are easy to read on the backs of books:

$$
\begin{array}{c}
9 \\
(44) \\
\text{"17"} \\
(001)
\end{array}
$$

tells a plain story, and the book is arranged by it without trouble. Translated into English, the UDC might have been received more favourably by British and American librarians had the tabulation been a greater improvement upon the DC.

Why has a classification maker not followed the example of the compilers of some telegraphic codes? Their notation problem is much like ours. Pronounceable words not longer than six letters are numerous enough to accommodate any schedules known to me. If only three digits are added to each word the range is enormous. A pronounceable

## CLASSIFICATION IN DISPLAY

code word is easier to remember than numbers, or a mixture of letters and numbers; for example:

|  |  |
|---|---|
| Baal | Babbla |
| Bab | Babble |
| Baba | Babbli |
| Babal | Babblo |

which can be uttered clearly and quickly, and remembered easily. With code words for subjects and three numbers (in a series like the categorical tables of the SC) for making common subdivisions, a great classification could be applied simply; for example:

| Baba 212 | BABA |
| Baba 345 | 821 |
| Babel 821 | |

## VI

Early advocates of subject classing pleaded that, if all the world adopted the popular DC, the same book everywhere would receive the same mark. It was hard to believe that librarians would class alike, or that all would welcome the fiat even of a great library. Agree that the foundation of a general scheme can only be well and truly laid in a great public library, and that of a special scheme only in a comprehensive subject library, then uniformity is a remote end, and is indeed only practicable if we abandon the ideal of grouping books for the convenience of particular groups of readers.

Compare the grouping of headings for the Textile Industries in the Patent Office tables, and their distribution in LC, and my meaning should be clear. The Patent Office co-ordinates the headings in one class, but in LC, intended for a large general library (though organized in departments) the same headings are spread over H (Economics), S (Agriculture) and T (Technology). Recognizing the high authority of the classifiers, we conclude that both arrangements practically are right, the one for the one library, and the other for the other. In the LC scheme law books are distributed instead of being grouped: mining law goes with mining, medical law with medicine. Class K (Law) is thinned down to jurisprudence and legal procedure, all special law being, as it were and oddly enough, radioactive! But in a subject library for lawyers the books would not be far-flung but would stand with jurisprudence in K. No scheme in fact is wholly appropriate for every kind of student. Point of view is all pervasive. Let me take you for a moment into criminal circles. The report of a murder trial in this country is generally a good example of the classing from two points of view: the prosecutor arranges the evidence in historical sequence, so co-ordinated that the facts pointing to the accused's guilt are given most prominence. The defending lawyer arranges evidence to give salience and emphasis to the facts indicating the prisoner's innocence. But I am able to note an equally apposite example from our own practice. Plays in pamphlet form, such as those published by Appleton, French, Gowans and Gray, Nelson and other firms, are filed in boxes or in a vertical cabinet. They are borrowed mostly by amateur players, who invariably ask the question: "What X-act plays have you for Y number of characters?" The form of the request most frequently made about certain kinds of books ought to determine the order of their filing. No published classification provides for the grouping of plays so that this question may be answered straightway. Indexing them under the numbers of characters will not do, for we have to pick them out of class order when the question is asked, and file them away again when it is answered. A reader has a right to expect all the plays for (say) five characters to be laid before him in the turn of a hand. So we file these plays first by language. All French plays are marked F; English E; Scottish S; German G and so on. Then they are marked by the number of acts: $E_1$, $E_2$ signifying English one-act and English two-acts. Afterwards they are marked for form: C = Comedy, T = Tragedy, F = Farce, and so on. Finally for the number of characters: $C_5$ = Comedy for Five characters. Thus the mark: $E_1 Y_7$ means an English One-act play for Young people playing Seven characters; and $S_2 C_5$ is a Scottish Two-act Comedy for Five characters. Thus all the one-act comedies in English for four characters are together in a bunch. No other types of marks are used but those given as examples on this page.

## CLASSIFICATION IN DISPLAY

Do any librarians adopt a scheme without modification or expansion? Even that DC stalwart, Mr. Jast, detected spots in the sun. He arranged biography in alphabetic order of the names of subjects, forming a class B. Unable to tolerate the distribution of history and travel, he changed 91 into T, so that T42 English Description followed close upon 942 English History. These alterations were permitted by the DC editors, but uniformity was lost. The Aberdeen and Edinburgh University librarians revised the notation, if nothing else, and I have indicated already the radical changes in UDC.

The few known extensions of DC and LC point away from uniformity.

The tables for Mining prepared by the Colorado School of Mines multiply the headings by about ten. The compilers state that "the original classification, though imperfect, has not been changed. This is because of the copyright restrictions. . . . The imperfections can be seen in the division of 'Drainage', but to attempt to change it would be inadvisable, because so many have already adopted it". Law apart, the explanation is unconvincing. How many libraries of the kind and standing of that at Colorado School had adopted DC when the extension was published? Why did the Colorado compilers hamper themselves with a notation which divides the material between 551 and 622? This school has multiplied by three hundred the headings in Metallury, Metallography and Assaying, and the marks frequently run to nine figures. Why not new tables, with a new notation, intended for all libraries of the same kind? Inco-ordinated and congested tabulation is a high price to pay for ephemeral and illusive "uniformity".

The University of Illinois extended DC for the Engineering Industries, the numbers adopted ranging from 330 Political Economy to 77 Photography, the major protuberance being at 62 Engineering. The compilers explain: "In the working out of the extension of the various subjects the main divisions and sections . . . have been retained unchanged. It cannot be denied that there are many glaring inconsistencies in the arrangement of engineering subjects. For example, no engineer of to-day would put electrical engineering as a division under mechanical engineering (621.3) co-ordinate with blowing and pumping engines (621.6); nor would he relegate concrete to an unimportant place under building materials. There is no doubt that a committee of competent engineers could vastly improve the logical arrangement of the class numbers for engineering subjects. However, the system as it is, with its faults, has been in use several years and has become more or less universal. . . . It is far better to accept the system merely as an arbitrary set of numbers corresponding to certain topics and resolutely dismiss rigid ideas of logical sequence and consistency." So for the sake of a false uniformity we are to put up with "glaring inconsistencies", co-ordination disapproved by "competent engineers", and "arbitrary sets of numbers". Conservatism of this kind, to which most librarians give allegiance, is but another name for paralysis.

The headings even of the voluminous LC are shouldered apart by intruders. A big extension for the British Isles, and particularly for Scotland, was thought necessary at Edinburgh. In LC 425 headings cover City Planning; the extension by Harvard University School of Landscape Gardening required about 1,400. The same school issued an eighty-page extension for Landscape Architecture. The more I study extensions the firmer becomes my conviction that the compilers should ground their drafts, as Mr. Hulme recommends, upon the areas of record before them for plotting. The Harvard School of Business Administration proceeded on these lines in making *A Classification of Business Literature*, 1937, and so I think did Mr. Cyril C. Barnard in *A Classification for Medical Libraries*, 1937: both are independent of general schemes, and each has its own markings.

I have written at length on uniformity for several reasons. A librarian committed to a general scheme is reluctant to revise any part of it, even for the benefit of readers with changing and developing interests. Dwellers in Coventry, for example, have lost their old-time intimate concern with silk-weaving and watch-making, and now want all that has been recorded about mechanical engineering, and the internal combustion engine. Again, when the librarian feels himself bound by a general scheme, new volumes of record force him to swell the tables beyond reasonable limits; remember how our Colorado and Illinois extenders hampered themselves. Above all, with

*Burke & Koretke*

DISPLAY WINDOW, WOODLAWN BRANCH
The Chicago Public Library

*Facing p.* 48 *(see p.* 151)

## CLASSIFICATION IN DISPLAY

Sindbad's old man of the sea on his back, he is hindered from forming the subject departments which I believe to offer the fullest opportunity for the development of librarianship. Nowadays subject libraries are increasing in number, though rather slowly. More and more general libraries in the United States are becoming aggregates of special libraries. In the Congressional Library divisions for Aeronautics, Bibliography, Fine Arts, Music, Chinese Literature, Slavonic Literature, Law and other subjects, are administered under specialist chiefs. New York Public Library has like divisions for American History, Genealogy, Art, Music, Economics, Science, Technology and other subjects. The Cleveland, Baltimore, Los Angeles and Rochester Public Libraries have carried the process of organizing books for the greatest use a step further by forming subject departments of amalgamated reference and home-reading stocks, and are therefore notable examples of the advance of specialization in bibliographical function. Even in this country a little headway can be recorded.

Having followed Mr. Hulme's path so far I ought fairly to add that he believed uniformity to be an attainable ideal, though remote. "From the above considerations," he writes, "it may be gathered that a degree of uniformity in co-ordination equal to that which appears theoretically to be attainable in the definition of classes is not within our reach. For it is evident that the methodical examination of the composition of book classes will reveal the existence of common subject-matter between a great number of classes, which will in turn suggest a correspondingly large number of places to which classes can be rationally allotted. Taking, therefore, into consideration the varying requirements of different institutions and the variation of personal idiosyncrasies, it seems probable that uniformity in book classification will be of slow growth, and that such uniformity as will be attained will be in deference to authority and experience rather than to the dictates of pure reason. . . . The Archaeologist, Chemist, and Art Manufacturer, for instance, will continue to co-ordinate the literature of glass and pottery from their respective standpoints. . . . But apart from these special standpoints due to the essential limitations of the requirements of the specialist collections, time and experience will

DISPLAY SLOPE AND READING TABLE
Morningside, Edinburgh

*Photo: F. B. Savage*

Facing p. 49 (see p. 103)

ultimately point to the desirability of uniformity" in all libraries which cater for the community from a catholic standpoint (*L.A.R.*, V. 14: 180–1). But Mr. Hulme's goal is surely afar off. In the large city library, if reference work, now uneconomic and restricted nearly everywhere, is to be developed equally with lending for home study, a series of departments by subject, and not by method of issue, must be formed. Small and middle-town general libraries would be more effective with one, two, or three subject departments. It would be absurd to organize as many departments in Coventry as in Baltimore, but first-rate special libraries of economics and commerce, science and technology, are greatly needed there. General librarianship will diminish, I hope rapidly, and the possibility of uniformity in classification will be more remote than ever.

## VII

While classification tends to disintegrate in great and special libraries, it becomes (for a reason other than that stated above) less regarded in small libraries, where variations in book grouping are finding more favour as methods of display are adopted.

When popular town libraries were inaugurated librarians assumed that brief catalogues, by the grace of Mr. Cutter, would connect a book with any reader who knew the author's name or the title or subject; would reveal to him what books a library had by any author, on any subject, or in any form of literature; and, if editions, sizes, dates and other bibliographical data were noted, would help him to choose the work most useful to him. Not too quickly they learned, or collided with the fact, that most readers in libraries are but children at school: they are bibliographically ignorant, and even students, off their own ground, look like glum and forlorn prospectors. At length, realizing that to hand out books by call numbers was not enough, that they must teach and guide, the admitted, at first with the cold welcome of a liveried footman to a tramp, readers to examine books at the shelves. To books arrayed by size, and date of acquisition? No; all that time-honoured organization must be scrapped. Bit by bit, guided

## CLASSIFICATION IN DISPLAY

classing became common. Some librarians stooped to conquer with a little personal guidance. (I don't want the young reader to get the idea that these things happened all at once. Die-hard denizens of the Athenæum Club are radicals beside the crusted tories of British librarianship, and progress was the slow, slow drift of a glacier.) In time, I say. Though the Clerkenwell Public Library first let astonished readers jump the counter in 1894, sparely guided classing was the only kind of display in British libraries until a few years ago. Now, decades too late, to our own methods we add some of those of the go-ahead bookseller.

These various methods may be described summarily:

(1) *Display by literary methods:* catalogues, in print or typescript, subject and author lists and indexes, bulletins, newspaper communiqués, and the like. Not a part of the subject of this book.

(2) *Display by personal guidance:* the art of receiving, helping and encouraging readers; making them comfortably at home in libraries. Perhaps the most important part of the function of expounding books, but, requiring a book to itself for its proper consideration and explanation, it cannot be dealt with here. It should be integrated with display. Lectures and talks are a part of personal guidance, but we have had too few to judge their worth finally. The two or three general broadcast talks on libraries and reading have not, to my knowledge, brought one new member to any library in my charge. On the other hand, the B.B.C. talks on new books are influential but embarrassing and injurious to public libraries because they lead to a sudden, heavy and brief demand for a few books already well-used and in short supply: our libraries cannot satisfy the demand for boosted books without over-buying, and inducing future staleness leading to future waste. Perhaps talks on groups of books on special topics: Philosophy, Religion, Biology and so on would be more profitable to us, but they have not been tried. (See the author's *Special Librarianship*, pp. 230–42, or *Library Association Record*, October 1936.)

(3) *Display by formal classification:* grouping books in any library, general or special, and, with the aid of bookcase labels and directions, arraying them in a visibly-intelligible order, so that they reveal their subject-matter to readers.

(4) *Display by exhibition of selected stock:* arranging books in interior showcases, generally illuminated, or in bookcases out of the run of the notation, or in cradles or on tables, to give them temporarily greater prominence; all the exhibits being immediately available for issue. An unprofessional method which no decent librarian will practice unless he wants to get books used.

(5) *Display by demonstration in reference libraries:* the exhibition of whole classes of books, or substantial parts of such classes, either in formal classed order, or in fresh groupings, under the personal guidance of a librarian acquainted with the relevant bibliography. The object of this demonstration, which however is superfluous in subject departments, is to reveal the contents of reference libraries, the buried wealth of which is advertised with particular difficulty.

(6) *Display by selective processes:* giving greater prominence to the best books for readers at a particular time by removing to reserve or depôt books which, however well classed, exhibited or advertised, are rarely borrowed because they are (1) seasonal and required only in certain months of the year, or (2) partly obsolete, or (3) out of favour for the time being, or (4) shabby, unattractive and not worth replacing. We cut the trees to reveal the wood. The selective process which reduces the displayed stock is as cardinal as the selective process which replenishes it.

(7) *Display by rotation of stock:* by changing all or part of the stock of small home-reading libraries, in other words by chain organization, readers are given a wider range of choice than stale stock allows them.

(8) *Display by advertising:* in corridor, entrance and external windows, the material being posters, showcards, non-literary exhibits, drapery and apparatus; books are rarely included. The aim is to draw people into the library. A vulgar practice, like all advertising, condemned by every librarian who hasn't a shop window, or wouldn't know how to fill it if he had.

In the following chapters I consider the methods numbered (3) to (7) in the above order, beginning with the preparations for receiving readers inside the library, and ending with the devices for drawing them in.

CHAPTER III

## 3. THE PRACTICE OF CLASSIFICATION: RELATIONS WITH CATALOGUING AND DISPLAY, PREPARATORY READING AND SCHEMES

I

MANUALS of cataloguing and indexing have been included in this series, and I cannot therefore deal with the literary methods of display, of introducing books to the people. Yet the value of this book would be greater if an account of the principles of cataloguing and indexing were included; for then it would be a comprehensive epitome of all the methods which ought to be reviewed together, as a whole, because they have an almost identical function. It is nonsense to say that one man is an expert in cataloguing, another in subject-indexing, and a third in classing, unless we mean also that absolute competence in the one method implies, as it does, equal competence in the others. I will content myself therefore with trying to make this integrity of function clear.

Cutter's well-known table in his *Rules for a Dictionary Catalogue* (the third edition was my first textbook, given to me in 1891, the year of its publication, by the U.S.A. Department of Education) is as follows. The Objects of cataloguing are, he tells us :-

(1) to enable a person to find a book of which either
    (*a*) the author
    (*b*) the title   is known
    (*c*) the subject

(2) to show what the library has
    (*d*) by a given author
    (*e*) on a given subject
    (*f*) in a given kind of literature

(3) to assist in the choice of a book
    (*g*) as to its edition
    (*h*) as to its character

The several objects are one: the exposition of a library's contents to a reader who has a clue to a book and requires advice about it, or who, having made up his mind about the subject of his reading, wants helpful matter on it. The objects of classification and of display are identical. The practice of teaching classification and cataloguing as independent subjects has veiled the near-identity of their functions. By tabulating the means of attaining these objects in (*a*) the dictionary catalogue, (*b*) the class or subject catalogue, (*c*) the classification and (*d*) display (in its narrow meaning, exhibition) I hope to demonstrate this functional integrity.

Here are the Means, the capital letters referring to the above Table of Objects. The asterisks indicate roughly the degree by which the Objects are attained.

A, THE AUTHOR BEING KNOWN }
D, BY A GIVEN AUTHOR

  \*\*(*a*) *In dictionary catalogue:* author entry

  \*(*b*) *In class or subject catalogue:* author index. If short title is added to author entry in index, as in Sonnenschein, *Best Books*, or to subject head, as in the *London Bibliography of Social Sciences*, two asterisks should mark this means.

  (*c*) *By classification:* Literature and Music when the works of authors and composers are grouped together in class order, and Biography when classed and indexed by personal subject.

  (*d*) *By display:* leading authors and composers whose works are thrust prominently into notice in clearly marked bookcases, whether the cases are isolated or not, and people whose biographies are treated similarly. (The display of authors and personal subjects isn't limited to music, literature and biography, but to authors in any class, e.g., Aristotle, Darwin.)

B, THE TITLE BEING KNOWN

  \*(*a*) *In dictionary catalogue:* title-entry if title is remarkable or distinctive.

## RELATIONS WITH CATALOGUING AND DISPLAY

  *(b) *In class or subject catalogue:* title-entry in index if title is remarkable or distinctive.
  (c) *By classification:*—
  (d) *By display:*—

C, THE SUBJECT BEING KNOWN
E, ON A GIVEN SUBJECT
  *(a) *In dictionary catalogue:* subject entry, and references.
  *(b) *In class or subject catalogue:* class entries and subject-index entries.
  **(c) *By classification:* grouping books by subjects adequately guided on open shelves; the subject-index to the classification; and correlative or liaison lists (see pp. 100, 106).
  *(d) *By display:* subjects which are temporarily and prominently exhibited in showcases or on tables.

F, IN A GIVEN KIND OF LITERATURE
  *(a) *In dictionary catalogue:* form, series, collection or language entries. (But even language entries are unusual, though desirable.)
  *(b) *In class or subject catalogue:* form and language groups; series and collection entries in subject-index.
  *(c) *By classification:* Literature when works are grouped by language and form; Music when works are grouped (mistakenly) by instrument and by kind of composition instead of by composer.
  *(d) *By display:* when groups by language or forms (ballads, poetry, etc.) or series or collections are displayed temporarily or permanently in isolated, guided cases.

G, THE EDITION OF A BOOK
H, ITS CHARACTER
  (a) *In dictionary catalogue:* giving edition, imprint, and descriptive notes—but notes are rare in general catalogues.
  (b) *In class or subject catalogue:* as for (a).
  **(c) *By classification:* giving readers access to shelves, where they may examine books.
  (d) *By display:* exhibiting recommended books under conditions enabling readers to examine them.

If the above table does not plainly indicate how nearly alike, how closely dovetailed are the functions of the three processes (classification, cataloguing, display) then I have failed in my object. Note, however, that the function of cataloguing falls short of that of classification, which more effectively introduces to a reader books he knows nothing about: authors and titles quite new to him, on topics he had no intention of studying. In this simple diagram, to illustrate the argument, the word display is given its comprehensive meaning, which embraces all three processes. The overlap of classing and cataloguing represents class entries and subject-index entries in the class catalogue and subject entries in the dictionary catalogue, all three of which have a common function.

```
+-------------------------------------------+
|                  DISPLAY                  |
+------+--------------+--------------+------+
|      |              |              |      |
|      | CLASS|ING    |              |      |
|      |              |              |      |
|      |       CATALO|GUING          |      |
|      |              |              |      |
+------+--------------+--------------+------+
```

The intimate relation between the three processes suggests that the following rules are administratively sound:

(1) an assistant should practise classing before cataloguing; oddly enough in most libraries he begins with cataloguing.

(2) the assistant classing a book should suggest the subject headings (in catalogue or index) for it.

(3) the assistant cataloguing a book should check the classmark before approving the subject headings.

(4) the displayer should consult classer, cataloguer (as well as the subject department head) before arranging a display.

Only by following these rules may we co-ordinate the work and attain the objects tabulated by Cutter.

# RELATIONS WITH CATALOGUING AND DISPLAY

## II

We note emphatically this integrity of function because classing, when looked at as a part of one general operation, falls into its right place as an ordinary method, no more formidable than choosing subject headings for a dictionary catalogue. And when we realize that book classification isn't an exact science founded on some "true order" of knowledge, but on a survey and measurement of literature, its study and application become far less difficult and complicated.

Here is an interview, imaginary but in common form.

The librarian takes up his 'phone. "Send Mr. Boffin in, please." Boffin enters. "Oh, Boffin, I want you to take over Lammle's duties at the classing desk on Monday."

Boffin hesitates. "But, Mr. Wegg, I haven't taken my classification exam. I think you must have overlooked that."

"Thank Heaven for that," replies Wegg; "there's hope for you."

"But I haven't classed books before, sir," objects Boffin.

"Now listen, Boffin, before you talk any more nonsense," replies Wegg. "How long have you been here?—you know the scheme we use, don't you? Thoroughly, eh?"

"Yes, I hope so."

"You've done a lot of subject cataloguing, haven't you? And I know that the subject headings you choose are generally right. At least, I agree with them. How do you get those headings?"

Boffin is silent. He wonders what Wegg is driving at.

"You get the right headings," continues Wegg, "because you're able to diagnose the subject of a book. In fact, you class the book. Subject diagnosis is three-quarters of the art of classing. D'you mean to tell me that, when cataloguing, you can ascertain a subject and find a heading for it, but when classing you *can't* ascertain a subject, and *can't* find a class mark in a scheme well known to you? Pack o' nonsense. Go away. Begin Monday."

Boffin, I'm sure, was not convinced: ten to one he left the presence looking as wooden as Dr. Richard Garnett when *Erewhon* Butler tried to persuade him that a woman wrote the *Odyssey*. But there is no flaw in the argument of Wegg, who no doubt wanted to pump confidence into him. Don't look upon a classer as a kind of medicine man. In part bad classing is the fruit of ignorance and laziness, in part of teaching and examining on wrong lines. When a business man arranges his papers, or an author the material for his book, does he bother about the logical bases of classification: the correlation of properties, the meaning of the five predicables, denotation and connotation, extension and intension (*summum genus* and *infima species*) the Tree of Porphyry and so on? I don't want to be misunderstood. It would not be unreasonable to expect librarians to read logic, a valuable study profitable in any walk of life. Careful and critical reading of Jevons, *Principles of Science,* or Welton, *Manual of Logic,* or Flint, *Philosophy as Scientia Scientiarum,* is fine mental discipline, and in particular a thorough knowledge of the theory of classification is indispensable to scheme makers. But the dribble of terminology and theory demanded by the Library Association Education Committee is no more wanted by the classer of books than by the cataloguer or the book indexer who chooses subject headings and attaches page numbers to them. The practical art of grouping books, in fact, has been turned into a craft-mystery by jargoneers and by examiners who ferret out conundrums to cow neophytes. At one time candidates sitting at the miscalled practical exam were not allowed to put forward alternative marks; or to refer to the classification index, though every chief requires his classers never to omit this primary check. That puerility is at an end. But not yet are they permitted to consult the reference books always at hand in their daily work, and still they are expected to class, not ordinary, everyday books, but *catalogue entries* of mongrel literature which can be grouped only after it has been examined and partly read; a practice which would stop dead if examiners were compelled, as they should be, to publish their own markings immediately after the exam. (Students tested in cataloguing must play a like guessing game, when they pick subject headings.) Any idiot may ask what nobody can answer: as a result many young people, even when through this silly exam, are obsessed by the fear that classing is full of traps and pitfalls, and they go to work as gingerly as firewatchers clamber over a roof in the black-out. Like the wicked Wegg I want to give the student confidence. After long experience of the DC I turned to LC, and found, rather to my astonishment at first, that I could class more accurately and rapidly by it. After a while I knew the reason: LC was made to measure literature, not the universe. To mark books on a scheme which isn't founded on literary warrant is like arranging classed books of all heights on fixed shelves.

Here are facts to uphold the foregoing argument. For a time, I had an account kept of the books (1) easy to class, (2) moderately difficult and (3) difficult. The results on 2,419 non-fiction books, taken as they came in the day's work, were 94·17 per cent easy; 4·6 moderate; 1·57 difficult, the classification used being LC. The figures in one department differ from those in another, though the all-over percentages are not affected by the variations; for example, *Art Library*: 88·31 easy, 10·4 moderate, 1·29 difficult; *Commercial*: 75·1 easy, 22·8 moderate, 2·1 difficult; *Music*: 98·97 easy, 0·9 moderate, 0·13 difficult. That a larger proportion of commercial books are difficult to class accords with my experience. But of *all* the books classed, no matter where or by whom, 94·17 per cent were easy.

### III

But though the task of marking books isn't difficult, and certainly should not be intimidating, librarians, if they are to apply effectively a classification founded on a survey and measurement of literary output, must have a firm background of bibliographical and general knowledge: a background, I may add, quite as necessary to cataloguers, and to librarians who undertake personal service or organize display.

In the large general library, into which accessions flow regularly in large volume, distribute the work evenly, and arrange that certain classes of books fall to the lot of the same classers. In Edinburgh the books on music are marked by one assistant, on local history and antiquities by another, on art by a third, on economics and commerce by a fourth, and on remaining subjects by others. Further dividing of labour is expedient when other subject departments are formed. I recommend the plan for general libraries which are not organized in departments by literary function: let one assistant regularly tackle science and technology, another religion and philosophy, and so on. When we are co-ordinating a library for the first time how much easier it is to mark at one and the same time all the books on Electrical engineering, or Shakspere, or British history. Parcel the work as recommended, and so get it done more accurately and consistently, and give a larger number of young librarians a more intimate acquaintance with the subject-matter of books added to the library. In the smaller general library the labour cannot be shared in equal degree, though every senior ought to have practice.

How is this background of bibliographical and general knowledge to be acquired? Breadth of knowledge is valuable to a librarian. By no means do I deprecate the discipline of profound study of one or two subjects which counteracts any baneful effects of half-learning. Nevertheless general rather than intensive knowledge helps him professionally. Time is well spent in reading reviews in special journals, informative articles in good general periodicals, and any miscellanies (*The Mercury Books*), biographies, memoirs and essays that interest him. But even shallow reading is the better for being planned. On this account I recommend some epitomes particularly useful to the general practitioner in classing, or for that matter in librarianship. I emphasize the fact that I have chosen them for general practitioners, because subject librarians must read more thoroughly: Gardner, *Art through the Ages*, is an excellent introduction for the art librarian, but only Michel, Venturi and other large and special works will content him.

I don't claim that these compends are the best. They are readable, and I hope they will be read, not studied, as for an exam. They may be inaccurate in some details, for authors writing on very broad subjects can hardly avoid error. A few seem to me out of balance: Singer, *Short History of Science*, good as it is, perhaps devotes too much space to ancient science and too little to modern. After comparing them with like books I believe their contents fill in the background required. Let me add that I have not read all of them; at my age, "fine confused feeding" isn't good for mental health. But I have read several through, and the modern parts of the remainder; the earlier parts I have examined carefully. The epitomes now recommended are better than those obtainable in my youth. Kellett, *Short History of Religions*, for example, is better than that of Dr. Menzies (1895); Haney, *History of Economics*, than that of H. D. Macleod (1896). But we older men had other advantages over my young friends of to-day. Cassell's *Popular Educator* and *Technical Educator*, Dr. Robert Brown, *Science for All*, and many other books, were issued in parts, which we could afford the money to buy, and the time (for they appeared monthly) to digest. These miscellanies were not scholarly, though some of the writers were well-known and competent, but they were excellent food, at that time, for growing librarians, and there is nothing now to take their exact place.[1] In these years, the eighteen-nineties, the magazines were full of good general reading, but *Chambers's*, *Cornhill*, *Macmillan's*, *English Illustrated*, *Century*, *Scribner's*, *Harper's* and others are now defunct or quite different in character; while there were more literary journals, *The Bookman*, *Literary World*, *The Academy* (admirable paper!), and *The Athenæum* ("The 'Athæneum', that was the name! Golly, what a paper!" And it *was* good and solid).

I can give an idea of the particular value of manuals to the classer by referring to the first book on my list: *A Short History of Philosophy*, by Dr. A. B. D. Alexander (third edition, revised and enlarged, XII, 648 pp.; Maclehose, Jackson and Co., Glasgow, 1922). This well-arranged summary of the history of philosophical thought, from ancient Greek to modern times, clearly indicates the relative importance of philosophers (a demonstration most necessary to the book selector), and traces their influence upon each other, knowledge indispensable to the classer, the displayer and the librarian who offers personal guidance. No part of it is beyond the careful reader. It will keep the classer out of bunkers. For example, logic is the science of the laws of thought. Hegel demands that logic and metaphysics shall be conceived as one. "Logic must deal with the whole kingdom of

---

[1] These books were *general*. In recent years books in parts have been on special subjects, e.g., Knight and Step, *Hutchinson's Popular Botany*, and Phillips and Steavenson, *Hutchinson's Splendour of the Heavens*—the latter, now out of print and up in price, being the best popular book on the subject. The few more general works of this type: *Outline of Literature* and *Outline of Art* are not so good.

thought. It must present the truth as it is in itself—the whole organism of being. It must, in short, reveal the very working of the mind of God." Yet often we find the *Logic* grouped with logical books instead of with his other philosophical works, of which it is an integral part. A smattering of historical knowledge would prevent the classer from distributing Herbert Spencer's *Principles of Biology*, . . . *of Sociology*, . . *of Ethics* instead of grouping them as parts of the Synthetic Philosophy. No other book on this history have I been able to read more easily, and with equal profit. It indicates clearly the powerful influence the leading philosophers have had upon the history and conduct of peoples; an influence by no means reflected in the handful of philosophical works commonly to be found in public libraries. The impact of philosophical thought upon political thought in Germany, for example, has been terrific.

*A Short History of Religions*, written by E. E. Kellett (607 pp., Gollancz, 1933) is intended "not to satisfy, but to stimulate, the interest of serious-minded people in its theme". It does not claim to be impartial: "absolute impartiality is not possible but I have", the author writes, "to the best of my power, tried to live up to the motto of one of the greatest of religious leaders, and to be 'the friend of all, the enemy of none'." The subject-matter includes: Religion, its nature and origin; Judaism; Roman and Greek religion; Germanic religion; Christianity; Mohammedanism; Zoroastrianism; Far Eastern religions; the Churches of England and Scotland, and the various sects. The book is written in lucid, compact English.

An associate professor and chairman of the School of Economics, University of Texas, Lewis H. Haney, has compiled a well-arranged *History of Economic Thought* (third edition, 827 pp., Macmillan Co., 1936). The first edition appeared in 1911, so that it is a well-established book. This critical account of the origin and development of the economic theories of the leading thinkers in the leading nations has a bibliography and footnote references; on the whole it was reviewed favourably, and in my judgment it is adequate for our purpose.

R. H. S Crossman, the Warden of New College, ably summarizes the history of political ideas and political practice in the brilliantly

## RELATIONS WITH CATALOGUING AND DISPLAY

planned *Government and the Governed* (xii, 306 pp., Christophers, 1939). "This spirited and challenging survey of the course of political thought from the Renaissance to the present age", wrote H. /A. L. Fisher, "is the work of a young apostle of democratic principles", I think it impartial, if a little fatalistic and pessimistic in temper. It is a readable account of political science from the beginnings of the modern state to fascism, including the English, American, French and industrial revolutions, national liberalism and imperialism, socialism and the Russian revolution. A bibliography is included.

Dr. Charles Singer, the professor of medical history in the University of London, and at one time visiting professor of the history of science in the University of California, recently put out a well-illustrated *Short History of Science to the Nineteenth Century* (xiv, 399, Oxford University Press, 1941). Persons, movements, advances and inventions are selected as illustrative examples. Notwithstanding the compactness of the narrative the book is written in such clear English that it may be truly described as simple. Psychological, social or abstract mathematical problems are not considered. "Dr. Singer's learning is always exact, as befits the senior British historian of science. His book is full of fascinating information, and will at once become a standard work . . . both for the man of science himself and the general reader" (*Nature*, V. 148: 179). A more popular book is Walter Shepherd, *Science Marches On* (420 pp., Harrap, 1939). I doubted whether to place it or Singer's book first; both are good for our purpose.

No single book embraces the vast, humming world of technology. Edward Cressy, *Discoveries and Inventions of the Twentieth Century* (third, revised edition, xxiv, 458, Routledge, 1930) hardly deserves to stand with the books noted above, but it covers a great part of the field in a popular style. The 350 illustrations are attractive and helpful. It is modelled on a similar book: Robert Routledge, *Discoveries and Inventions of the Nineteenth Century* (thirteenth edition, 836 pp., 458 illus., Routledge, 1929, now out of print, but obtainable second-hand). Cressy and Routledge, with Sir William Tilden, *Chemical Discovery and Invention in the Twentieth Century* (sixth edition, revised and enlarged by Dr. S. Glasstone, xvi, 492 pp., 143 illus.,

Routledge, 1936), in my opinion are the best books for reading, though not for reference.

With more confidence I recommend *Art through the Ages* (revised and enlarged ed., 820 pp., 891 illus., Bell and Co., 1936), by Helen Gardner, an author in charge of instruction in the history of art in the School of the Art Institute of Chicago. Her book covers architecture, painting, sculpture and the minor arts, from the remote days of the glacial age in Europe, through the successive civilizations of the Near East, Europe, America and the Orient, to contemporary art in Europe and America. Written in an engaging style, it is profusely illustrated, has a bibliography for each section, and at the end a list of selected books on esthetics. A briefer book is André S. Blum, *Short History of Art* (edited and enlarged by R. R. Tatlock, Batsford, 1926), but I prefer Gardner.

Percy A. Scholes, author of *Oxford Companion to Music*, a tip-top reference book for the classing table, has written an excellent book for any "concert-goer, pianolist or gramophonist", with a course of study for adult classes in the appreciation of music, in *A Listener's History of Music* (fourth edition, 3 vols. in 1, with an encyclopaedic index, xiv, 180 + xii, 225 + xii, 165 + iv, 54 pp., Oxford University Press, 1933). Part 1 tells the story up to Beethoven, part 2 continues with the romantic and nationalistic schools of the nineteenth century, and part 3 hurries us to a rackety and detonating finale among the composers of to-day, the impressionists, neo-romantics and anti-romantics; a most "readable and friendly" book, and containing little beyond even my low degree of comprehension. Dr. Harvey Grace, in the *Musical Times* (V. 70: 517) expresses the opinion that "these intensely interesting and lively volumes mark the summit of Mr. Scholes's work on behalf of the listener". A bibliography of further reading is printed as an appendix. H. C. Colles; *Growth of Music: a Study in Musical History for Schools* (Oxford University Press, 1931) is shorter, but I vote for Scholes.

As librarians are expected to study English literature thoroughly for their professional exams I have looked about for a well-grounded epitome of general literary history, and after much deliberation I have chosen Ford Madox Ford, *The March of Literature from Confucius*

EXHIBITION BOOTH, Designed by Mathilde Kelly
Hild Regional Branch, The Chicago Public Library

Facing p. 64 (see p. 166)

*to Modern Times* (xiv, 878 pp., Allen and Unwin, 1939). It is a stimulating book. "I must write only about the books that I have found attractive," the author tells us:

"because if I lead my reader up to unreadable books I risk giving him a distaste for all literature. Too many of the classics that the learned still mechanically ram down the throats of their pupils or their readers have lost the extra-literary attractions that once they had and so have become but dry bones, the swallowing of which can only inculcate into the coerced ingurgitators a distaste for all books.... So there may well be here certain omissions that may astonish you until you reflect upon the matter".

An attractive book in Harrap's New Geographical Series is J. N. L. Baker, *History of Geographical Discovery and Exploration* (new edition, revised, 552 pp., 1931). The author, a lecturer in geography in the University of Oxford, has written an excellent narrative, clear, concise and always interesting, illustrated with numerous sketch maps, and he introduces us again to many books of travel, once read with pleasure and now forgotten. An alternative, less compact in style, but perhaps more readable, is Sir Percy Sykes, *History of Exploration from the Earliest Times to the Present Day* (illus., xiv, 374 pp., Routledge, 1933). Sir Percy Sykes' meat however, is less solid, and he recognizes Baker's book as the standard. I find these accounts of receding frontiers deeply interesting. A general modern geography should be read. Chisholm and Birrell, *Smaller Commercial Geography*, will do, but the student will fare better if he tackles boldly Chisholm, *Handbook of Commercial Geography* (latest edition, Longmans), which is a mine of general knowledge, and a fundamental work in education.

In spite of the almost intractable material G. P. Gooch, *History and Historians in the Nineteenth Century* (vi, 600 pp., Longmans, 1913) isn't difficult to read. "The object of the work is to summarize and assess the manifold achievements of historical research and production during the last hundred years, to portray the masters of the craft, to trace the development of scientific method, to measure the political, religious and racial influences that have contributed to the making of celebrated books, and to analyse their effect on the life and thought of the time." James T. Shotwell, himself an historiographer,

SHELF PLACARD

Facing p. 65 (see pp. 101–2)

described this as "the best introduction to the modern school of historians".

Am I immoderate in advising this preparatory reading? Is it too much for a classer of Philosophy and Religion to read Alexander and Kellett?—a classer of Art and Music to read Gardner and Scholes? By no means. At any rate a librarian cannot do without a firm groundwork of reading and of general knowledge. To put good books in charge of an ill-read librarian is as silly as entrusting good food to a bad cook.

No classer will attain confidence unless he habitually consults reference books. Near the worktable, within reach of his arm, he requires enough of the most trustworthy books to answer all queries except the most uncommon; so equipped, he need make few journeys to the general reference library. I will be content with indicating the kind of books required, without printing a list which would quickly become obsolete. Prefer handy volumes, if otherwise good. The size and general accuracy of *Everyman's Encyclopaedia* are about right; one volume is a clear World Atlas. Brewer's books, *Phrase and Fable*, and *Reader's Handbook*, are useful, though not indispensable. Good summary reference books on Philosophy and Religion are few. Calderwood's old *Vocabulary of Philosophy*, and Mathews and Smith, *Dictionary of Religion and Ethics* are the handiest. For answers to social science questions we must go to the reference library and consult: Seligman, *Encyclopaedia of the Social Sciences*, Watson, *Encyclopaedia and Dictionary of Education*, and Pitman, *Business Man's Encyclopaedia*; but *Pitman's Business Man's Guide* is a trustworthy desk-book. Handy dictionaries of the Greek, Latin, English, French, German, Italian and Spanish languages are requisite. I find Ostler's *Little Oxford Dictionary* the best book in which to find quickly the more usual meaning of a word. There are few handy Scientific and Technical reference books: Henderson and Henderson's *Dictionary of Scientific Terms*, and Chambers's *Technical Dictionary* are commendable. Hourticq's *Encyclopaedia* and similar works in the reference library must help us in Art, but Scholes' *Oxford Companion to Music*, though bulky, ought to be at hand. Quite a number of reference manuals to General and English Literature have been compiled; the

## RELATIONS WITH CATALOGUING AND DISPLAY

revised Manly and Rickert's *Contemporary American Literature*, and *Contemporary British Literature* are excellent. I have found a pocket volume, *Brief Biographical Dictionary*, by Charles Hole, most useful, although it gives only the name, description and birth and death dates of each person in a one-line entry. Phillips' *Dictionary of Biographical Reference* (o.p.) is a similar book, but larger, and it contains references to fuller literature. I think Phillips contains more names than any other biographical dictionary. Chambers's *Biographical Dictionary* and the Concise *D.N.B.*, with a volume of *Who's Who*, and the several volumes of *Who was Who*, will keep any classer straight. Abundant reference material on Geography and History exists. We want a Gazetteer, a Geographical dictionary, an Atlas; a dictionary of dates, and dictionaries of English history, including Gretton's *Modern History of the English People*. For bibliographical reference the London Library *Catalogue* is necessary, particularly the Subject-Index, but most queries on this subject must be answered in the reference library.

### IV

As the schemes of classification can be properly understood only by the student who has their prefaces and tables before him, I shall hardly do more than name, and take my examples from, those which are generally in favour in America and this country.

The *Decimal Classification and Relative Index*, first published in 1876 as *A Classification and Subject Index for Cataloguing and Arranging the Books and Pamphlets of a Library* (the words "decimal" and "relative index" did not appear in the title until 1885), reached its fourteenth edition in 1942. Used in a great number of libraries all over the English-speaking world, it is likely to remain in favour for a long time. No other book has had a more powerful influence upon library administration than this invention of Melvil Dewey, a celebrated American librarian. Puck-like, he put a girdle round the earth with his "damned dots" (as Lord Randolph Churchill bluntly described something he didn't understand) and with them American library methods were carried from Albany to the Antipodes. When applied in Europe and in South America its tabulation has been largely modified, and nearly everywhere alterations are recorded. That it needs fundamental revision is generally accepted. Two versions are wanted: one continued and improved in detail on the current plan for present users; the other radically altered, to mend dislocations, to give living room to protuberant parts, and to expand the notation, while retaining the best features. If recasting is undertaken I hope the editors and publishers won't hesitate to copy admirable details of other schemes, for it is annoying that librarianship should be prevented, by legal barriers or by reluctance to pool ideas, from obtaining all the advantages of co-operation.

The clearest account of DC is in the preface.

The DC has been expanded in *Classification Décimale Universelle*, the full edition being published in 1927–32, in three volumes and index, by the Institut International de Bibliographie, Brussels; it is often spoken of as the Brussels classification. This revision was first adumbrated in *Manuel du Répertoire Bibliographique Universel* (1905). It has been applied to the card catalogue of the Engineering Societies Library in New York, to the Science Museum Library, South Kensington, and to a few other libraries; but more generally as a tool in documentation, for the arrangement of cards in indexes of periodical and similar bibliographic material. It is significant that the I.I.B. is now known as the Institut International de Documentation. Probably the scheme would have made more headway had it been translated into English, and had the LC not adequately filled the need for a great classification. A translation into English, under the title *Universal Decimal Classification* (UDC), was in course of publication when war broke out (1939). Some parts are well adapted to the co-ordination of special libraries. Dr. S. C. Bradford founded upon it his *Classification for Works in Pure and Applied Science in the Science Museum Library* (third edition, 1936), and Dr. A. F. C. Pollard partly translated it for a Universal Bibliographical Repertory of Optics, Light, and Cognate Subjects (Camb. U.P., 1926).

The late H. V. Hopwood's article on UDC (see p. 21) is worth reading, though rather old. The best account in English is Dr. Bradshaw's section in Sayers, *Introduction to Library Classification* (6th ed.),

## RELATIONS WITH CATALOGUING AND DISPLAY

1938, an excellent book. Those who read French should go directly to the scheme itself and study the preface, notes and tables.

In 1898 or thereabout the Library of Congress adopted a scheme for class E-F, *America: History and Geography*, and the preliminary and provisional tables for this class were published in 1901, about two years before the *Outline of the Scheme of Classes* (1903). Although the whole tabulation is not quite complete, 27 parts, nearly all of which rank as volumes, are now in print. (For some extensions, see p. 48.) Parts are revised from time to time: E-F, *America*, which filled about 47 (95 pp. printed on one side of leaf only) pages in 1901, required 298 in 1913. The tabulation, good from the beginning, has improved in later parts. Class B, pt. II, BL-BX (1927) is far and away the best ordering of Religion in existence; turning over the 337 pages and remembering the few pages devoted to this great subject in early editions of the DC, I find it difficult to believe that progress has been so rapid. Class H, Social Sciences (621 pp., 1920) is an example of encyclopaedic scheduling on a soundly co-ordinated basis, with ten tables, varying in range, of geographical divisions; it is impregnably solid and thorough.[1] P-PA, Philology, Linguistic, Classical Philology, Classical (Greek and Latin) literature (447 pp., 1928), PQ French Literature (185 pp., 1936), PQ Italian, Spanish and Portuguese Literature (223 pp., 1937) and PT German Literature (312 pp., 1938) are comprehensive, accurate, well-digested and methodically codified, so they serve not only as tables for grouping books, but as incomparable synopses of the history and development of European literature. The continuation PJ-PM, Languages and Literature of Asia, Africa, Oceania, America; Mixed Languages; Artificial Languages (246 pp., 1935) with the Index to Languages and Dialects in P-PA, PB-PH, PJ-PM (57 pp., 1936) apart from its function, is a valuable reference book; no other work on philology has equal scope. The tables for S, Agriculture, Plant and Animal Industry, Fish Culture and Fisheries, Hunting Sports (99 pp., 1928)

---

[1] The admirable *London Bibliography of the Social Sciences*, published by the London School of Economics (4v., 1931-32), is a catalogue of a library classed on this scheme, though the DC geographical divisions are used instead of the LC.

and U, Military Science (95 pp., 1928) would give any librarian, in a general or special library, an unbreakable grip on these topics.

Each part of LC has its own index. While we await the promised general index, *Subject Headings used in the Dictionary Catalogues of the Library of Congress* is a limited substitute, because many headings are marked for class.

The notation is clear, separable, expansible and introceptive to over six million headings, if need be. Librarians and readers carry PR 2298 in the mind more easily than 942.421; why I don't know, but perhaps the decimal point is grit in the oil: for example, DA 86.21 will lead to more mistakes than DA 8621: or perhaps letters and figures in contiguity help the memory. The Home Office, after many tests of registration marks for motors, decided that two letters and four figures were more quickly apprehended than six figures. An LC mark is as separable as a DC mark:

    DA         942
    962        421

as expansible, because a decimal point or a Cutter mark may be added anywhere, while its range is vaster than that of any other scheme.

LC has grown rapidly in favour in the greater libraries of the U.S.A. In this country the National Library of Wales, the University Library of St. Andrews, the London School of Economics Library, the Edinburgh and Cardiff Public Libraries and the Wigan Reference Library are the most prominent adherents. Its future is guaranteed: the Library of Congress is deeply committed to it, and must therefore continue to revise, develop and print it, even in this unstable age.

> "What's not destroy'd by Time's devouring hand?
> Where's Troy, and where's the Maypole in the Strand?"

No adequate account of LC has been written. A work running to 6,300 pages demands a manual to itself. I recommend the student to consult the *Outline of the Scheme of Classes*, and to analyse one part, T Technology or J Political Science being perhaps the most enlightening for this purpose.

## RELATIONS WITH CATALOGUING AND DISPLAY

The *Subject Classification*, compiled by James Duff Brown, was published in 1906; the second edition, revised, in 1914, and a third edition, revised and enlarged by Mr. J. D. Stewart, in 1939. Its basis is wholly theoretic, for like the DC the headings and co-ordination have inappreciable literary warrant. Brown apparently forgot that he had to arrange literary record. Here he was penny-wise with headings, there prodigal in the unwanted: for example his plotting of Aeronautics is ridiculously inadequate, but he is the only classifier I know who has provided a heading for a—hiccough! The scheme is divided into five main groups: Matter, Force, Life, Mind and Record, but

> "What is matter?—Never mind.
> What is mind?—No matter,"

and grouping by subject-matter is abandoned in large areas, where individual biography, poetry, drama, essays and other forms are ordered alphabetically by names of biographees or authors, without regard to period or language, so that novels by Hughes, Hugo and Cutcliffe Hyne, plays by Shakspere, Schiller and Shaw, or biographies of Lamarck, Charles Lamb, the Princesse de Lamballe, Lancaster and Lanfranc stand together; in the average home-reading library classed on this "Subject" scheme about 60 per cent of the books, including novels, are in alphabetical disorder—the queerest arrangement imaginable. No; not the queerest. The zoologist is astonished to find horse racing and Ruff's *Guide to the Turf* among the Ungulata. The great class music, because it is a division of sound, splits Physical Science in half; the art of the composer goes for nothing! Even Dr. Johnson, who thought music the least disagreeable of noises (but he did not know anything like the horrors of our high-brow, strepitant modernists of Tin Pan Alley), would not have classed the foghorn with the flute. I wonder Brown did not put politicians and bagpipes under Pneumatics. Under Meteorology we find flying machines, blowing engines, bellows—and even time and clock making, which on his principle of making every development depend upon its origin, should belong to Astronomy Well, well!

"Pretty! in amber to observe the forms
Of hairs, or straws, or dirt, or grubs, or worms
The things we know are neither rich nor rare,
But wonder how the devil they got there."

POPE: *Prol. to Satires.*

It is applied, usually with modifications, in about sixty libraries in this country, but it has had no favour abroad, which is hardly wonderful. The best account of it is in the preface.

If I have nothing to say about the *Expansive Classification* of Cutter, the *Bibliographic Classification* of H. E. Bliss, and the *Colon Classification* of Mr. Ranganathan, it is because they have been applied in few libraries anywhere, and, excepting Cutter, which has (or had) four adherents, to none in this country.[1]

---

[1] Te failure of Cutter to win general acceptance for his admirable scheme is damentable. But he was tardy in getting it into print. He first adumbrated the scheme in a 36-pp. pamphlet entitled: *Boston Athenæum: How to Get books, with an Explanation of the New Way of Marking Books*, by C. A. Cutter (Boston, Rockwell and Churchill, 1882). In part the scheme was published in the *Library Journal*. Its systematic publication began in 1891: *Expansive Classification: pt. 1, the First Six Classifications* (Boston, 1891-93). The seventh classification was in progress in sheets in 1904. I am indebted to Mr. D. J. Haykin, Chief of the Subject Cataloguing Division, Library of Congress, for these facts, which I print here because the history of this scheme has nowhere been given accurately and fully on this side.

CHAPTER IV

4. THE PRACTICE OF CLASSIFICATION: RULES AND CODES

I

Was Melvil Dewey the first to draft rules for classing books? No matter. His rules, being the most familiar and having guided many a librarian, claim consideration, and will be viewed in the light of Mr. Hulme's main thesis.

Take his second rule first: *Content or real subject of which a book treats and not form or accidental wording of title, determines its place.* Mr. Sayers' variant of this rule is: *Class by subject, then by form, except in pure literature, where form is paramount.* Mr. Merrill is more cautious: *Class a book ordinarily by subject.*

What is the subject of a book? The answer is taken for granted, quite wrongly. It is defined as "that which forms or is chosen as the matter of thought, consideration or inquiry". Again: "that which it is the object of the author, artist or composer, to express; the scheme or idea of a work of art"; "the theme of a literary composition; what a book, a poem, etc., is about". Now all the rules agree (and librarians generally accept them) that subject-matter is to be preferred as the characteristic for classing or grouping books. And obviously any co-ordinated arrangement is easier to understand and to follow if the same characteristic or principle is applied throughout. Clearly too, more knowledge is revealed when division by subject is consistent.

Every literary or illustrated work is on a subject or subjects. I can imagine no exception. It follows that all such works, other than an inconceivable book with subject-matter *wholly* unlike that of any other book existing, may be grouped by likeness of subject-matter, their nearness (as it were) to each other being determined by degrees of homogeneity. If this argument is sound, as I believe, why should there be any exception to a class or group by subject? Is there not confused thinking as to what may be the subject of a book?

The subject of Jevons, *Elementary Lessons in Logic*, is Logic, its principal, its only theme. The subject of Brown, *House Decoration and Painting* is clear from the title, which truly describes the book. Suppose a book of Essays on Philosophy and Religion; the subjects therefore are named. How do we mark this book by DC?—040, General collected essays, 104, Essays on Philosophy, or 204, Essays on Religion? Not in 040, which is too broad a place. Then 104 or 204? Suppose the essays to be unrelated, half on Philosophy and half on Religion. We class in 104, on the principle that half a loaf is better than none; we rely upon classification and the catalogue to reveal the essays on Philosophy, and upon the catalogue to reveal those on Religion. Again of these unrelated essays if those on Religion form the greater part, the mark is 204, because it reveals more. If the essays are related, being for example on the Philosophy of Religion, 201 is the mark. Form does not affect the marking at all. We mark the book either to indicate the first part of its subject-matter, if the two parts are equal, or the principal subject, if the parts are unequal. LC, I may add, based on literary warrant, has a special place for just this kind of book.

Take the following works as examples:

*Encyclopaedia Britannica.*
Seligman, *Encyclopaedia of the Social Sciences.*

The subject of the *Britannica* is the sum of all the articles in it. An attempt at a synthesis of all knowledge, it is grouped in DC 03, General Works, and it stands comfortably beside other pantological works. But form does not enter into the arrangement. Seligman compiles in exactly the same form, but he limits his subject to Social Science. The subject-matter of the *Britannica* is nearly unlimited; that is the only difference.

We come to closer grips when we mark Sampson, *Concise Cambridge History of English Literature*. Literature is not a form, but just as much a subject as Music, Art or Painting. English literature, sometimes loosely described as a form, is a subject embodying the

## PRACTICE: RULES AND CODES

thought and expression of the minds, the spiritual and psychological history, of English men and women. Sampson's book is the history, interpretation and criticism of the *writings of the English people*. On the *dictum de omni et nullo,* or "whatever can be asserted of every member of a class can in like manner be asserted of every sub-class contained in that class", it follows that the subject of Shakspere's plays is that which he, as English author and artist, expresses; his spiritual and psychological history; he is one voice, revealing the English mind, at a particular time. It is inexplicable that this view of an artist's standing and function should be dimmed even for a moment, because it is a principle of criticism. Hegel has written: "Every work of art belongs to its time, its people, its environment."[1] Taine was of the same opinion. Therefore the logical order is:

> *English Language
>   English Writers (Literature)
>     English writers at a certain period
>       Shakspere
>         His Works
>       *Writings about him

Omitting the lines marked with an asterisk, this order is that in Sampson's *History* and in every other well-arranged history of literature; why depart from it? Mr. Sayers' variant of Dewey's rule cannot be right. He tells us to class by subject, then by form, except in pure literature, where form is paramount. But form is not paramount, even in literature, in any scheme known to me except the oddly-named *Subject Classification*. Even the DC, which lays undue emphasis on form, first differentiates Literature by language, so that all the English writers fall together. Mr. Sayers' rule is not correct in another particular. "Class by subject then by form" is a direction contrary to general practice. In many parts of every scheme Language, Country, Period, Date of publication, Relation, or Alphabetic order is preferred to form.

To show clearly how inapposite to rational grouping is the principle

[1] "So dann gehört jedes Kuntswerk seiner Zeit, seinem Volke, seiner Umgebung."—*Aesthetik*.

of division by form, let me compare the treatment of Literature in DC and LC. In the LC differentiation by language comes first, then period, afterwards author, the stages being:

| | |
|---|---|
| P | Literature |
| PR | English literature |
| PR 1804–2165 | Anglo-Norman. Early English |
| PR 1850–1954 | Chaucer |

At PR 1850 therefore are grouped the whole of Chaucer's works (originals, adaptations, translations, selections), miscellany about them (periodicals, dictionaries, indexes, etc.), biography, authorship, sources of his works, his influence, criticism and interpretation, language and style—in fact every separate printed item by or about him is grouped in one place on the shelves, while in the class catalogue, in addition, analytic entries for all the essays and articles on him, in miscellanies classed elsewhere, augment the entries for the separate items. At this point therefore we form a Chaucer Collection; and so, for every English writer, we form a collection within his period and under his name. I can imagine no more revealing arrangement.

The arrangement in DC is far less satisfactory, the steps being:

| | |
|---|---|
| 8 | Literature |
| 82 | English literature |
| 821 | English poetry |
| 821.1 | Early English poetry |
| 821.17 | Chaucer |

Consider this arrangement. All the early English poetry is together, unless it be in dramatic form; but at no one point shall we find all early English literature, for it is cut into chunks, distributed and labelled Poetry, Drama, Fiction, Essays, Letters, or Satire and Humour. Now the usual (not the only, but the most usual) approach to the study of English literature is by period, and to distribute period literature by form is contrary to the policy of grouping books for the convenience of the greater number of systematic readers. Worse is to follow. Although Chaucer's poems are grouped at 821.17, biographies of him and criticisms of his work are tucked away in 928, or in alphabetical order at B, and a book about his England, even if the greater part of it is extracted from the *Canterbury Tales*, at 942.037 or even at 914.21. It is common to observe in libraries arranged by DC that Shakspere's works are in 822.33 (Elizabethan drama) his poems in retreat at 821.39 (Elizabethan poetry, minor, yes *minor* writers) his life in a crowd at B (in alphabetical order of his name) or at 928 (Biography of Literature) and his literary landmarks in another corner at 914.248 (Warwickshire)—the oddest hide-and-seek arrangement ever conceived by any human being outside a circumlocution department. True, the DC editors are not happy that their tabulation should be more out of joint than Hamlet's times, and they have compiled author tables, by which "all material regarding author and his work is provided for under his special number, but *complete* table is *preferably* used only for authors on whom library is making a special cóllection (e.g. Shakspere, Dante and Goethe)". But why? Group Shakspere, by all means, but why not Donne, Ben Jonson, Dryden, Bunyan and other writers? In many places DC makes fun of classification!

This partiality for form (*pace* Mr. Sayers) leads to some diverting howlers. John Donne is grouped among the satirists and humorists, not as a poet!—I wonder what Donne rhapsodists think of that.

> "Come live with me, and be my love,
> And we will some new pleasures prove
> Of golden sands, and crystal brooks,
> With silken lines, and silver hooks."

John Marston, too, is a satirist, not a playwright! and he (in 827.34, Elizabethan satire and humour) is far away from Ben Jonson (in 822.34, Elizabethan drama) a greater satirist whom he attacked in his plays. As my readers hardly need more examples of these antics to convince them that classing is not segregation it will be enough to add that the Deweyite last ditchers tuck Goldsmith into four, and Meredith into five holes. I believe the reason for the muddle is doubt as to the *principal* subject-matter. The form-lovers argue that as we can't class *Hamlet* with the history of Denmark, the play has no subject. But that conclusion is absurd: Shakspere has poured his mind and art into the play, and his mind and art are the subject-matter: the subject is Shakspere. Analogously, the great picture of the surrender of Breda is a record of an historical event, but the principal theme is the mind and art of the painter; the subject is Velasquez.[1] The Pastoral Symphony illustrates country life, but the principal subject is the mind and art of the composer: it is Beethoven.

To sum up. All literary works have subject-matter. If we adopt subject as a principle of division it follows that they may be grouped by likeness of subject, and co-ordinated by degrees of homogeneity. No other principle is applicable, if we are to be consistent, until division by subject is exhausted. And as the matter of books may be on several subjects, related or unrelated, we must class by the predominating subject, the *principal theme*. Dewey's rule, therefore, isn't precise enough, and Mr. Sayers' variant of it is incorrect, illogical and misleading. The following rule is a clearer guide.

*Class every book by its principal subject from the point of view of your readers, under the heading which most nearly describes the meaning and scope of that subject. When division by subject is no longer possible, and further subdivision is desirable, divide by language, period, literary form, alphabet, date of publication, or other characteristic, choosing first that characteristic which has most significance in revealing the knowledge in the book.* This rule is extended on p. 81.

I have debated this second DC rule first because the principle by which we divide our books, once accepted, cannot be departed from without grave inconvenience.

II

Now for the first Dewey rule: *Put each book under the subject to the student of which it is most useful, unless local reasons "attract" it to a place still more useful in your library.* Mr. Sayers' variant is: *Place*

---

[1] Some time after I had written this passage I read the following in *The Note-Books of Samuel Butler* (1918), p. 107: "A great portrait is always more a portrait of the painter than of the painted. When we look at a portrait by Holbein or Rembrandt it is of Holbein or Rembrandt that we think more than of the subject of their picture."

## PRACTICE: RULES AND CODES

*a book where it will be most useful.* Dewey's rule, in fifteen words (for the qualification is nonsense: can there be a "more useful" place than the "most useful"?) shatters the argument that a subject grouping of books can be parallel with a classification of knowledge, a "true order" of the sciences, and that uniformity of marking in all libraries is possible, probable or desirable. But nobody denies the necessity of a "most useful place" rule, properly understood. The judge of the most useful place is the librarian who has worked among the readers for whom the library, general or special, is intended. Can anybody apply this rule, or formulate any code for classing books (about this point more later), unless he has actually served the people coming to his library? Of course, he cannot. The rule emancipates from thraldom to any scheme; it allows, urges, compels adjustment of any part for the benefit of readers. English literature is arranged for greater convenience first in periods, then by author, all the works (whether his own or other people's) revealing his life, mind and art standing together: familiarity with readers teaches me that this co-ordination is perfect, and the rule allows me to adopt it, whatever the DC tables require. Whether Beethoven expresses himself in concerto or quartette is of secondary importance: experience persuades me that his works should be together, no other arrangement will do, and the rule permits it, whatever the DC tables may ordain. (Rule or no rule, I should think first of the convenience of my readers; but for the moment I put myself in place of the student learning these rules and of the tiro applying them).

But is this rule drafted with enough particularity? For donkey's years the DC has printed two rules side by side: (1) Put each book under the subject to the student of which it is most useful, and (2) Real subject of which a book treats . . . determines its place. The two rules don't hang together. Sense can be made of them only by expressing (1) differently. If the mark—for what else is meant by the word "place"?—is determined by the principal theme of a book, how can there be any more useful mark? What Dewey was trying to express in (1) is this: Although a book must be given the mark for its principal theme, a subject-group, the relation of which to other subject-groups is debatable, may be co-ordinated in any progression that is convenient to the people studying it; in other words, the groups generally used together must stand together. Dewey could have meant nothing else. For example, he could not have meant this, as some of his admirers seem to think: "Put a book, when you are in doubt about its principal subject, in the most useful place"; because doubt about subject prevents certainty about the most useful place. Clearly these two irreconcilable rules have worried Mr. Sayers, who has given up the conundrum. Therefore *he* orders us to class by subject. Then, reflecting, questions of interrelation and point of view begin to weigh with him, and he says with aplomb: *Place a book where it will be most useful,* which is much like ordering one-way traffic in a street, and then telling motorists to do what they darn well please!

As I have said, the question which the words "most useful" beg is not prompted by subject classing to the limit, and by the coherent grouping of subjects: such methods are never inconvenient to readers. The doubt arises only about the order in which unrelated or doubtfully related groups are best arranged to reveal the knowledge in them to a particular community of readers. We determine this order by experiment. Here, for example, are books which are not borrowed. Why? Is the selection right? Yes; as good as we can make it. Are the books shelved in the right *place* to attract attention, not to be overlooked? (No; I am not wandering. My subject, from beginning to end, is display. The moment a book is classed and shelved it is on exhibition. *The books in an open-shelf library form an exhibition, and we try to give all of them, at once or in turn, the greatest possible prominence.*) Very well then; is the exhibition-stance well placed? Yes; *no* books are in dark coops or obscure alcoves or on shelves before which we must grovel, or up to which we must CAT-BURGLE. (This question, by the way, rarely can be answered with the word "Yes", though bad shelf arrangement is a grand way of hiding books. Here I answer affirmatively only to raise the question and get rid of it.)

Content with our selection and stance we then ask: Are the subject groups arranged in the order most useful to the majority of readers? Since 1898, when my chief put the third edition of DC into my hands and told me to "go to it", I have been experimenting to resolve

## PRACTICE: RULES AND CODES

doubts about grouping. I have room only for three of the greater examples. I have discovered (1) that the grouping of (a) Biology, Zoology, Botany, Agriculture with Horticulture, and of (b) Language with Literature are the most useful *to all classes of readers*, and (2) that the grouping of (a) Electricity and Magnetism with Electrical engineering and (b) Chemistry with Chemical technology are the most useful *in industrial communities*. Mr. Bliss writes: "The most adequate classifications are, generally speaking, those that are most consistent with the organization of knowledge relevant to the interests in view." Mr. Sayers' opinion is similar: "A satisfactory classification is an arrangement of things in the order in which those who know most about them habitually think of them." In other words Messrs. Bliss and Sayers abandon uniformity, and throw all "true orders" into the dustbin, together with DC, SC and all conventional schemes not based on literary warrant. They could not have done a better thing for the healthy future of classification.

I have now cleared the ground to extend my rule, which I give in tabular form, so that I may mark with letters the parts which will be referred to when I consider Dewey's other rules:

(A) *Class every book by its principal subject from the point of view of your readers*

    (B) *under the heading which most clearly describes the meaning and scope of that subject.*

(C) *When division by subject is no longer possible, and further subdivision is desirable,*

    (D) *divide by language, period, literary form, alphabet, date of publication, or other characteristic, choosing first that characteristic which has most significance in revealing the knowledge in a book.*

(E) *and when, by this process, all the books have been grouped in the order determined by the scheme of classification,*

    (F) *vary or adjust that order as may be necessary to display the books to the best advantage of your own readers.*

## MANUAL OF BOOK CLASSIFICATION

This one precise rule fills the place, not only of Dewey's first two rules, but of all his rules, apart from (10), which is a check on procedure rather than a rule of procedure, referred to in the next section.

A sentence or two on those parts of the rule lettered (D) and (F). (D) Which characteristic, of those enumerated, has the most significance in revealing the knowledge in a book? A few examples should make the answer clear.

| Book | Hierarchy of Marks | Comment |
| --- | --- | --- |
| 1 History of England, 1837–1900 | History, Country, Period, Author | All books on the civil history of the Victorian era are exhibited together |
| 2 Victorian Statesmen: Short Biographies | History, Country, Period, Form (biography), Author | Collected political biographies are exhibited in a group following the formal Victorian histories |
| 3 Victorian Scientists: Biog. Essays | Science, History, Period, England, Form, (biography), Author | Science books for this period are exhibited together, the biography supporting formal history |
| 4 Victorian Chemists: Biographies | Science, Chemistry, History, Period, England, Form (biography), Author. | All history of chemistry is grouped by period and country. *Note:* in 3 and 4 period takes precedence of country, as the science of a period "hangs together" better than that of a country |
| 5 Howells, *Italian Journeys* | Italy, Description, Date of journey, Author | All the books on Italian travel of the same period stand together |

PRACTICE: RULES AND CODES

| Book | Hierarchy of Marks | Comment |
|---|---|---|
| 6 Aeroplane Design | Science, Mechanical engineering, Heat Engines, Aeronautics, Aeroplane design, Date of publication | After division by subject is exhausted, the next preferable characteristic is publication date, this arrangement, on shelves and in class catalogue, revealing latest knowledge |
| 7 History of American Literature | English Literature, American, History, Author | Author takes precedence of date of publication, even were division by that characteristic necessary, as the critic is more important than the period of the criticism |
| 8 Critique of Shakspere in German | English literature, Period, Shakspere, Criticism, Language | All German critiques are exhibited together |

Other examples will be found on pages 42–3 and 132. These illustrations probably will be enough for my purpose. Common sense, rather than rule, determines the order after dividing by subject is completed. The orders above, by the way, are not always those followed in classification schemes. I add that the minute subdividing illustrated above is desirable only in a reference or a special library.

(F) Variation or adjustment of order to display knowledge in books to the best advantage of readers, is considered fully in Chapter V, pp. 90–114.

Let me run through Dewey's chief rules:

(3) *Always remember that the question is not "where will one*

83

*probably look for a certain book*", but "*under what subject is the book of greatest value?*". Unnecessary: covered by A.

(4) *Give every book most specific number which will contain it.* Unnecessary: see B. Limiting the number of digits in a mark is a bad error in classing a developing library.

(5) "*Predominant tendency*" *or obvious purpose of a book usually decides its number at once. Still a book often treats of two or more subjects. In such cases put it where it will be most useful.* Unnecessary: covered by A.

(6) *If two subjects have distinct page limits, generally class under first and make analytic [catalogue] entry under second; but if second is decidedly more important or much greater in bulk, class under that, with analytic entry under first.* Unnecessary: covered by A.

(7) *Consider not only scope and tendency of each book, but also nature and specialties of each library.* Unnecessary: see F.

(8) *If a book treats of a majority of the sections of any division, give it division number, instead of most important section number with added [catalogue] entries . . .*" I don't fully understand this rule. The interpretation seems to depend upon the weight given to the words "most important". As far as I understand it the rule is covered by A and B. (Dewey's example is as follows: "Class a volume on light, heat and sound under head most fully discussed". LC, based on literary warrant, has a heading for these three subjects treated together—QC 220). The grammar of this rule seems a little rickety. If the book goes in the division are added entries not recommended? The editors should alter this rule.

These examples indicate that all Dewey's rules, with the exception of the "check on procedure" rule, are incorporated in the comprehensive rule on page 81. Note the lumber we have got rid of. It has been shown that nothing but an accidental relation can exist between the co-ordination of books and the "true order" of the sciences; that like books may be grouped and co-ordinated with like groups, but anything resembling exact classing, as that word is defined in logic, is impossible. These statements being accepted, one simple rule has been formulated for applying marks to books. Our American friends, at one time, were eager students of "true orders" and logical principles

## PRACTICE: RULES AND CODES

of classification: Dr. Richardson especially: but they dropped it years ago, and Margaret Mann's *Introduction to Cataloguing and the Classification of Books*, Grace Kelley's *Classification of Books*, and other manuals, contain no trace of this early pedantry, which, superficially treated, is of no practical and little educational value. However, the conservative Education Committee of the Library Association still compels exam candidates to mull irrelevant theory around in minds which would be better employed in acquiring bibliographical knowledge.

### III

Dewey's master check on procedure, so-called rule 10, is thus stated: *To secure uniformity, make for future reference full notes of all difficulties and decisions, for it is more important to put books on same subject* together *than to put them in a more nearly absolutely correct place.*

How *can* there be "a more nearly absolutely correct place" than with other books on the same principal theme? The Editors of the DC should not allow their respect for Melvil Dewey to hinder them from clearing up obscurity.

The notes of difficulties and decisions should take two forms.

First, the subject-index. Every library should have a subject and name index to its own arrangement of books, for the index to the classification isn't specific enough. The new edition of Edinburgh's Subject-Index, now awaiting print at the end of the war, runs to 65,600 entries in 32 volumes of foolscap manuscript, not counting supplements for departmental libraries. It is an index much like the relative index to DC, except that

(1) the entries are narrowly specific, e.g.,
    Greenock, Old West Kirk                                XDA 1722
    Grosmont Castle, Monmouthshire                         DA 680.19 G
    Growth, form and, biology                              QH 511
    Guardian and ward, Scot. law, case of Sir Robert
        Gordon                                             XK
    Guides (Queen's Own Corps of Guides)                   DS 442.5

(2) names of biographees, authors and music composers (as subjects), places (included in broad headings) and other names are included.

## MANUAL OF BOOK CLASSIFICATION

| | |
|---|---|
| Green, Capt. Thomas, master of the *Worcester*, 1705 | XDA 805 |
| Grimes, Absalom, Confederate mail runner | E 467.1 G68 |
| Shakspere, William, dramatist | PR 2750–3112 |

The classification index is the key to the subject divisions in it. The library index is the key to the subjects, personal and otherwise, in the classed stock: a subject not represented isn't indexed; a more specific subject than that represented by the classmark assigned to it is indexed. For example here is a comparison of the number of index entries in DC (thirteenth edition) and in the Edinburgh Libraries index under the following headings:

|  | DC | EPL |
|---|---|---|
| India | 7 | 156 |
| Insurance | 53 | 149 |
| Shakspere | 1 | 176 |

The comparison is not intended as a criticism of the DC index, which only reveals the headings. The library index reveals both the headings and the books under them. It follows that any highly specific subject-index to a library's collection is also an index to the classer's placings and decisions. No better preventive of inconsistent classing than this internal index has been devised.

And pray don't index on cards. Write entries on foolscap on every fourth line, and insert new entries in the spaces. It takes less time to re-write congested pages than to fiddle with a card index, not to speak of the bother of getting up from one's chair frequently to consult it, whereas the foolscap sheets, if filed in grip binders, may be kept on the classer's table.

In addition to this internal index every library should have a code for classers, as well as a code for cataloguers. Mr. W. S. Merrill has compiled a *Code for Classifiers: Principles Governing the Consistent Placing of Books in a System of Classification* (second edition, A.L.A., 1939)—an excellent model to follow. It isn't necessary to consult a code often, and as the ordinary $5 \times 3$ card is too small to take long directions, of which there are many, I recommend sheaves. Here are typical entries on sheaf slips:—

PRACTICE: RULES AND CODES

---

PERIOD

WORKS COVERING MORE THAN ONE HEADING OF THE TABLES

Class under the heading in which the earliest date of the substantive narrative is included.

Macaulay, *History*—DA 450, the intro. to his detailed narrative being ignored

MacCarthy, *Hist. of the Georges*—DA 498

Bateson, *Med. England*, 1066–1350—DA 175

---

The direction follows the practice of UDC, in which the actual dates are the subdividing marks:

| | |
|---|---|
| 9(42) "1485: 1939" | England, history, 1485–1939 |
| 9(42) "1660: 1837" | ,,   ,,   1660–1837 |
| 9(42) "1914.08.04" | ,,   ,,   8 Aug. 1914 |
| 9(42) "1927" | ,,   ,,   1927 |

The word Heading on this slip, and throughout the Code where it is unqualified, means class, division, subdivision, section or subsection.

---

COMMON SUBDIVISIONS
DATES OF PUBLN

SCIENTIFIC WORKS

After classing fully by subject (incl. period in the case of historical works) use Biscoe numbers to mark dates of publication of first editions.

Makins, *Concise Flora of Britain*, 1939—QK 306 T9

---

A like slip is necessary under the caption TECHNICAL WORKS: Durney, *Machine Shop Practice*, 1941, being marked TJ 1160 U1, in which U1 = 1941.

These slips are arranged in alphabetical order of the catchwords at the top right-hand corners in the above examples.

It may be asked: Why a Code if the specific subject and name index records the decisions? The answer is simple: while the index records decisions it is not a reliable guide to parallel cases. We class

87

## MANUAL OF BOOK CLASSIFICATION

a book on *The Influence of the Cinema upon Reading* under Reading, and index so:

> Reading, cinema's influence upon
> Cinema, influence upon reading

Any other book on this topic will receive the same mark if the classer refers (as he should) to the internal index. But when again he has a book on the influence of one thing upon another, the index gives him a clue only if he can remember one of the "influence" books already classed. The Code however is a faithful guide. For example (I quote from Merrill):

> RELATION
> When a book treats of more than one subject, or of the relation existing between two or among several subjects: Determine what this relation is and class according to the following rules.
> (*a*) If the work treats of two factors, one of which is represented as acting upon or influencing the other: Class under the subject *influenced or acted upon* . . .
> (*b*) If one factor is represented as the source, cause or formative agency of the other: Class under the factor so derived or resulting . . .

And so on through (*c*), (*d*) and (*e*).

The Code also gives general directions which cannot be indexed or recorded in the tables. I have already given one example (not by Mr. Merrill) which requires scientific and technical works to be arranged in order of publication dates. Here is another. Mr. Merrill's *Code* advises as follows:

> EDUCATION PSYCHOLOGY
> Class in education, if system permits.

This is a good example of a direction relating to the co-ordination of groups. I choose it, also, because it suggests two comments. (1) "If system permits"! But it should permit. If Education is the place most convenient to readers, there it must go; the system which prevents our doing so must be altered *by the user*. We cannot be bound by any system. (2) Is Mr. Merrill's direction right? My experience

## PRACTICE: RULES AND CODES

is that the people who read Psychology are much more interested in Educational psychology than educators. The point is arguable, and I refer to it only because it indicates that nobody should class books who has not served readers in person.

Mr. Merrill's *Code* is valuable for a number of uses, three of which I will note:

(1) Written with precision and clarity, it may be adopted as a Code by any librarian who marks in an interleaved copy the directions he prefers, when alternatives are given.

(2) It may be followed as a model by a librarian who prefers to compile an internal Code free from alternatives and qualifications.

(3) It may be studied with great advantage by classers engaged in practical work.

Here are two entries from it:

> QUANTUM THEORY
> Works on the quantum theory of the atom: Class in physics. E.g. (1) *The Quantum Theory of the Atom*. By George Birtwistle (Cambridge, Eng., 1926). (2) *Term Structure of the Non-Collinear Triatomic Molecule of type $X_2Y$*. By Alexander V. Bushkovitch (Philadelphia, 1934).
>
> Examples cited are classed: (1) by LC in *quantum theory* (QC 174) under physics; by DC in theory of physics (530.1). (2) by LC in *triatomic molecule* (QC 174.5) under physics; by DC as in (1).
>
> GEOPHYSICAL PROSPECTING
> Works on geophysical methods of prospecting, especially for oil: Class in economic geology—(John Crerar Library). E.g. *The Principles and Practice of Geophysical Prospecting*. By the Imperial Geophysical Experimental Survey (Cambridge, 1931).
>
> LC classes *geophysical prospecting* (TN 269) under mineral industries. DC classes it in mining engineering (622.1) or according to the point of view—(DC editors).

Together the internal index and the code, in which all decisions and general directions are registered, cannot fail to ensure consistency of marking, if the classers refer to both before using the tables, the index always and the code when necessary.

# B. DISPLAY FOR PARTICULAR PURPOSES

CHAPTER V

## 1. THE HOME READING LIBRARY AS AN EXHIBITION OF BOOKS

I

CLASSIFICATION of our kind being a mechanical time-saving device for the discovery of knowledge in literary works, it follows that any classed library is an exhibition; even one to which the public are not admitted, though in it knowledge is revealed only to the staff. A classed open shelf library however, from one end to the other, is nothing but an exhibition. Think of it so, and the point of view is quite fresh; if classing is display, if the formal array of books is but an exhibition, why may we not copy the methods of museums, art galleries, shops and stores to heighten its effect?

We can say of many British librarians, as Leibnitz said of his famed monads: "They have no windows through which anything might come into them or go out of them." If this quotation looks aggressive, why not?—it is a cut and thrust at our Blimpishness, our unctuous complacency with things as they are, and our conviction that nothing but money and more money, not brains, forethought, hard work and enterprise, is required to improve a grand service! Everything new has met with stubborn obstruction, and display, like the classing of which it is an extension, was bound to have its opponents. I am surprised however to observe that Mr. J. D. Stewart, a go-ahead librarian, wobbles on the subject. He writes (*L.A.R.*, 4th ser. V. 1: 353): "Kept within reasonable limits, the segregation and special display of selected groups of books has extremely good results, and I imagine that it is now employed in most progressive libraries. It is directed chiefly to the casual reader, who does not mind very much what he reads, but who likes to find something pleasing with the minimum of trouble. If carried to extremes, however, it is the negation of librarianship. There is little use in classification, cataloguing, or in any of the methods of systematic library arrangement, if too many of the books are taken from their ordered places for the purpose of being exhibited in bins, display racks, or ranged upon occasional tables, just because they happen to be hot from the press or garbed in bright colours." He jumps in, let it be noted, with that question-begging phrase, "within reasonable limits" on his lips, but what limits are reasonable? After this cautious beginning he tells us that the extremely—extremely, mind!—good results of display, "now employed in most progressive libraries"—progressive no doubt within reasonable limits!—consist in luring the casual reader, "who does not mind what he reads, but who likes to find something pleasing [in spite of his indifference?] with the minimum of trouble". If Mr. Stewart does me the honour of reading this book he will learn that display is no more directed to the casual reader than is the co-ordinated array of books. Anybody who doesn't care a hang what he reads will pick up from any corner a book he fancies. But why is our critic snooty about casual readers? By pondering a moment he will realize that even a method "directed chiefly to the casual reader" can also have "extremely good results", for have not young "casuals" been led to study merely by having access to books? Is it not the librarian's business to give prominence to his best books? Mr. Stewart's "ain dear land" might not have had a national poet if Burns's father had not got together an armful of books. And remember John Clare with Bible and Prayer-Book, the old volume of essays with no title, the manual on farming, *Robin Hood's Garland*, *The Scotch Rogue*, *Robinson Crusoe*, the sixpenny romances, and the penny sheets of Robert Tannahill and other song-writers. It isn't everybody who begins at college; some begin in the public library, some at the penny bookstall Why this contempt for other than pukka students and novel-eaters —yet I suppose the casual reader who would like to begin on something, but doesn't quite know what, will always be derided.

Again, if Mr. Stewart reads me, or visits a "most progressive" library—Baltimore, for example—he will learn that books are not displayed "just because they happen to be hot from the press or garbed in bright colours". Show copies which are fresh and not dog's-eared. Choose bright colours for leather bindings instead of poorhouse uniforms. Give out new books in publishers' jackets to protect the cloth covers. Only indurated tories would prefer the humdrum and the drab. But "books hot from the press"—well, let Mr. Stewart refer to the list on pp. 159–61.

But Mr. Stewart unwittingly indicates his irrational thinking when he says that "if carried to extremes", display is "the negation of librarianship. There is little use in classification . . . cataloguing, or . . . systematic library arrangement, if too many of the books are taken from their ordered places" for exhibition.

"Nae cauld faint-hearted doubtings tease him",

yet in the paragraph before the passage I have quoted Mr. Stewart advocates relegating "faded rows" (why *should* they be faded?) of "indispensable but lesser-used (*sic*) volumes" to internal stores. "*No great hardships, and many advantages,* result from this plan of a *selected display* (oh! Mr. Stewart!—my italics, of course) for the shelves to which readers have access, and the transfer of the rest of the stock to a store from which it can be obtained when required." Then again, from the home reading library, about one-third of the books are always lent. Now, Mr. Stewart, "there is little use in classification, cataloguing, or in any of the methods of systematic library arrangement", if faded rows of "indispensable but lesser-used books" are in store, if readers have access only to a *selected display*, and if besides they are allowed to co-operate in this "negation of librarianship" by borrowing books for home reading. Let Mr. Stewart look upon classification as display, and upon an open home reading library as an exhibition of books, and then all his difficulties (which are imaginary) will vanish, and his prejudices (which are arbitrary) will be overturned.

This book exhibition is in a number of parts, a few or all of which may be present:

(1) The formal display

(2) Methods of enlivening formal display

(3) Books from the formal display
    (i) re-grouped to exhibit distributed relatives
    (ii) lifted into greater prominence
(4) Interior showcases
(5) Reference books

## II

In the early days of open shelves the bookcases were generally a little more than seven feet high. Boards or cards, framed or unframed, bearing the names of the principal classes, and here and there tables of divisions, were cocked up on the tops of the bookcases, or hung from them, looking as if they had been thought of after the cases were made. Indeed the furniture of early open libraries was often adapted from that built for indicator compounds. Even later, when bookcases a little over 6 ft. in height became more common, the guiding was both too finikin and too general to be effective. Librarians played around with wee shelf labels, in tin or xylonite holders, the lettering ungainly, shy and retiring. Even when architects lend a hand they fail, because, whether men of genius or just competent, they expect readers to carry binoculars. To be frank I don't think guiding has improved in late years. No library here, none I have seen in America, reaches a high standard in labelling an exhibition of books; I haven't attained it myself. Either we are afraid to let ourselves go, or we knuckle under to the aesthetic timidity or illegibility of architects; we uphold the dignity of public buildings and let readers down, or are obstructed by unimaginative committeemen.

Let me try to put myself in place of a reader borrowing for the first time—and make a few assumptions. Well stocked with good books, the library bears no resemblance to a central depôt for a chain of twopenny or county libraries. The books are grouped to the limit of the subject principle. The reader cannot follow the arrangement, cannot fairly be expected to learn it, and perhaps is better not to try. He has no Virgil to conduct him through the nether regions, for the staff are too few in number to offer guidance. Now what help ought he to expect in a library, where ordinarily the rows of books are packed with hardly a break in their flat run?

Look elsewhere, and we may get a hint. A customer entering a big store is directed to the lift and told the number of the floor carrying the article he wants; he is reminded of this direction by the lift attendant who intones the main classes of goods at each floor; and as he walks out of the lift he plainly sees the stalls, each with a whacking sign (for it *does* hit you) to tell him the goods it bears. And here he is at the right stall "like a lamb dumb before his shearer".

Now how is the reader to be got to the Pierian spring, to the sacred oak of the golden fleece, or to the right book on rearing a pig?

(1) Detach main classes or groups of classes, if practicable. For example, here are eight groups:

| General Works . Reference Books | Art . Music |
| --- | --- |
| Philosophy . Religion | Language . Literature |
| Social Science | History . Travel |
| Science . Useful Arts | Novels |

If one of the main groups is unduly large, because the library has a bias, make other detachments: for example, Mechanical Engineering, English Literature, British History, and other groups which are big enough. A library may be divided into a number of groups of nearly equal size, if the names of the principal classes are ignored; for example, drop the class heading Literature, and use

| General Literature |
| --- |
| Foreign Literature |
| English Literature |

Mark off the small special departments so formed by alleys in

## HOME READING LIBRARY

which tables are ranged at intervals. At Baltimore the departments are in roomy alcoves, an arrangement not practicable in cramped libraries. Too much regularity isn't homely and inviting, but clumps of bookcases, with alleys between them, break up the library conveniently for guiding, and significantly to readers.

(2) Mark each detachment with a whacking signboard; the letters being artistic in style (Trajan Roman will do) but vulgar in size. Vary the size with the area of the room; in a big apartment have ten-, but nowhere less than six-inch letters. Harmonize the colours of the board and the letters with the ground they will be seen against in natural and artificial light: the conditions being unknown particular suggestions are futile. In a twilight apartment illuminate the signs.

(3) Let the bookcases be not more than 6 ft. 6 in. in height so that the large signs, all of which should face the counter, may be seen from the entrance.

As noted above, personal guidance is unfortunately not a part of the organization. I have used these big signs only in one library. There, the alcoves being deep and the bookcases 7 ft. 6 in. in height, too much matter was required on each sign, so that the letters were not more than four inches tall. As the signs had to be read with the light behind them, by day and night, I framed opaline glass, and left the letters white and translucent on a ground of black. Though too small, they were effective enough to convince me that big signs are better. I now regret not using more of them, but I was a long time before I concluded that they were needful, first because I depended on personal guidance, which I encouraged, and which might have been neglected, when, with a careless nod towards a big sign, librarians might leave readers to their own devices: the public service is a prolific begetter of jacks-in-office.

What signs ought the reader to find at the division to which he has been guided?

(4) Letter each bay (tier) of four or five shelves. A double-sided bookcase 6 ft. 3 in. long, with two 3 ft. bays on each elevation, will have four signs, or five or six if there are one or two shelved ends or haffits (see p 109). The lettering of each bay ought to be definite; as we class a book under the most specific heading, so above the bay

MANUAL OF BOOK CLASSIFICATION

we paint the heading which indicates, with particularity, its contents. For example, here are the subjects painted above eight adjoining bays which contain a part of Religion.

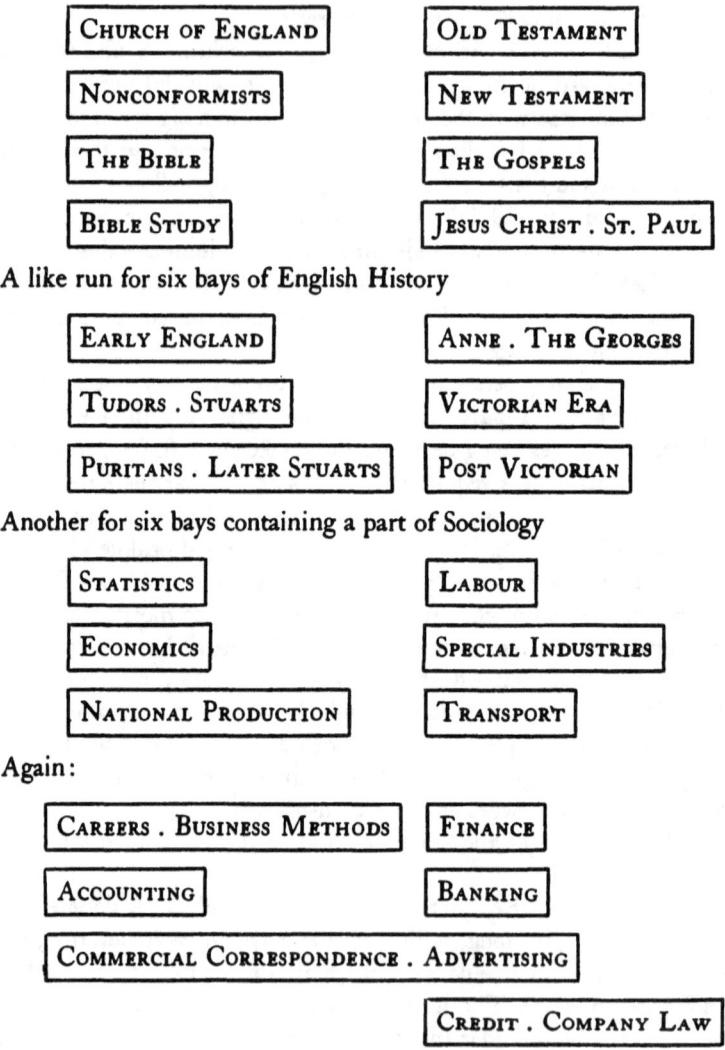

A like run for six bays of English History

Another for six bays containing a part of Sociology

Again:

*Photo: C. S. Minto*

## ILLUMINATED DOUBLE-SIDED BOOK SHOWCASE
Fountainbridge, Edinburgh

*Facing p.* 96 (*see p.* 111)

## HOME READING LIBRARY

I have given other examples of specific guiding in my book on *Special Librarianship*, p. 248. My object in citing a number of examples is to underline clearly the need of definite headings, and to express the opinion that a library cannot be adequately stocked if like detail is impossible in it.

Be plain as well as specific. Prefer ANIMAL LIFE or ANIMALS to ZOOLOGY; STUDY OF MAN to ANTHROPOLOGY, ETHNOLOGY or ETHNOGRAPHY; FARM AND GARDEN to AGRICULTURE AND HORTICULTURE; WEATHER to METEOROLOGY; WARFARE to MILITARY SCIENCE. If groups are small choose plain and specific terms rather than general; INSECTS . BIRDS . ANIMALS, not ZOOLOGY; HUGO . BALZAC . DUMAS, not FRENCH LITERATURE, 19TH CENTURY. The homelier terms are more attractive, and usually briefer.

Movable bay guides are sometimes preferred, but, if large enough, and even when of uniform length, they cannot be changed without scarring the bookcase. Lettered specifically, they rarely describe accurately the contents of the bays to which they are moved, because books are generally re-arranged to accommodate added stock. On the other hand lettering painted on the bay panel may be cleaned off, and the new headings written in at moderate cost, which is well repaid by the more uniform result.

Changes will be less frequent if no lettering is painted until the library has "settled down", about nine months after its opening. Arrange and re-arrange the books until you are content with the look and allotment of them. Write each trial heading on a card 2 ft. by 9 in. Bend the card at right angles 3 in. from one of the sides. Pin the 3-in. part to the bookcase top and let the 6-in. part hang in front of the cornice without any fixing; so the front of the case will not be marked. Allow the trial cards to remain for any period extending well into the reading season, that is for not more than nine months. By this time the proportion of each class and division likely to be on the shelves at any time will be known. Then re-arrange the books, putting in each bay a number as nearly equal as the run of the grouping permits. Choose a signwriter with care, and instruct him to paint letters not less than $2\frac{1}{2}$ in. tall, in a form drawn by the architect, and approved for legibility by the librarian.

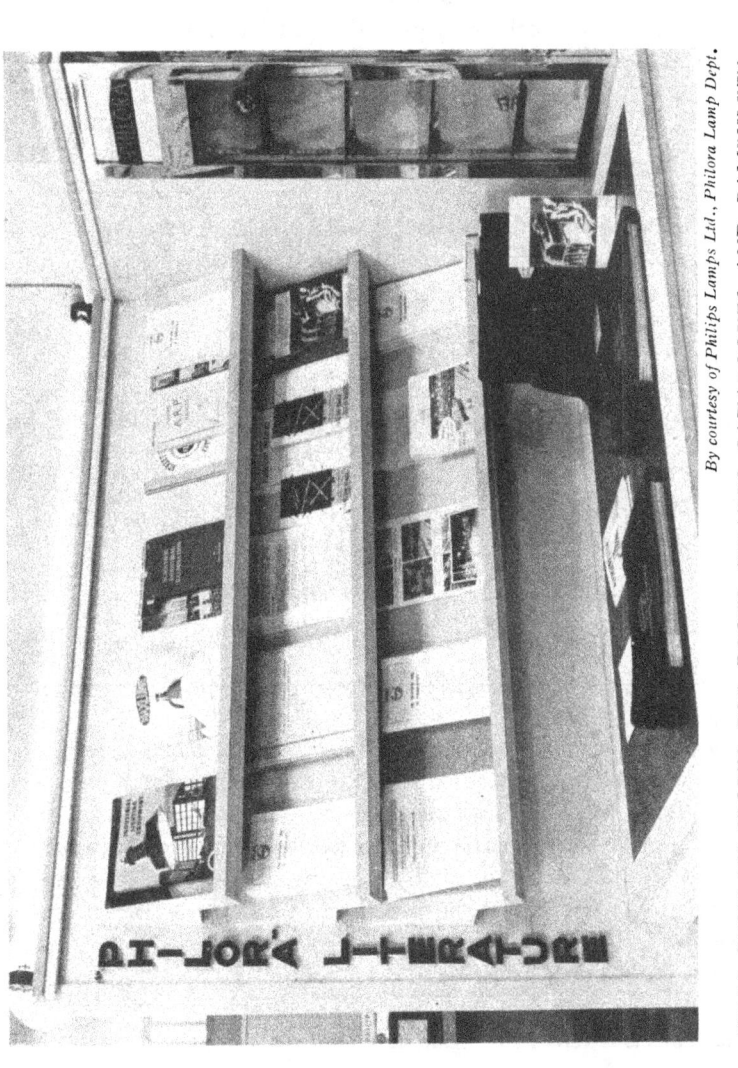

*By courtesy of Philips Lamps Ltd., Philora Lamp Dept.*

WALL DISPLAY SLOPES FOR BOOKS, TRADES CATALOGUES AND PAMPHLETS

With lights under slopes the effect of this form of display is enhanced

*Facing p. 97 (see pp. 103, 134)*

## MANUAL OF BOOK CLASSIFICATION

If the cornice of the bookcase is 8 in. the bay panel will be about 5 in. wide. In what colours should the panel and the letters be painted? I have tried a number of combinations:

| Finish of Bookcase | Colour of Panel | Colour of letters | Effect |
|---|---|---|---|
| Pale (not golden) oak | Polished mahogany | Leaf gold | Bold, rich |
| ,, | Black | ,, | ,, |
| * ,, | Apple green | Biscuit | Gay, for cold room |
| ** ,, | Iceland poppy | Sunshine | Colourful, brilliant |
| ,, | Leather, Tan Brown | Tussore | Clear, cold |
| * ,, | Marine green | Iceland poppy | Gay, clear |
| **Dark oak | Iceland poppy | Sunshine | Gay, rich |
| ,, | Dark oak | Leaf gold | Bold, rich |
| * ,, | Sunshine | Iceland poppy | Bold, cheerful |
| ,, | Primrose | Imperial red | Bold, dignified |
| *Dark mahogany | Dark mahogany | Iceland poppy, w. gilt outline to letters | Bold, rich, expensive |
| ,, | ,, | Leaf gold | Bold, rich |
| ,, | Orange | Leather | Bold, gay |
| ,, | Pale blue | Imperial red | Clear, cold |
| * ,, | Straw | Apple green | Clear, cheerful |

In order that the colours may be identified I use the names given to the Petragloss paints of Messrs. John Line and Sons. Refer to the Petragloss card when choosing colours by other makers. All the above colours are glossy, and permanent in outdoor light. The combinations marked with an asterisk are highly recommended, for they are gay and colourful, while the letters, if painted in good body colour, are legible. Iceland poppy is a grand flame colour, but only Petragloss make the shade which is just right.

The contents of a bay need not be limited strictly to the books on the subjects lettered. For example if three bays are allotted to

| Insects | Birds | Fishes |
|---|---|---|

## HOME READING LIBRARY

the books on INSECTS may run over into the BIRDS bay; it is enough that the majority of the books named are below the right sign.

The reader, directed by the big signs and the bay guides, now stands before the books on his subject, and if his interest in them is general he makes his choice without more ado. But if he wants a book on a highly specific part of the subject he refers, not to the classification index, which reveals only the table headings, but to the library's own index, which reveals the topic dealt with in any one book (see p. 85). Put the index before him in every corner; fit to each bookcase haffit a tiny slope bearing a copy of it. Wanting a book on the coalfields of Kent he turns up in the index either KENT, COALFIELDS, or COAL, KENT and obtains the classmark. If the marks upon the books are plain he quickly withdraws the work he needs. After a Heath Robinsonnade pilgrimage in search of the best method of marking books I am satisfied that the only clear and tidy way is to number them, as a binder does, in gold. The tools are not expensive, and the handling of them may be learned quickly by any deft man or woman. Written tags, painted and even stylo'd numbers remind me of the ticketed articles in cluttered shops in poor quarters. Down with Tags!

The reader now has the book he wants. At home, opening it at chapter one, he may find a printed list of other books on the subject of his book or on related subjects. Any list intended to introduce a reader to other books than that he has borrowed, or to books not on the shelves at the time of his visit, should be printed on a slip or leaflet which may be "tipped into" a crown octavo or any larger book. Librarians rarely put into their books these correlative lists, which are of capital value as publicity, though for a century or more publishers have printed similar lists, either in the advertisement pages or on the jackets of books. But publishers are business men, not public officials; however, I must refrain: *de mortuis nil nisi bonum*, and I myself have left undone those things which I ought to have done.

An earlier form of the liaison or collateral list, but less comprehensive in scope, is that given in annotations. Here are two examples from *The Reader's Guide*, at one time issued by the Wallasey Public Libraries:

JAMES, WILLIAM. Meaning of Truth: sequel to Pragmatism. 1909.

The pragmatist philosophy may be summed up thus: "When once the question has arisen concerning some actual belief 'Is it a true or a false belief?' how do we in fact decide the question? The answer of pragmatism is that if the belief furthers the purpose which led us to ask the question, it is regarded as a 'true' belief; if it fails to further the purpose it is regarded as a 'false' belief." Or in other words: "True ideas are those that we can assimilate, validate, corroborate and verify. False ideas are those that we cannot." For a review of Pragmatism see *Edinburgh Review*, v. 209-363 (R Z296). Other books by Prof. James are: *Varieties of Religious Experience* (E B27); *The Will to Believe* (E B11X25J); *Human Immortality* (E B45A381); *Talks to Teachers on Psychology* (E L34) and *A Pluralistic Universe* (E B11X25J).

While the above example illustrates references to books by the same author, that following draws attention to like books by other authors:

WALLACE, H. F. Stalks Abroad: account of Sport obtained during a two-years' tour of the World. *Illus*. 1908.

*Author* is a fellow of the Zoological Soc. *Subject:* Experiences in the U. States, British Columbia and the Rockies, N. Zealand, Japan, India and British East Africa; out of 266 pp. nearly 100 deal with the last country. *Treatment:* Popular. Well illus. Books of a similar kind are: Storey's *Hunting and Shooting in Ceylon* (S W51); Kirby's *In Haunts of Wild Game* (E Y39); Neumann's *Elephant-Hunting in East Equatorial Africa* (E Y34); Baldwin's *African Hunting* (E Y41); Schilling's *With Flashlight and Rifle* (E Y30); Brown's *Stray Sport* (E N58); Selous' *Travel and Big Game* (E N58); and Dickinson's *Big Game Shooting on the Equator* (S Y34).

When the reader wants a book by an author known to him by name, his approach is by way of catalogue. Having turned up the entry he has to find the book, not by the *name* but by the *mark* of its subject. Therefore on every bookcase indicate plainly, in letters about 6 in. high, the first and last classmarks in it. Adaptable number signs are particularly convenient. If DC is employed have the numbers 0 to 9 printed in black on cartridge paper. Cut the numbers out as required, mount them on fairly thick cards of uniform size, and arrange them in the necessary order in a framed slot which juts well above the top of the bookcase

| 8 | 2 | 0 | - | 8 | 2 | 5 |

The dotted lines indicate that each number is on a separate card, but

## HOME READING LIBRARY

the numbers may be cut out and pasted side by side on one strip of card. If LC or SC is applied letters must be printed to use with the numbers.

Here is another method of guiding a reader to the name or mark of a subject. Letter or number the bays arbitrarily, 1, 2, 3 and so on. Draw a plan of the layout of the bookcases, and mark these letters or numbers upon it. Print on a card a clear block of the plan above or beside an alphabetic index of the principal subjects; and when the books are arranged, neatly print the letters or numbers of the bays containing the subjects after the names of them in this alphabetic index. Frame and hang a number of these directory plans where they cannot fail to be seen by readers, or better still mount them in covers, rather like periodical cases, and lay them on the readers' tables in the library. Arbitrary letters or numbers are brief, clear, easily remembered and are therefore more convenient for use on the directory plan than classmarks.

If personal guidance is continuous and liberal all these methods may not be required. But continuous and liberal? However good a librarian may be as a cicerone, he can attend to only one reader at a time, and at a busy hour, if unaided, he must leave others to fend for themselves. Again ciceroni are not uniformly successful unless they are *naturally* good at it; even a man well-trained in guiding may not be temperamentally fit, or acceptable in personality, or broad enough in sympathies to place his mind alongside the minds of other readers, so various in their outlooks, interests and mental capacities. Yet in personal guidance lies the brightest hope of success.

### III

A few other guides are desirable even if they hint at much ado about nothing. But who am I to reject toys which gratify the people —and wheedle them to borrow? They require little in hard cash and hard work.

The shelf-placard enlivens display, and introduces points of interest in the flat array of books. (*See illus. facing p.* 65.) Have made

## MANUAL OF BOOK CLASSIFICATION

a rectangular wooden box, enclosed on all sides, 9½ by 8 by 8 inches, and finished to match the bookcases. The base is ⅞ and the top ¼ inch thick. On the shelf, of which it is the same depth, it presents to the reader a front 9½ in. high by 8 in. broad, with narrow flanges at top and bottom, the rebates of which hold the placard. Take a card 8 in. wide by about 9 in. high, mount upon it a relevant picture, and letter it to indicate a group of books. This group is on a narrower subject than that painted on the bay. For example, under the bay heading GEOLOGY are books on Scottish geology. Mount a small coloured geological map or a coloured picture of strata on the card, letter it at the top SCOTS GEOLOGY, at the bottom paint an arrow directed to the left, and slip the card into the holding flanges in front of the box, which should be placed just after the last book of the group on this subject.

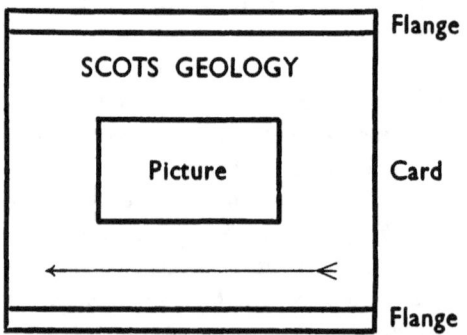

The colours of the card and the lettering should harmonize with the colours in the picture. So in the PHYSICS bay we may put a placard for LIGHT; in the SOUTH ENGLAND bay one for DEVON; and in a DOMESTIC CRAFTS another for COOKERY. Let the cards remain until all the books are out, or for about a fortnight, then move the boxes to advertise other subjects with appropriate pictures and signs. Twelve placards will "light up" twelve subjects at a time, and many in the duration of a year. The cards, all of the same size, may be wrapped up and filed away for later use. If the method is to be successful the boxes should be well made, the pictures bright and relevant, the letter-

## HOME READING LIBRARY

ing clean, legible and artistic, and the colouring brilliant and harmonious.

Two boxes, with a different picture on each, may be used as book ends for subject displays on tables. For this purpose I like them better than cradles. The placards are larger than the lettered signs on cradles and strike rather a brighter note. The cradle is better employed in holding the books returned by readers. When filled at the counter remove it to a table, and put an empty one in its place. This shuttling has a number of advantages: readers looking for books have no inducement to crowd near the entrance wicket; returned books are taken quickly out of the way of the assistants who have discharged them, and are immediately available for reissue; labour is saved because many books in the cradles go out again with little delay, while the remainder can be restored in notation order as time permits. Much business is lost if returned books are held up at the counter.

Bench and some forms of table displays are anathema to me. Books laid in rows on their fore-edges become misshapen in a few hours, and will be damaged by readers who ram an open book round the back of another. In the most untidy library I ever saw (and how I recoil from untidiness in a library) the books on their fore-edges were ranged in three rows one above the other on wall banks, much as they are sprawled on a penny stall in a country market. Stepped benches, in which books stand upright upon the treads and before the risers, should be fitted upon low tables, and should not be more than three steps high. I don't recommend them, for they cannot be kept tidy, and borrowers will lay books on the tops of others.

Books lying flat and supported by broad ridges on steep, narrow slopes (*see illus. facing pp.* 49, 97) attract attention, particularly if lights are concealed under all the slopes but that at the top. I hid some rococo columns in an old library with these slopes, and the books laid flat upon them quickly went out.

Here are some other playthings.

Take a good coloured Mercator map of the world not less than 30 by 24 inches, and hand-print over each country the classmark for it in neat open letters, that is, in outline not filled in. Treat a map of the British Isles likewise. Frame and display them on walls near the travel and topography collection. In the thirteenth edition of DC a poor outline map has country numbers printed upon it, but a map which is interesting to readers for its geographical information, and large enough to take many class numbers without overcrowding, is far better. Maps with clean sharp outlines, the most legible names, and soft transparent colours are preferable.

Messrs. Faber and Faber publish a chart, $21\frac{1}{2}$ by $17\frac{1}{4}$ in., of British artists from 1560 to 1860. Mark upon it the class numbers of the artists, and frame and hang it near the art books. Mr. Herbert Bedford took seventeen years to prepare a large chart of Architecture, Sculpture, Poetry, Painting and Music (Kegan Paul, 1938). Treat it in the same way. Mr. R. R. Bowker's publications include an eight-colour picture map of the Holy Land, 22 in. by 32 in. Significant events are noted in print close to the places where they occurred. Index the geographical features and the historical notes, and attach class-marks to the entries. On a sheet copy the index and marks, in letters of the style of those on the map and frame it with the map. So treated it advertises books on the Bible, Biblical history, Palestine, Arabia, and Egypt, and is an attractive object of interest. The same firm publish a Picture Map of France, a Map of America's Making, the Booklovers' Map of America, the Booklovers' Map of the British Isles, and the Map of Great Adventures, some or all of which are worth indexing and marking for libraries on this side.

Anything to avoid the humdrum. For more ephemeral indexed displays use a big screen or notice board. In 1937 was published a large coloured map of British Empire Shipping, with little blobs on it to represent our ships, and the names of the commodities produced in the countries linked by sea routes. Take a large sheet of paper, index on it in bold letters the commodities and the headings relating to maritime commerce, add the classmarks, and pin it up on the board along with the map. Let it remain until readers no longer pay attention, and then file for use another time. The Navy League Sea and Air Map of the World may be exhibited in the same way. The Newspaper Directory Map of the British Isles illustrates journalism. The *National Geographic Magazine* published a map of the Classical Lands of the Mediterranean, overprinted in red letters with historical and literary notes. Index, mark and display as recommended; but if the library is strong in the classics the map is worth a frame.

Always bear in mind that any chart or map must be interesting and attractive to the readers for any matter in it, apart from the marks the librarian adds.

I have noted only a few of the many ways of guiding a classed library. The paramount aims may be stated in a few sentences. Let the reader be sure of his way about the moment he enters. Use low bookcases so that each bay delimits a fairly small number of books. On the cornice panels name specifically the chief contents of the bays. "Light up" important groups not indicated on the panels by using shelf-placards. Don't be afraid of big lettering if it is artistic, or of gay colour if in harmony. Let the painter, the signwriter and the placard maker know that nothing but the best workmanship will do. Avoid the drab, the flat, the humdrum and the official. Get the whole staff to think up new ideas and fresh attractions. Life, movement, colour, intelligence, sales initiative, all belong to the art of librarianship.

## IV

Books may be regrouped temporarily to reveal fresh relations, or be lifted out of the formal array into greater prominence.

In the rule for classing on p. 81 I affirmed that the principal theme determines the place of a book, and that the convenience of the readers for whom the library is mainly intended determines the co-ordination of groups, when their relation to each other is debatable. The wisdom of this part of the rule is generally admitted, though in practice a scheme, once adopted, is often applied bureaucratically, without imagination, as though it were of universal validity. The catalogue must reveal what classing fails to reveal; so we are told, quite truthfully. But the work of the classer, when merged in that of the displayer, suggests other ways, not to be neglected if only to counteract present-day shortcomings in cataloguing. As noted already, the early advocates of open shelves broadcast the wicked heresy that card catalogues were good enough for readers admitted to choose books at the shelves: they opened a door and threw away a key. Yet memory tells me that the old double-column title-a-liner, though produced at a loss, was consulted by readers regularly and frequently. Any return to it, now that printing costs are so high, is beyond the dreams of hope. Yet it is easier to lure an old trout with a fly than to tempt the majority of readers to fiddle with cards. The card catalogue is an obstacle rather than a means. Reference students as a rule *must* find their way through its jungle of cards before they can rifle the treasury of the temple, but readers in an open branch library look upon it as the Ark of the Unfathomable.

The books referred to in this section are mongrels for which there are alternative classings. In fact I am suggesting the exhibition of distributed relatives, a phrase which looks sinister, but is only a little pedantic—and if a writer is not pedantic on the subject of classification he had better go flap a Laputan—for it means, in plain words, display to reveal the secondary themes, the themes rejected when the primary themes were chosen for marking. On p. 99 I described correlative lists, so called because they included entries of books on related subjects, and because a copy was "tipped in" every book on these subjects. Their function is the same as that of the exhibitions now to be recommended, but is more enduring in action because they remain in the books a long time, and more direct in appeal because they go straight into the hands of readers already interested in their subjects. They keep the converted informed. But the exhibitions, by broadening the appeal, may attract readers to these subjects *for the first time*, and are worth while for that purpose alone.

Let me note some examples of the ways in which classed books may be regrouped to reveal more knowledge, or to attract more readers.

Biographies are written as memorials to more or less celebrated people, but many librarians prefer a mass burial of these tributes, in alphabetic order by names of personal subjects. In this levelling process Sir J. D. Hooker, a world-famous botanist, whose life illustrates and amplifies the history of botany, is taken out of the way of botanical students, and becomes just—Hooker. However we must recognize that order by alphabet is a common way of "negating

## HOME READING LIBRARY

classification" (to use Mr. Stewart's phrase in a connection which will delight him) and we mitigate some of the harm by removing biographies temporarily from Abecedarian disorder to bearings where they are re-introduced to readers.

For example, pick out all the biographies of Labour Leaders, and show them in a bookcase apart from Abecedaria. At Edinburgh I have used small rolling cases like that depicted in the illustration facing p. 193. The coaks of a frame for movable signs fit into holes in the top of the case. For this exhibit the sign would be FRIENDS OF LABOUR, or LABOUR LEADERS, or LABOURISTS, SOCIALISTS and COMMUNISTS. Other groups may be formed of lives of: MEN OF SCIENCE; PHYSICIANS AND SURGEONS; GREAT ARTISTS; COMPOSERS AND MUSICIANS; ENGLISH POETS; ACTORS AND ACTRESSES; NAVAL COMMANDERS; GREAT AMERICANS. Even better is it to exhibit biographies in company with books on the themes they illustrate: lives of Labour Leaders with histories of Labour, of Naval Commanders with Naval History and so on.

A well-advertised feature of DC is its relative index. The kind of display I am considering now includes all the related entries which would be grouped under one heading in the DC index, and all entries under the same heading in the library's internal index. Books on India are in Ethnography, Economics and a half-dozen other places, by the rule of principal theme. For a little while we unite in one bookcase *all* the books on India: ethnography, description, history, biography, antiquities, economics, social life, literature, religions, missions, folklore, art and even novels about the country. Isn't it an intelligent thing to do? Wouldn't it be useful to bring together, for a month or two, the various kinds of books, and the illustrations from the Picture Collection, about all the countries bordering the Mediterranean? We are indolent or lump-headed if we neglect these methods.

Many readers have a taste for books of adventurous travel. Tambs, *Cruise of the "Teddy"*, Paterson, *Man-Eaters of Tsavo*, Robinson, *Deep Water and Shoal* (a grand book, equalled only by another by the same author, *Voyage to Galapagos*), Graves, *Lawrence and the Arabs*, Tomlinson, *Great Sea Stories*, Smythe, *Kangchenjunga*

*Adventure*, Shackleton, *Heart of the Antarctic*, *Tschiffely's Ride* and hundreds of others are distributed by country or ocean: why not collect and show them under the label: *Books of Adventure?

Another show, this time to demonstrate that books contain much knowledge positively valuable to humanity, and not of the kind that may be turned readily to evil uses. *The Benefactors of Mankind —a grand subject!—Ambroise Paré, father of modern surgery; Harvey and his researches into the circulation of the blood; van Leeuwenhoek, discoverer of bacteria; Florence Nightingale and nursing; Simpson and chloroform; Lister and antiseptic surgery; The Curies and radio-activity; Pasteur and antitoxin; Reed, Carroll, Lazear and Sir Ronald Ross, the enemies of yellow fever and malaria; Luther Burbank, breeder of new fruits and flowers; Braille and Moon, and their systems of reading for the blind; and the rest of them. It is well to remind people that Gutenberg's invention is a means of spreading meliorative knowledge as well as knowledge about pirates and robbers, cheats and politicians, spies and quislings.

Again *Mountaineering books, if distributed by country, should be exhibited together, not once but several times in the course of a few years. Here are sixteen examples among hundreds of distributed subjects which may be exhibited under the following captions:

1. Authorship and Journalism
2. Psychology for Everyman
3. *Missions
4. Careers for Boys and Girls
5. Business Books
6. *Inventions and Discoveries
7. *Handicrafts
8. *Dramatic Production
9. Fine Poetry
10. Recommended Plays
11. *Great Novels
12. *Literary Landmarks
13. Scots Vernacular Verse
14. Selected Books of Travel
15. Guide Books
16. The Sea and All About It

Show examples from the Picture collection in the exhibits marked with asterisks. Authorship and Journalism covers books on the art of writing, newspaper production, editing, and the lives of authors and journalists; Psychology for Everyman, psychology and special psychology for educators, labour managers, and others; Dramatic

## HOME READING LIBRARY

PRODUCTION, theatres, stage design, management, play production, scene painting and lighting, make-up, costume and the lives of actors and producers; THE SEA AND ALL ABOUT IT, oceanography, fish and fisheries, sea life and sailors, voyages, naval warfare and the like.

Books on topics of the day are rarely worth exhibiting, as readers need no inducement, at the time, to borrow what they want.

Although so far I have not gone beyond the temporary exhibition of distributed relatives, I don't hesitate to recommend the practice of giving prominence, either permanently or for a time, to groups and series of groups which ordinarily stand upon the shelves as a coherent body of literary information, whether with related subjects elsewhere or not. I divide this kind of exhibit into two categories (1) selected books for temporary or permanent display, and (2) minor groups of particular importance.

First the selected books. Take from a large group or series of groups the works which may be recommended without reserve. For example, pick out the best novels in French, and display them upon a plainly labelled bookcase which is rolled into position near the formal array of French Literature. (These rolling cases, by the way, first designed for a travelling library headquarters, and afterwards used in an accession department, are among the displayer's best equipment. *See illus. facing p.* 193.) Many other subjects may be similarly treated. What are the best works on British History for certain purposes? For a time at any rate we can let the reader know by displaying them apart from the general body of several thousand works on this subject. Throw up the best on Philosophy, Psychology, Biblical Studies, Political Science, Economics, Education, Business Books, Physics, Chemistry, Plant Life and Culture, Engineering, and on a hundred other subjects in a well-stocked library. Indeed I have found it profitable to keep books on subjects of perennial interest in bookcases out of the normal run; on Shakspere, for example, Burns, Scott, Good Juvenile Books, Great Novels, Recommended Novels, Short Stories, Selected Plays and Fine Poetry.

Now for the category of minor groups of particular importance. For many years it has been my practice to shelve the ends of double-sided bookcases. About 18 in. wide, the ends take five shelves, with a lettered panel above them, in an elevation exactly like that of a side. If asked: Why not broaden the side elevation by 16 in. so that the same number of additional books may be displayed on the sides as on the ends?—I reply: True, but breaking up, not storage, is the object. Lift out of notation order and give prominent homes of their own to such minor groups as:

| English Grammar and Composition | Angling |
| English Anthologies | Ballads |
| Photography | Art of Reading |
| Shelley | Swedish Literature |

A group is too large for an end if the number of books likely to be "in" at one time exceeds sixty. If practicable, groups should be allotted ends near the main classes to which they belong. But no matter where we put them they are out of notation order, a dereliction of textbook preachments no sensible librarian would commit. However, the books of small well-defined groups, boldly labelled, go out more often from case ends than from case sides, and as long as that happens all my colleagues are welcome to call me daft.

The more special the library the greater the display value of case ends and other small receptacles, as I hope to prove in Chapter VII.

*Every book in the various exhibitions described above may be borrowed at sight; none is reserved even for an hour.*

## V

So far ordinary bookcases have been the equipment for my displays; in them the books stand in rows with their backs to the reader, and in notation order, though some of them are lifted out of the general run of it. Hitherto I have been rational in methods of expounding books, and now I become anarchic, for I shall plead guilty to dis-

## HOME READING LIBRARY

playing them in showcases without regard to order, and I shall promise no amendment.

In case-shows books not only appear in the ordinary way with their backs to the onlooker, but more often they are arranged to display front covers, if they are lettered, or the jackets on them, or the title-pages and frontispieces; and they may be in rows, or groups, or in units, upright or flat or tilted.

Unlike the exhibitions linked with the formal classing and the window displays recommended in Chapter VIII, the internal showcase in a home reading library ought to contain no book which isn't available for issue at sight and on demand; as the contents of it come and go, there must be more regularity, less care for centres or points of interest than in an outside, entrance or corridor window, in which the display remains for two or three weeks. The lettering in internal showcases should be telegraphic in brevity; the placards few in number, though they can't be dispensed with altogether. On the other hand a showcase ought to be well-made, perfectly adapted for its work and very, very good to look at.

The showcase illustrated (facing p. 96) depicts the last of several forms, each of which was an improvement upon an earlier model. The first, introduced by me into the Wallasey Public Library in 1911, is illustrated in my *Special Librianship*, together with later forms, all now ruined by enemy action! The latest is double-sided, one elevation fronting the entrance alley, the other the library room beyond the barrier; another like it is a wing at the outgoing end of the counter; and each elevation contains four bays of shelves and one showcard board. The windows are locked doors, with keys to pass. The front of the bookshelves is 9 in. behind the glazed doors. The fixed shelves are 31 in. long and 8 apart, except that the uppermost shelf is 13 in. from the lower surface of the top, and the lower surface of the bottom shelf, reserved for taller books, is 10 in. from the floor of the case. As all books are shown open, or sideways with the front board or jacket toward the reader, the shelves are but 4 in. deep. A ridge projecting at the front edge of the shelf, $\frac{1}{4}$ in. above its surface, aligns the books. These dimensions are for one side of a double case which is $28\frac{1}{2}$ in. from side to side. Midway between each shelf a horizontal line of angling gut, thin, strong, translucent, and hardly noticeable, is stretched taut to keep the books upright. Strong lights are hidden near the roof of the case, each end of which is fitted with ventilating panels to draw off the heat emitted by the lamps. Long ago I abandoned strip lamps because they were always giving trouble. The middle bays in each elevation are of unpainted cork, and take showcards which are changed frequently; in the case illustrated at p. 96 there are:

(1) A Subject card, 21 in. by 8 in., lettered PSYCHOLOGY.
(2) Six Book cards, 21 in. by 4 in., each bearing the name of the author and the brief title of a good book on Psychology.
(3) A Picture card, 21 in. by 12 in., mounting a coloured illustration intended to be an attracting point.

The cards, the sizes of each kind being always the same, are slipped behind two perpendicular lines of gut, and are supported at their bottom edges by the tiny brass eyelets through which the gut passes.

The cases look gay at all times, particularly in the evening, when illuminated. They can be kept in apple-pie order at the busiest times, for a book, guided and held in place by the shelf ridges and the taut gut lines, may be taken out and replaced by another in a moment. I have never observed any trace of untidiness in a properly-fitted showcase.

The expense of providing showcases, and the trouble of keeping them filled, is always thoroughly repaid if the following rules and conditions are obeyed and fulfilled:

(1) The supply of good quality non-fiction stock must be ample. The case is not intended to advertise books for tired business men or for novel-eaters. (Why are business men the only people to get tired?)
(2) Show only fresh, clean stock.
(3) Indicate plainly that any book in the case may be borrowed immediately.
(4) Show in the case every new book, even if it goes out next minute.
(5) Keep the case spotlessly clean and bright; and use efficient clean lamps.

ART DEPARTMENT PLACARD
By T. S. Carruthers
Card, cream. Large Letters, red. Small letters, primrose green. Picture, sepia.
Size 22 × 16 in.

*Facing p.* 112 *(see pp.* 146, 221*)*

# HOME READING LIBRARY

(6) Take *all* the books out at least once a week, and lay them apart until the case is filled with others from the shelves. Then shelve the books taken out. Don't show any books longer than a week at a time. Don't allow any residue of "non-starters" to accumulate in the case.

(7) Let all the desk assistants take a turn at filling the case, and so avoid "groovy" displays.

A word or two more. The rolling cases and bookcase ends are better for subject displays, and interior showcases are generally filled with a miscellany of books. If a showcase is used for exhibiting a group of books upon one subject care must be taken (1) to keep all the related books together and (2) to replace a borrowed book by another on the same subject.

Interior cases are generally lit up only in the evening, or during overcast days, but if the library is a dull hole let the lights burn all day, for the cost is justifiable and not heavy.

## VI

When the crossword puzzle boomed in the U.S.A. the Baltimore and Ohio Railroad, to aid the solvers, provided dictionaries in their main line coaches. But in how many home reading libraries in our country is a dictionary to be found, let alone a body of supporting reference books? Such a reference collection is *necessary* only in home reading libraries which do not adjoin the main reference library, but is *desirable* in all of them to encourage readers unfamiliar with the value of reference books to use them, to aid those who, knowing their value, need references when choosing books, and to sustain librarians in the duty of personal guidance.

This reference collection, if practicable, should occupy a central position in the home reading library. Letter the case plainly: REFERENCE BOOKS FOR USE ONLY IN THIS ROOM. Not more than three hundred volumes are required. Include an encyclopaedia; atlases; dictionaries of the Bible, languages, dates, biography, literary history, quotations, civil and political history, gardening, science and technology; concordances; guides to books, aids to readers, general

MUSIC DEPARTMENT PLACARD
By T. S. Carruthers
Card, cream. Large letters and staves, orange. Small letters, green. Notes, black.
Size, 30 × 25 in.

*Facing p.* 113 *(see p.* 143*)*

bibliographies (*English Catalogue*, Whitaker, and the rest) and some yearbooks. Of the foregoing the more important are the bibliographies, concordances and dictionaries. But acquire any book that will help the librarians to answer inquiries, and the readers to look up facts.

"What has this reference collection to do with my subject?" I am asked.

"Because it contains, or should contain," I reply, "the literary tools necessary to expound other books, to reinforce display, to help the librarians in their work of guiding readers. These books save time in discovering knowledge in books. Their important function, from our point of view now, is the same as that of classification schemes, catalogues, indexes and displays. They are indispensable."

"But would they be used?"

"Why not?" I reply. "If I were told, after these books had been provided, that few people used them, I should be sure that personal guidance was faulty and inadequate, or that the library was little better than a fiction shop."

## VII

I know that this chapter on the home reading library considered as an exhibition is inadequate. But without space for more examples, I have restricted myself to those indicating the general lines on which the exhibition should be organized. And let me end with a warning. The classification, if minute and well co-ordinated, and if the marks are applied with discrimination and accuracy, is the ground-work of the exhibition. But from the point of view of readers the crowning point of the organization is the directive apparatus; to them the classification is nothing, guidance everything. Classification is a mechanical time-saving method which reveals knowledge in books. True, but only to librarians who understand it. To readers, unless the co-ordination is well guided, it is but a map of unknown country without lettering and without a scale.

CHAPTER VI

## 2. GENERAL REFERENCE LIBRARIES

### I

EVERY well-managed reference library with miscellaneous contents (and in this chapter I have only general libraries in mind) is divided into two parts: the stack and the open shelves. In addition the British Museum has exhibition galleries (the King's Library, the Grenville Room and the Manuscript Saloon) and study rooms for manuscripts, maps, and large and controlled books (the Manuscript Room, the Map Room, the North Library and the Oriental Students' Room)—but this account is exemplary rather than complete. The reference library of a smaller city should have the departments proper and necessary for its work. For example the central reference library at Edinburgh ought to be supported by rooms for (1) quick-reference books (2) study —we have but one—(3) exhibitions and (4) demonstrations.

About the quick-reference room I have written already in *Special Librarianship*, pp. 47, 140–57, and study rooms or carrells are nc part of my subject.

### II

In the Exhibition Gallery we generally find displays of rare books, MSS., documents, maps, prints, collectors' books (which "give character to a library") and others on "topics of the day".

They may be divided into two categories (1) unique, rare or irreplaceable items, and (2) other items, the showcases for each being different in appearance and strength. Too often the cases are massive strongholds, arranged in dim, lofty rooms. In

>    "arched walks of twilight groves
>    And shadows brown"

"hide me from day's garish eye": the whole effect is lowering and brings *Il Penseroso* to mind. Cases holding rarities must be nearly burglar proof, and books containing paintings and coloured engravings ought not to be exposed to strong daylight. Yet even book rarities will be fairly safe in metal cases of light structure. Anyway why need all the cases be alike? The showcases in the exhibition room of the Manchester Central Library are unobtrusive, though, in my opinion, not well adapted for displaying books. Certainly the items in the second category may be shown, and illuminated by internal lamps without harmful effect in well-ventilated cases, even if of slight, gracile design. I recommend lights hidden within the cases. The cost isn't wholly an addition, for less general lighting is required when the cases are illuminated, and the total bill for current isn't extravagantly higher. An exhibition room with the general lighting wholly reflected, and the local lighting hidden, is bright and alluring, yet not garish, tranquillizing and alleviating, yet not too cold and scientific. But let there *be* light; don't keep one eye glued on the meter.

Beautiful things ought to be exhibited always in lightly built, unobtrusive cases, quite suitable for them. Not many years ago I happened to see an exhibit, one of fine printing, on two occasions in two different settings: first in slender-framed, graceful cases arranged under good natural light, and then in heavy mahogany cases in a room nearly as dim as a gothic cathedral, where the loss in exhibition value was such as I could never have imagined, or believed had I been told, unless I had seen it with my own eyes. I have no love of standardized furnitures in libraries. For one thing they suggest poverty of ideas, lack of imagination, and want of care in adapting a fitting not only to purpose but to environment. Odd that a librarian who—in peacetime at any rate!—sniffs at reach-me-down clothes, is willing to buy a reach-me-down book- or showcase or display trough. He should have no trouble in getting cases designed for each of the several kinds and values of exhibits in his charge.

Here are two types of exhibition cases.

SHOWCASE FOR BOOKS. The deck of a double-sided case, at the edge which touches the waistcoat of the onlooker, should be 30 in.

## REFERENCE LIBRARY DISPLAY

above the floor, and should slope gently, not more than 2 in. in 20 towards the centre line of the case. Let the two slopes be not more than 20 in. from front to back, so that in section they form a gable about 40 in. wide and 2 in. higher at the apex than at the sides. Five feet is a convenient length. Glaze the protecting frame above the deck at the top, front and ends, and have no lateral division between the ridge line of the deck and the underside of the glazed top: so daylight floods in at all angles, with much advantage and no drawback in exhibiting books. Hide lamps, if required, under the middle lateral bar of the glazed top. Let the deck be made of polished hard wood, which is easily kept free from dust. Cover it with a loose strip of good quality felt or velvet, or of homespun canvas or fabric of an attractive but subdued pattern; and vary the hue or pattern in each case, choosing an accordant setting for a particular exhibit. The deck covers may be rolled up and shaken and brushed out of doors. A case should be immaculately clean, and the interior cannot be kept perfectly free of dust if the lining is of adherent fabric. Although I have recommended gentle slopes a flat deck is desirable if the showcase is narrower than that recommended above. In Coleman, *Manual for Small Museums*, a flat table case is illustrated facing p. 202. Its dimensions are: length 60 in., width 24 in., height of deck from floor 30 in., and height of glazed metal frame 8 in. This case takes two rows of open books, and will serve as a wall case, with both rows laid the same way, or as an island case, with the rows facing opposite ways. But avoid book showcases with steep slopes. At Edinburgh I had a gigantic mahogany case 15 ft. long, 4 ft. wide, with a slope of 22 in. in 24!— weighing I know not how many tons.

MAP AND CHART SHOWCASES. Exhibit small maps, charts and prints in a book showcase, but large and rare ones behind glass on an upright screen, or one which slopes very abruptly. The glass should be several inches in front of the screen. The best glass is the non-reflecting, curved K-Ray glass. Hidden lights at the top rail of the screen, with a switch controllable by visitors, are desirable, and not harmful if the space behind the glass is ventilated.

I will deal more fully with exhibitions when I come to the chapter on special libraries. At the same time I don't want to over-emphasize the importance of the exhibition gallery. Its function is to win publicity for the Reference Library, and for some of the rarer and more interesting contents. But I doubt whether the publicity is of the unerring kind. Are the visitors who wander in to yawn and chatter over "collectors' books" not inclined to associate libraries with museums, the functions of which are different?[1] When I reflect upon this subject I mentally compare the ordinarily rather idle sightseers in the King's Library of the British Museum, with the hard-working crowds in the Main Reading Room and the North Library. Besides, I attach most value to an exhibit which advertises the book as a tool rather than as a curiosity and a rarity. "A museum is seldom a cheerful place," writes Pater—"oftenest induces the feeling that nothing could ever have been young; and to Browne the whole world is a museum; all the grace and beauty it has being of a somewhat mortified kind."— *Appreciations: Sir Thomas Browne*, pp. 137–8. There's a deal of Browne in many librarians.

A word or two on labels. They are rarely large enough, being either in ordinary typewriting, or in fine-cut old-face type which is beautiful, but eye-fatiguing. Why not broad, plain but not ornamental lettering in india ink, the capitals being never less than $\frac{3}{8}$ in. tall, and the lower-case letters never less than $\frac{1}{4}$ in. These are minimum sizes, and the lettering should be broad, not hunched.

## III

More important than the Exhibition Gallery is the Demonstration Room, in which nearly the whole stock of the reference library is displayed, class by class in turn.

For these demonstrations a room is required, or a run of open shelves, or one or two alcoves in the main reference library. The room is preferable. The accommodation needed depends upon the volume of the whole collection. In a library of 100,000 volumes few

[1] "My wish is that my drawings, my prints, my curiosities, my books—in a word these things of art which have been the joy of my life—shall not be consigned to the cold tomb of a museum, and subjected to the stupid glance of the careless passer-by."—*Will of Edmond de Goncourt.*

## REFERENCE LIBRARY DISPLAY

classes of books (long runs of periodicals being left out of account) comprise more than 10,000 volumes, or if they are greater in number they are divisible into sections which may be denominated by comprehensive headings. The demonstration room therefore should accommodate about 10,000.

For example, in this general library there would be fewer than 10,000 volumes on religion. Here is a plan of operations. In the demonstration shelves show all of them, apart from obsolete books and from periodical sets other than the first and last volumes of each. Provide screens, slopes, showcases and tables for pictures, rarities and large books. Select pictures from the Illustration Collection, the use of which will be described on placards, and others from portfolios of unbound illustrations or facsimiles, such as the set reproduced by the American Bible Society and the British and Foreign Bible Society to illustrate the history of the English printed Bible at its quatercentenary. Display big books, for example *The Book of the Dead* and David Roberts, *The Holy Land, Syria, Idumea, Arabia, Egypt and Nubia*, on the slopes and tables; and manuscripts and rare volumes in the showcases. The demonstration being ready, announce in the press to ministers of all denominations, lay preachers, missionaries and teachers that it will be open for inspection *and criticism* for three months, a shorter period for a big collection being undesirable.

If the advertising is forcible and of the right kind, the labour of moving the books for the demonstration will be rewarded by good fortune. But the policy of demonstrations won't succeed unless it is continued year after year, for a long time, indeed as a regular item of reference policy. In my experience the ardour of committees and librarians is too quickly chilled if the public response isn't immediate and overwhelming. Intermittent drives against public inattention are not effective. Keep at it, and still keep at it.

I have deliberately taken as my leading example, Religion, a class which makes the poorest (but yet a good) show, and attracts the fewest people, because I want it to be abundantly clear at the beginning that demonstrations are not primarily stunts to lure the saunterer and the passer-by into the library, but are intended to "open out", a class at a time, the contents of a department most troublesome to advertise.

# MANUAL OF BOOK CLASSIFICATION

An autonomous, open, special department is a demonstration; what I recommend is a passing substitute for it, not by any means adequate, but well worth all the labour and energy devoted to it, when the stone and steel bonds of an old-fashioned building prevent us from enjoying the ideal.

A summary review of the classed stock will indicate how wide is the range of demonstrations, which may be planned in any order. If the room is large enough, then any subject in small capitals in the following list should be exhibited as a whole; if not we must be content with parts, with groups of allied minor subjects. To these subjects and groups I have prefixed the DC class, division or section numbers, omitting the unwanted noughts.

| | |
|---|---|
| 1 | PHILOSOPHY |
| 14, 18, 19 | History of Philosophy |
| 2 | RELIGION |
| 22 | The Bible |
| 22, 23, 24 | Christian Theology |
| 209, 21, 27, 28, 29 | History of Religions |
| 3 | SOCIAL SCIENCES |
| 31, 32, 33 | Political and Economic Science |
| 331, 335 | Labour, Socialism, Communism |
| 13, 15, 37 | Theoretical and Practical Education |
| 38, 65 | Commerce and Business |
| 4 | PHILOLOGY |
| 5 | SCIENCE |
| 52, 53, 54 | Physical Sciences |
| 57, 58, 59 | Biological Sciences |
| 6 | USEFUL ARTS |
| 62, 67, 68 | Engineering and Manufactures |
| 333, 58, 63, 71 | The Land: Economics, Botany, Agriculture, Gardening |
| 64 | Domestic Science |
| 54, 66 | Chemical Science and Technology |
| 72, 69 | Architecture and Building |
| 7 | FINE ARTS |
| 74, 76, 75, 73 | Graphic and Plastic Arts |
| 77 | Photography |

## REFERENCE LIBRARY DISPLAY

| | |
|---|---|
| 78 | Music, Theatre and the Drama (as platform entertainment) |
| 796–799 | Sports and Games |
| 8 | Literature |
| 81, 82 | English and American Literature, including Language |
| 83, 84, 85, 86 | European Literature, including Languages |
| 87, 88 | Classical Literatures, including Languages |
| 9 | History |
| 91 | Geography and Travels |
| 92 | Biography (from all parts, if classed by subject) |
| 93, 47, 87, 937, 48, 88, 938 | The Ancient World |
| 914, 94 | Europe |
| 914, 942 | Great Britain |
| 915, 95 | The Orient |
| 916, 96 | The African Continent |
| 917, 97, 918, 98 | The Americas |
| 991–996 | Eastern and Southern Seas |
| 998–999 | Conquest of the Poles |

The material is ample for a great series of demonstrations, continuous, too, for they can and should be repeated.

"Won't it take a long time to run through all this lot?" a critic will object. "The first will be forgotten long before the last is shown."

"True. But if the room's large enough the demonstrations may be of whole classes. The length of the list is determined by the size of the room. The bigger the demonstration the better. Small demonstrations need not be open so long."

"But I'm not clear as to what you're getting at with your demonstrations."

"A demonstration boosts the reference library in the most effective way known to me," I reply. "Take religion. The people interested in religious books have an opportunity of inspecting the whole lot of item. As they have in a home reading library. All of them, at one time. And the parts of religion can be shown up in a striking way by attractive title and guide cards. As in an open home reading library, in fact."

"Why not throw open the whole reference library?"

"Why not? But we're assuming that's not possible? Of course all the books of a small reference library should be on open shelves, and in some towns the plan of the library allows this to be done."

"The large reference library will have its open section, though?"

"Yes. In one way the open section makes demonstrations more necessary. It has a drawback. Readers are inclined to depend upon it. They overlook the far greater collection in the stack. The demonstration broadens their outlook. It exhibits all the strength of the library. As in this subject of religion. Isn't this good advertising?"

"I doubt it," replies the critic. "I don't see much advantage in persuading a number of people to walk in, and look round a collection at a time, likely enough, when they're not wanting to use it."

"That objection applies to *all* publicity. But that reminds me I haven't told you about the librarian in charge of our demonstration. A different librarian is chosen for each big demonstration, or for smaller demonstration, as far as the numbers on the staff allow. Every librarian picked for this job has a chance to show what he can do in arranging attractive displays. Another point: he must make himself familiar with the books, so that he can act as cicerone when visitors come. When necessary he should be relieved by the librarian who has helped him to bring the display together."

"The demonstration, at any rate, should advance the bibliographical education of the staff."

"Undoubtedly. More. It does help the visitors to have librarians there. Remember that criticisms are invited. The class demonstrated must be improved by the criticisms of the visitors. Not to speak of those of the staff."

"Yes, I follow that argument. The staff particularly. Librarians can't arrange a demonstration of such a kind without noticing gaps."

"Quite. Who likes showing a class full of holes? They'll fill some of them up at any rate. They'll have the books cleaned, too, repaired, rebound. Amazing how the quality and condition of stock improves when it's transferred to open shelves. But don't underrate visitors' criticisms. No librarian, unless he's an utterly fatuous fool, would presume to select books for a whole townspeople. He wants sugges-

## REFERENCE LIBRARY DISPLAY

tions from as many people as possible. If the curator of the demonstration is observant and receptive the outside criticism will be powerful to shape the collection to the needs of the community. That's proven. Ask any librarian who has had charge of a special collection."

"I think you're right in saying that," the critic agrees. "It seems to me too that the visitors will be encouraged to offer gifts."

"Naturally. Especially if a notice is displayed at the demonstration asking for them."

"I can imagine that some of the demonstrations might be more attractive than that of religious books."

"Depends upon the point of view, of course," I reply. "Need any demonstration be dull? I can't admit it. No. I would rather say that it's easier to make *some* more interesting than others. No doubt some demonstrations, if well arranged and illustrated with pictures, maps, plans and diagrams, make fine shows. Physical and Biological Sciences, for example. The Land. Chemistry. Architecture and Building. Fine Arts. British History. All grand material. Remember, however, that the chief aim isn't to make raree-shows. We demonstrate a library's contents."

"Let's look at your list again," the critic says. "I note in your smaller demonstrations you group books in other relations than those provided by the classification tables."

"Of course. These regroupings are illuminating both to the people and to the staff. I haven't indicated one-fiftieth of the cross classifications that may be revealed. Books may be demonstrated under all sorts of fancy headings."

### IV

Minor displays may be arranged in the Reference Library to draw attention to books on topics of the day, or helpful to students attending lecture courses. One of the most felicitous developments of reference work at Croydon in my years under Mr. Jast were exhibits of this kind. Generally only a modest case is required for each, and there may be a number of topics displayed at one time. Often attention is drawn to books which haven't been looked at for years. For example, when Mussolini romped into Abyssinia all the forgotten books on this country, which hasn't a rich bibliography, were referred to again; some of them would have been asked for, display or no display, but a fillip quickens and broadens interest. Lectures seem to have had their day. About twenty or twenty-five years ago, eminent, or at any rate competent lecturers, visited towns and delivered courses of lectures on "Six selected plays of Shakespeare", "The Life and teaching of John Ruskin", "British history in the eighteenth century", and many other subjects. The B.B.C. titbits talks and the listening groups have not filled the gaps left when these courses became fewer and fewer. Most University townspeople may take advantage of endowed lectures: at Edinburgh, for example, there are the Rhind Lectures: and displays on the matter of them are appropriate features of reference work.

In many reference libraries an alcove or a bookcase is set apart for recent additions. As it is desirable to keep the bookcase full, room is made for new books by relegating to the stack others which have been a long time exhibited. For many years the practice has been followed in the Picton Reading Room at Liverpool, the additions being arranged round the central heating and lighting unit under the dome in the rotunda. When at Wallasey this display, which I examined regularly, helped me in selecting books which were not in stock at the bookshops. About the utility of such exhibitions, a matter of routine in good reference libraries, there can be no doubt.

Many librarians are half-hearted in gathering valuable material if the demand for it isn't good right at the beginning. Maps, for example: a map assistant is a glutton for file money and wall space if he gets a free hand, and the results are not computable all at once. Yet maps of all kinds and all countries are worth buying, and many may be got without charge by writing for them. Good coloured maps leaven the demonstrations already recommended. Here are other uses. Frame a coloured map of the world, about 32 by 24 in. Hang above it a typed index, also framed, of the maps in the file, with the class or call mark attached, e.g.,

| Aberdeen | 914.125 |
| Abruzzo, Italy | 914.571 |
| Adirondacks, U.S.A. | 917.4753 |
| Africa | 916 |

## REFERENCE LIBRARY DISPLAY

An index too copious for one frame may extend to two, one on either side of the attention-drawing map; or if too voluminous for this restraint it may be on cards or on sheaves, above which the map and an abridged index hang. Copies of a printed index distributed or shown on tables in all departments and branches will attract use, but the typed index is as effective, more economical and more readily corrected.

An atlas-index is a quick and handy way of advertising a collection of moderate volume. Get a thin folio atlas, a good school atlas, if possible, rebind it with ruled paper interleaves, on each of which write an alphabetical list of the filed maps and town plans showing *in larger scale* parts of the proximate map. Letter the atlas: *Index to Some Maps in the Reference [or Commercial] Library*. An index of this kind is advertising of the most direct kind. Unfortunately, atlases with maps printed only on one side of the page are uncommon nowadays, but there are others in which maps on verso and recto are independent.

Maps occupy too much wall for a convenient demonstration of them when opened out. They reach us in various states: rolled; cut up and mounted with a gap about $\frac{1}{8}$ in. all round each section; and folded, with puckers at the folds. Most maps may be rolled, and I prefer this way. On a large table a map may be unrolled and referred to without inconvenience if it is held down by flexible weights, the most accommodating being gunshot or tiny ball bearings in washable leather bags of the size and shape of a pre-war sausage, two of which are strung together by a cord about 5 in. long: the soft leather bags of fluid weight are kind to any broadside, and may be laid down at any angle. Rectangular cloth-covered tubes store rolled maps economically on narrow shelves. If the contents are lettered boldly on the side of each tube, a case of shelved tubes forms a demonstration quite as good as any case of books, particularly if a few maps are opened out as "points of interest". Both "sausages" and tubes are fine examples of fusspottery, but all the best librarians I have known have been fusspots. It's an old maid's job, librarianship!

No need to add to these illustrative methods, of which there are many, because I am only leading up to the remark that every central library building, in a large or middle town, ought to include a map room. For years I have hankered for one, and now—alas! The map collection at Edinburgh is near a lumping adolescence, but it has never got itself a room, and a separate room is a collection's best advertisement. Maps and illustrations may conveniently and economically be in one room.

## V

A reference library should have the largest open collection that can be accommodated in the general reading room.

In this country perhaps the oldest (certainly the best known) is that below the gallery of the British Museum rotunda. There are grouped by subject all the indispensable works, not only of ready reference, but the fundamental collectanea, such as the *Monasticon*, the *Patrologia* of Migne, the *Foedera* of Rymer and the *Géographie Universelle*. People who use the Museum Library only now and then may be a little intimidated and confused by the bulk and range of the collection, but if they consult the plan, and make themselves familiar with the books on their own subjects, they will soon realize how vast is the wealth of information within their grasp, particularly if they take advantage of the courteous help of the officials. And here a question jumps to mind. Ought we not to expect greater use of the open collection than it gets? Certainly. But too often, thinking that no more is required, we are content with granting access. The truth is that *open shelves are not a substitute for librarianship, but an opportunity for the better application of it.*

Only librarians of long experience can form an open reference collection. Even they must vary it with the needs of the people most frequently using the library. The truly rewarding procedure is to include all the books best adapted and most often needed for quick reference; then watch use, eliminate neglected books, and substitute others until the whole responds to the heaviest demands.

A plan of the open collection is indispensable. That in the British Museum is a model, but in a library where changes in the places of

## REFERENCE LIBRARY DISPLAY

books are frequent one more accommodating is desirable. Draw a plan of the layout. Mark the alcoves or groups of bookcases with letters, and the bays or tiers with numbers. Reproduce the drawing in a block about 10 in. square, and print it on a card at the head of an abridged subject index (see also p. 101). The books being arranged, write the directive letters and numbers in permanent red ink against the index headings. So readers are provided with a compact guide to subjects, a library directory. When the books are rearranged fill in the new directive letters and numbers on fresh cards, which should be in frames with movable backs. Here are examples of several directory-plan-index forms: one a general directory, another of bibliographies, and a third of dictionaries of languages and literatures, author concordances and indexes. Following are specimens (the plans being omitted) of the indexes on two of these forms:

### DIRECTORY—PLAN—INDEX OF BIBLIOGRAPHIES

The numbers on the left-hand are the marks for the class. The figures in red indicate the alcoves or sections where the classes may be found. The letters in red indicate divisions in the alcoves or sections.

| Classmarks | Subjects | Numbers and Letters in red |
|---|---|---|
| Z 5063 | Aeronautics | 4C |
| Z 3518 | Africa, South | 4C |
| Z 5095 | Almanacs | 4D |
| Z 1201 | America | 3F |
| Z 1601 | America, South | 3F |
| Z 1225 | American Literature | 3F |
| Z 5971 | Angling | 4D |
| Z 1041 | Anonymous | 3E |

*And so on*

At the foot is a note informing readers that the Index is abridged, and that other bibliographies will be found by referring to the catalogue, or by inquiring at the counter.

## MANUAL OF BOOK CLASSIFICATION

DIRECTORY—PLAN—INDEX OF CONCORDANCES
DICTIONARIES OF LANGUAGES AND LITERARY
AND OTHER INDEXES

*Note as in former example*

| PA 3888 | Aristophanes | 8E |
| PQ 1799 | Balzac | 8L |
| PR 1588 | Beowulf | 8P |
| BS 10 | Bible | 5 |
| PR 4245 | Browning | 9B |
| XPR 4345 | Burns | 11K |
| PA 6276 | Catullus | 8E |
| PR 3383 | Cowper | 8S |

*And so on*

Writing about these forms I am reminded that it is sometimes desirable to regroup books, to break class order. Certain groups are better apart from the bulk on the open shelves. Examples? Here are some.

1 General Biography ⎫
2 British Biography  ⎬ separately, or as one series
3 Foreign Biography ⎭
4 Atlases (unless there is a Map Room)
5 Yearbooks
6 Indexes, Concordances, and Quotations
7 Bibliographies

Collect all the dictionaries or miscellanies of concise biographies of the British people, such as the *D.N.B.*, *Athenae Oxoniensis*, *Alumni Cantabrigiensis*, Fuller, *Worthies of England*, Lodge, *Portraits*, Boase, *Modern English Biography*, *Who's Who*, *Who was Who*, Anderson, *Scottish Nation*, and Crone, *Irish Biography*. Arrange them apart in a bookcase upon which is painted in large, plain and beautiful lettering the words BRITISH BIOGRAPHY, or LIVES OF BRITISH PEOPLE. Treat General and Foreign Biography similarly.

Another example. The rules of classification and the laws of

## REFERENCE LIBRARY DISPLAY

common sense require us to keep concordances with the words concordanced, and indexes with the works indexed. Break the rules, and let the laws go hang! In an independent bookcase group all books which analyse, in index form, the contents of other books: concordances, indexes, literary dictionaries, anthologies of quotations and the like. Alternatively put the indexes in one case, and concordances and quotations in another. When general indexes of periodicals, series, collected works and other publications are "lumped", much time is saved, and a possible source of information not overlooked. Develop the index group by acquiring duplicates of indexes to volumes of bound periodicals. Bind one copy with the parts it indexes, file the other and its successors in a box, pamphlet pocket or grip cover until there are enough to make a volume. Ten annual indexes of *Engineering* bound together, the end of each being marked by a coloured leaf, form a reference volume so handy that it cannot fail to develop the use of the periodical. True, such additions to the index collection are in formation years before we get plenary benefit from them, and alas, I admit that competent indexing of periodicals is far less common than in the good old days; yet the plan repays adoption.

Here are some examples of the kind of indexes which may be brought together:

> *Notes and Queries*
> *The Times*
> *Glasgow Herald*
> Carlyle, *Works*
> *Old Edinburgh Club*
> *English Historical Review*
> Walpole, *Letters*

Concordances and anthologies of quotations form a natural group. A concordance is an admirable guide to quotations, for if only one keyword of Shakspere is remembered Bartlett puts us on the track of the whole passage. The general indexes to Carlyle and Walpole, noted above, though not concordances, naturally belong to the group, as they too expound authors; for this and for other reasons I prefer the one group for the three kinds of books.

If the above categories are grouped and displayed in the way I recommend, a directory-plan-index for them isn't required.

## VI

What am I driving at in the last section? Just this: a large open collection ought to be broken up into groups which can be distinctively named and thoroughly advertised.

Imagine a general reference library in any big room open to full view, without alcoves, oriels—or chancels! The open collection is arranged in wall-cases. If the architect hasn't planted columns in front of the wall, or partly concealed in some other way the clear run of the bookcases, then it is possible and desirable to indicate the principal subjects in letters readable by any but purblind visitors the moment they enter the room, as we may "spot" any shop from the other side of a square by reading the signboards. Is there any reference library with signs large enough to be read afar off? Good heavens, no! You must not be vulgar and blatant in a reference library: the thing isn't done! I have seen a rotunda with a trite literary quotation finely and clearly lettered round the base of a dome; you could read it with pleasure—and with ease if the library committee would provide some tilting and revolving armchairs under the centre of the dome! But to read the case guides from the entrance you needed Sam Weller's telescope. Nearly all architects of public buildings avoid designating a room, hall or bookcase in letters which are readable at a distance or even readable at all.

If the guiding of the collection is provocative and in high relief, the display of particular groups is less urgent, although some groups, like those I have cited as examples, rivet people's attention more surely if they are lifted out of the general run and displayed in bold isolation. The whole art of display for a general reference library, or a home reading library for that matter, lies in the intelligent application of three rules:

(1) *Break up the heavy mass of books into the smallest sections that can be indicated without confusion by legible signs.* Dewey decimated

## REFERENCE LIBRARY DISPLAY

knowledge by chopping it into ten classes; the classes into ten divisions; the divisions into ten sections; the sections into ten subsections; and librarians, charmed by the pattern, looked upon his regimented summary and found it good. But they were misled. There are more than seven wonders of the world, not all equally wonderful in every eye; more than ten main classes of knowledge, none foremost to everybody alike. Why use lettering of the same prominence for 62 Engineering and 76 Engraving because the headings for them are in type of equal emphasis in the DC tables? To do so is infantile. If our selection of books is right the importance of a subject *to our readers* is to be measured, not by the value and range of notation DC gives to it, *but by the space it occupies on the shelves.* So, in lettering, thrust into high relief the well-represented subjects, those of the greatest service to your readers, even if you must ignore some which are printed in black-face in DC. Take the sequence

> Engineering
> Mechanical Engineering
> *Steam Engineering*
> *Electric Engineering*
> *Air and Gas Engines*

If the collection warrants it prefer *main* lettering for the subjects in italics, rather than for the more general subjects. STEAM ENGINEERING implies Mechanical Engineering and specifies Steam. Apply this rule to the whole classification: in a British library ENGLISH LITERATURE and BRITISH HISTORY are *main* classes; in a university city PHYSICS, CHEMISTRY, BIOLOGY and ZOOLOGY are main classes; in a commercial city STATISTICS, ECONOMICS, COMMERCE and BUSINESS; and in every town MUSIC. *Main classes, in fact, are determined by volume of stock*: an unphilosophical dictum of, I claim, the profoundest common sense. I only give some examples of the rule that, just as we choose and co-ordinate our books for a particular community (see p. 79) so *we must carry the emphasis of selection and co-ordination into our labelling*. If Dewey chose to give equal value to Comparative Philology (41) and to North American History (97) we need not be such docile and torpid bureaucrats as to follow his example in our lettered guides.

(2) *No matter what the classification requires, group books which support each other.* For example 01 BIBLIOGRAPHY, 09 BOOK RARITIES, 655 PRINTING and 02 LIBRARY ECONOMY, the four together, are worth designating as a *main* class. BOTANY, AGRICULTURE and GARDENING, if grouped, advertise each other; so, ECONOMIC GEOLOGY and MINING ENGINEERING, or DESCRIPTION and HISTORY, country by country.

(3) *Use the classification tables to the fullest extent.* This recommendation is in fact but a continuance of the process of "breaking up". By differentiating one book from another we display both. An ideal class mark ought to embody signs representing all the catalogue headings (apart from analytics), as well as signs which cannot be revealed by headings. For example the mark in UDC for a book on *Varnishes used in the Manufacture of Violins in Italy* is 787.1 : 667.7 (45), which represents the catalogue headings for Violins—Varnish—Italy. Again the mark for *History of Marriage Law in Scotland* is 347.62 (41) (09), which represents Marriage Law—Scotland—History, the last not a catalogue heading. Finally a *History of Astronomy in France in the Sixteenth Century* is marked 52(09) "15" (44), which represents Astronomy—History—Sixteenth century—France, only two of which call for headings. If therefore we employ the tables of a great scheme to their fullest extent we go far to isolate a book from its neighbours. The whole art of classification consists in so differentiating or displaying the matter in books.

CHAPTER VII

3. SPECIAL LIBRARIES

I

It may be asked: After describing formal classing and display in home reading and reference libraries, is there anything left to say about methods in special libraries?

Yes, because we look at the subject from a different angle. As a rule, the classing is more minute in a special than in a reference or home reading library, not because it is the practice to make it so—the practice should be uniform in all departments—but because a lot of the material is highly special, more varied and more niggling, though for all that not unimportant. Again, the users of a special library won't respond to the displays which attract people to the home reading or to the general reference library, but they will to more informing displays, on more intensive themes, and of a more distinctive type.

To begin with let it be clear that the libraries referred to in this chapter include both reference and home reading books.

II

I take my first examples from technical and commercial libraries, which may be considered together, the support they give each other being of the strongest.

These departments house material not commonly found, at any rate abundantly, in general departments. And that which readers do not expect a library to possess should be prominently displayed. Trade catalogues leap to mind because they are rarely collected, and because they contain detailed information and numerous clear illustrations not always in books. Asked for illustrations of pumping engines I should turn forthwith to the catalogues, where I should quickly find many of that high quality which advertising manufacturers can afford, and publishers often cannot. And so readily found. File the catalogues in boxes in alphabetical order of the names of firms, using Cutter or another Alphabet Table mark. Index the goods in them on cards which give the makers' names and the catalogue call numbers. It is simpler to file catalogues than to make them known, and it is vain to advertise unless plenty have been accumulated. Slopes fixed one above the other on a wall, with tiny lights hidden in the angle with the wall, underneath all the shelves except the bottom, will display catalogues aggressively, if one co-ordinated group at a time is chosen, and is followed quickly by others. (*See illus. facing p.* 97.) Above the shelves hang a bold sign describing the volume and multiformity of the collection, and adding a note on the worth of trade catalogues, and on the utility of the library's index to them. But external as well as internal publicity is required. We are lucky if we have an outside lobby or corridor window at our service.

Let us try to arrange a window.

Make a number of placards, each with an illustration as its centre of interest, like that shown on the opposite page.

Nearly one hundred British firms make electric fittings and apparatus. There isn't room for all their names. The displayer therefore should class the catalogues, and include in a placard only the names of those making one kind of article: for example, Electric heaters, or Dynamos, or Transmission. The aim isn't to display any complete list of the firms, but to advertise the catalogues as a whole. Add a copy of the sign which hangs above the slopes, and some eye-catching pictures or photographs of technical operations of the kind readily obtainable on loan from big firms. With a pedestal or two, dwarf platforms and tables (all being stock properties usable over and over again) the material makes a good show. At one time librarians, had they displayed catalogues, would have been charged with advertising private trade, but to-day, opinion being more liberal, no objection is likely to be raised in large technical or commercial libraries where all kinds of catalogues are filed. After all we file publishers' catalogues for readers' use in reference libraries.

SPECIAL LIBRARIES

The treatment of this specimen of uncommon material will serve as an example for: Banking house journals; Pamphlets; abstracted Technical articles and separates; Commercial and Technical illus-

---

*Picture*

**TRADE CATALOGUES OF ELECTRIC POWER TRANSMISSION**

FIRMS

Cheeryble Brothers
Codlin and Short, Ltd.
Dodson and Fogg
Spenlow and Jorkins
Gruff and Tackleton, Ltd.

*And so on*

---

**LIMBERTOWN LIBRARIES COMMERCIAL DEPARTMENT FILES OVER 25,000 TRADE CATALOGUES OF ALL KINDS OF GOODS**

---

trations; Economic maps; Trade statistics; Economic reports on overseas countries; and collateral material.

With a policy to guide us in displaying we make a greater success of it. Attract people to subjects upon which the library can throw light. Advertise it only indirectly. This sort of thing, "The Public

Library is the People's University?" No, no! Numbers of people don't want university education, which anyway has a more limited curriculum than a great library. The public library hasn't too good a name: it is, people believe, the resort of snuffy antiquarians; fact-hunting writers; tramps and loafers, because we started the newsroom and can't be rid of it; novel readers, because we grouped our novels apart, and must now squander our heritage upon the outpourings of nincompoops to entertain nitwits—a weak and detrimental policy. We can give the library a higher reputation by attracting people who don't now come to us, who would take heavy toll of its abundant resources, who would learn that it is not only an instrument of blackcoat culture, not only a repository of Homer's *Iliad* and Sir Fretful Plagiary's verse, of *Tom Jones* and Rosa Dartle's novels, but of information on all the arts and crafts, all activities of the mind, and all skill with the hands. Hence the need of a policy. Demonstrate that authors are teachers, that books are media of reliable information on hundreds of topics. In the commercial department let us take one important subject at a time, and trim our display to drive home a lesson of such authority that people will talk about it, and cannot help associating it with the library. The Trade of the World! Upon agriculture and other industries, upon the prosperity of trade, the livelihood—the standard of living—of all depend: parson and plumber, doctor and dressmaker, librarian and labourer. With the aid of statistics, abundant in official returns and commercial periodicals, we can make displays of high educational value. That they will certainly be talked about, and may lead to more library business is of secondary importance, the main purpose being to ram home useful knowledge. Diagrams of imports and exports, covering one or two decades in the industrial history of the greater nations, are readily made of coloured paper laid down on large cards. (*See illus. facing p.* 144.) If the diagram for each country is of identical scale and of the same kind, the comparison is clear to the narrowest parochial shopkeeping mind, and it will suggest to the merchant that there is thought behind a display, the concomitant motive of which, publicity for the library, he thoroughly understands. Diagrams comparing merchant shipping, air communications, coal and mineral production of the chief nations, are also illuminating. Other diagrams on agricultural production and imports are easy to make, and quite as attractive and informative to thoughtful people. Economic journals regularly publish commodity price charts which are

---

| *Picture of Vertical File* | **ORGANIZED INFORMATION** | *Picture of Vertical File* |

*Business man:* "Your library can't help me much, Mr. Librarian. I must have the latest information."

*Librarian:* "Surely you can get it in newspapers and journals?"

*Business man:* "Aye. But you can't keep piles of papers. And think of the trouble of looking through them all for what you want. Sometimes I cut out pieces of interest to me until my pockets are full, and then I throw them away."

*Librarian:* "But we librarians not only cut out. We file to find. Do you know we have over 25,000 articles and cuttings on commerce and business at the Central Library? Call and ask our file a question."

*Business man:* "I didn't know you had got that sort of service. I *will* call or ring up when I want something next time."

*Librarian:* "Good! Remember, too, that we bind journals, and that they're indexed."

**EDINBURGH LIBRARIES COMMERCIAL DEPARTMENT**

---

cut out and filed because they are valuable for comparison, particularly over long periods. Coloured and mounted in series on placards, with appropriate lettering, they contribute not only to the education of the passer-by, but will probably encourage him to remember the library when he wants information.

Other profitable material in commercial and technical libraries are clippings and pamphlets in the information files. Generally clippings for these departments are stored, unmounted, in folders, because most of them are ephemeral in value. In this state they cannot be displayed. But why shouldn't a selection of them be mounted on cartridge paper and arranged upon a board in our windows? Better still, why not put a few in every display? For example, the diagrams of imports and exports may be accompanied by articles and newscuttings interpreting or supplementing the information in them; so for other diagrams. But when introducing them always add a bold placard telling the onlookers that they are but a few of many thousand clippings on all kinds of commercial and technical matter. In addition to these side displays, make placards advertising the file, if it contains enough information to answer many questions. An example is shown on p. 137. There's persuasion in such copy. But if, after issuing it, you befool the inquirer, don't expect him to believe you again.

For nine years I was in charge of a good technical library (now wholly destroyed: the heavens fell and justice was undone) at Coventry, but unfortunately the central building had no room for a well-organized subject department, and showcases and windows were not to be jammed into any corner of a building thronged with books. In a technical department with adequate display equipment, my enthusiasm would run away with me because manufacturers will give fine photographs and pictures, and lend examples or models of machines and tools, all of which make forceful points of interest in cases and windows advertising the library's contents. Why librarians don't let themselves go on display I can't imagine. I know that old or unaccommodating buildings cage activity. Yet even in late years every grand new library shows to the passer the dull, heavy, uncommunicative rock-like front of a national bank or a county jail.

> "May no rude hand deface it
> And its forlorn *hic jacet!*"

Journals, too, can be displayed effectively, in a mass or by subject. I prefer to insinuate them as side lines. For example a show to advertise books on Mechanical Engineering would include one or two

## SPECIAL LIBRARIES

machine tools, pictures of machinery, directory-index cards to the books in the library, samples of vertical file material, and a placard on the mechanical engineering journals; so for Automobiles, Heat engines, Economics or other topic. General advertising never has the punch of specific advertising. Periodicals take up a lot of room and any publicity for them hits the mark only in a subject display. Moreover, isolate each periodical, or arrange two or three in a group; don't put all of them together, even if on the same subject. Find an attractive page, lay the periodical down flat and wide open on a tilted board. Cut out the title on the front cover, and mount it above the open copy. Display only new copies of journals. Arrange them with neatness in symmetrical precision. Slovenly exhibits do more harm than good.

Many other displays, similar in kind, suggest themselves to the energetic librarian with initiative and mother wit. Any display which leads an onlooker to reflect upon a subject may lead him to study it. Run through some of the divisions in the commercial library—Banking, Shipping, National production, Foreign trade, Money, Exchange—are they and others not of vital concern to all of us, as I have said? Ought we not to induce people to read up subjects so intimately connected with the nation's welfare; to study them, not in a narrow, bigoted party spirit, but with a real effort to understand the best policy for us all? And Technology? Have we no contribution to make? Isn't it our business to help our technicians and workers to turn out, under the best conditions, the most marketable articles at the least cost? Upon British commercial and technical ability our hope of prosperity, of better things for everybody, wholly depends.

### III

A science department offers exceptionally good opportunities to the imaginative displayer. Star maps, fine photographs and beautiful illustrations fill out displays on astronomy; simple apparatus, borrowed instruments and pictures, those on Physics and Chemistry; local specimens, maps and illustrations, those on Geology and Palaeontology. On Biology, Botany and Zoology the material is ampler and better than on any subject but Fine Art. He may even tackle Mathematics without tears: a group formed of a cone, a cylinder, a sphere, a pyramid and a prism, is a good centre of interest for a display, in placards, of the ramifications of Mathematics (in astronomy, crystallography, drawing, economics, engineering, games, geography, navigation, physics, recreations and so on) of portraits of great mathematicians (Napier, Kepler, Newton, Leibnitz, Maclaurin, Euler, Lagrange, Laplace, Gauss, Sir William Hamilton, Cayley and others) and of some of the chief algebraic formulae (addition and subtraction: $n + (- m) = n - m = - (m - n)$ . . . multiplication, division, fractions, powers and roots, and so on) which, reproduced on a large scale, will bring any algebraic juggler up all standing, in goggle-eyed or smiling attention.

Our aim in displaying scientific books is to lead young men and women of the right turn of mind to study one or other branch of science, either as a life work or as an attractive hobby. Most of the friends with whom I went walking in my youth were mad about botany, gardening, natural history, geology, physical geography or astronomy. Being only a bookful blockhead I sometimes found them dry companions away from a pub, but they enjoyed themselves so thoroughly that I was often envious. They got a kick out of country life denied to me. To-day most young people know nothing of these pleasures. The specialist reigns supreme, elbows the amateur away. Few men have the time to learn all about a subject. Are the rest to be deterred from pursuing knowledge? Are there to be no "pickers-up of learning's crumbs?" If we can't identify all the plants, are we to know none? Surely our job is to encourage the happy amateur as well as the professional? Effective displays are good means to a desirable end. At any rate, it's a poor lookout for young librarians if they have to spend their lives handling the novels of Rosa Dartle, and the romances of Dedlock Bucket.

## IV

Music, the Theatre, Ballet, Dramatic production, all material on the platform and the stage, the show industry from the gaff and the circus to grand opera—could there be a more delightful department

## SPECIAL LIBRARIES

to care for and develop? We might welcome funny people who now never enter our doors: actors, revue artistes, film stars and other spotlight folk who throw prelates, prime ministers and municipal mace bearers into the shade. My experience is limited to music, but I have always longed for room to take in everything back of the footlights.

This department also accommodates matter which readers don't expect to find in it: prospectuses of conservatoires; catalogues of music publishers and gramophone record makers in all parts of the world; clippings; illustrations; facsimiles of music manuscript; playbills; plates of theatrical costume; photographs of ballet dancers in action; theatre programmes; and so on.

Let us try a display on Johann Sebastian Bach. What is there? Engraved portraits of Bach and his patrons and friends; pictures of the statues of Eisenach and Leipzig, the birthplace, inside and out, at Eisenach, the churches at Ohrdruff, Lüneburg, Arnstadt, Mülhausen, Lübeck, Weimar, Hamburg, of the ducal castle at Köthen, of the church and school of St. Thomas at Leipzig, of the keyboard of the St. Boniface organ now in the Rathaus at Arnstadt; not to speak of autographs, facsimiles of his manuscripts and many other items. Where are we to get these exhibits? Begin and develop a music picture collection with energy and vigilance, and it is surprising how much good stuff will be got together in a brief period. We can also take enlargements of pictures in books, use them in displays, and file them for future reference. The British Museum and other libraries, here and in the U.S.A., own original manuscripts of scores, and photocopies of typical pages may be obtained for pocket money. To this material add a few good library placards, and we have a show which will set the musical town talking.

Again we won't shirk difficult subjects. What can be done to display musical education? No subject ought to be out of the reach of a librarian who has deliberately and unremittingly laid up material for display. Why not portraits of famous teachers?—Liszt, Joachim, Leschetizky, Wilhelmj, Boehm, David, Czerny, Moscheles, Spohr, Wieck, Matthay, Holst, Stanford and others—why not index placards to books important to learners of music?—title-pages of instruction books, old and new, celebrated and ordinary?—illustrations of famous conservatoires?—prospectuses of modern conservatoires here and on the continent? The most unpromising subject can be publicized, though with less effect than we would like.

In this department the gayest displays are those on the theatre. The material is copious: portraits, playbills, illustrations of costumes, theatre programmes, designs for scenery and all kinds of other alluring things.

But here the critic, looking over my shoulder, interrupts me. "You're getting into a groove," he cries. "You're still talking about displaying by subject. Aren't you losing an opportunity?"

"Why? How's that?"

"This Music and Theatre department of yours; wouldn't you depend more on a treatment of the whole room as a display rather than on periodical subject shows?"

"The books are the prime contents of the room."

"Yes, yes; I know. Let it be a library, but something more, something different. A place with character, suggesting Music and the Theatre: the orchestra and the footlights, the music chamber and the greenroom, the song and the dance. Keep green memories of music, musicians, players and the play. Glamour! Let the room be warmly welcoming, with portraits, pictures, mementoes, facsimiles in every corner and on every wall. The whole room, I mean."

"Oh, antiquarianism?"

"No. Keep antiquarianism in its limited place. Don't collect only or even largely for collectors, but for living musicians, lovers of music, the opera and the drama."

"Perhaps you're right," I admit. "Indeed you are, if there's wall space. And screens and tables. But you wouldn't shut out group displays altogether, would you?"

"No, no. Change is desirable. But give the room unity, an air, a feeling that it's an anteroom to the stage. And so far you have written about the displays inside this room. You still have to get people into it."

"Yes, there's that. Recommendation does much, very much. Actual outside publicity may be in external show windows, if there are any; or it may take the form of specially designed placards."

"Placards?" demurs the critic. "Well, perhaps. But don't advertisers ask people to *read* too much?"

"Try something different. What about a placard with the caption GREAT SONATAS above bold—not niggling—scorings of themes by Haydn, Mozart, Beethoven, Schubert and other composers? (*See illus. facing p. 113.*) That'll catch the eye of a music lover quicker than any copy in words. Remember what I wrote about algebraic formulae on p. 140, and how you snorted!"

"Not very colourful, is it?"

"Why not? Cream card. Thick staves in brilliant orange. Big notes in black. The caption and name of the library in green. Quite a good combination, I think. The scoring occupying the greater part of the placard, of course: boost the subject, not the library."

"And a theatre window? Play pictures, I suppose. Costume designs. Portraits of your funny people, eh?—opera singers, ballet dancers, actresses, revue artistes. You're crazy."

"Crazy. I wish we were all crazy. Why half the women and all the clergy of the town would buzz round the window. The trouble is we're not half alive."

## V

When I drop into a library, and note how the librarian has exhibited his local prints, I am delighted to meet a supporter, yet irritated because he does not extend the practice to other departments. One of my brethren was quite entertaining in his ridicule of display. Too much good nature is one of my weaknesses, and I neglected to remind him that the walls of the main stairway of his central library were almost hidden by framed prints, of which he was inordinately proud.

But while display has been accepted as a tool in the local collection, I am not content with its quality. All the prints should be exhibited in the local room in class order, one subject at a time, with the items chronologically arranged. Having decided upon Edinburgh Castle and its precincts as the subject, hang the plans and pictures, not in balanced groups by size, but by date; only so can we reveal changes and developments. General views of Edinburgh? Group in order of dates those taken from the same point of the compass, to enable the beholder to follow the city's changing panorama. What was Edinburgh like when Walter Scott as a boy played on the surrounding hills and in the Grange fields?

> "Blackford! on whose uncultured breast,
> Among the broom, and thorn, and whin,
> A truant-boy, I sought the nest."

and when as a man he walked in the old and new town? Bring together all the prints of his time: plans, general views, pictures of hills, valleys, rivers, bridges, streets, public buildings, portraits of local characters, and the record of passing events of the time. Put all material of a kind together, and arrange it by date. Then we see Edinburgh depicted as Sir Walter saw it in reality.

These displays are in the room with the local collection, or in an adjoining room; the related books near them. Here let me note that in these days of photo-reproduction a modest collection may contain facsimiles of rare documents and books in other libraries. Nearly every Edinburgh manuscript in the British Museum and the Bodleian has been copied for our collection. Now that we are well into the dark ages, no opportunity should be lost of acquiring photo-copies of unique or rare items.

For approach or outdoor publicity arrange window shows in corridors, and in front of the building—if you are lucky to have windows instead of a mausoleum façade!—contribute paragraphs to newspapers, and reproduce prints on the bills of fare of public luncheons and dinners, and on reception programmes.

Six or seven good prints, carefully annotated on labels readable two yards away, a few choice books, and some placards on the collection as a whole, will fill adequately and effectively a window in a corridor or outside the building.

Newspaper paragraphs! Young librarians should be taught to write them. Nobody bothered to teach me, and I never learned. But a colleague comes to the rescue with this:

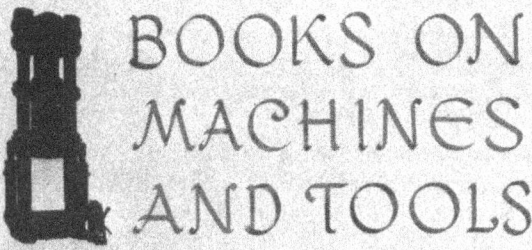

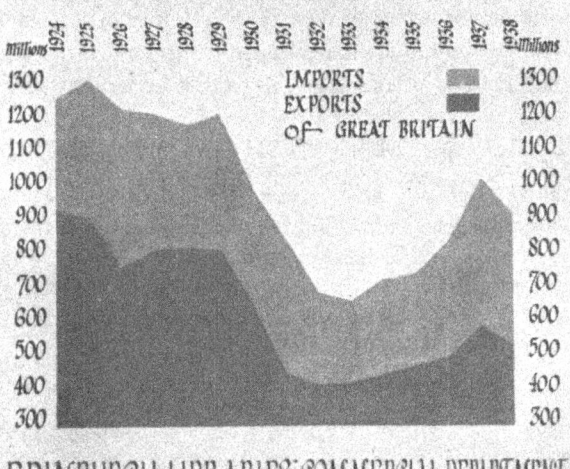

TECHNICAL AND COMMERCIAL DEPARTMENT PLACARDS
By T. S. Carruthers

*Facing p.* 144 (*see p.* 136)

## SPECIAL LIBRARIES

William Burke, an Irish navvy, murdered fifteen men and women, brought ruin on a famous Edinburgh surgeon, and was hung amid public execration, bequeathing a new word to our language, and gaining for himself a place in the *Dictionary of National Biography*. For years Mr. Grimwig, our local antiquary, has been collecting books, documents, illustrations and everything he could lay hands upon about the Burke and Hare Crimes. . . . Now he has handed his collection over to the Public Library. . . .

And so on. The first sentence rivets attention to a paragraph which is lucid, compact, and easy to read in a moment of time. (A. E. Coppard, the well-known short story-teller, wrote the opening sentences of his tales inimitably.) Many editors don't like publishing a veiled advertisement, but they are readier when it has news value, and is written with gusto and point. They are generally willing to reproduce original drawings or rare prints, and to acknowledge the source of them.

When the mayor or the provost gives a dinner or a reception, isn't it a good idea to reproduce a local print on the bill of fare, or on the programme? Here is an example, the picture being omitted:

EAST VIEW OF EDINBURGH CASTLE, ABOUT 1750.

This may be taken as a very accurate representation of the Castle about 1750. The vacant ground between the entrance to the Castle and the houses at the head of the Castlehill was formerly at a considerably lower level than the present esplanade, and was used by the citizens as a recreation ground. A group in the foreground is represented engaged in the amusement of "putting the stone."

*From an Etching by Paul Sandby in the Local Collection,*
*Edinburgh Public Libraries.*

The italic note is our publicity, for the print will certainly be well talked about by the guests. Some mayors refuse the offer to embellish menus or programmes, but the librarian should always try to lead them astray.

Now and then, say once in five years, an exhibition of large numbers of the prints may be shown in a gallery or hall apart from the library. Keep it open for a month or two. Arrange it in the same way as the smaller displays: hang all the prints of the same subject in a

*Photo: C. S. Minto*

## FOUNTAINBRIDGE BRANCH, EDINBURGH

With visible interior

*Facing p.* 145 *(see p.* 152*)*

group, and stick to chronological order even if, in general appearance, the exhibition is rather the worse for it.

One other direct means of advertising ought not to be overlooked. When a public building is about to be erected, or an improvement scheme is in prospect, offer to exhibit in the local room the plans and drawings, including all competitive drawings. Unfortunately proper accommodation is often lacking, the approach to the room is inconvenient, while the town council don't always welcome too much publicity for their schemes, perhaps because they cannily fear the spread of opposition. From our point of view a show of this kind is expedient, for it attracts visitors to the room and persuades them that we are concerned as much with modern developments as with antiquities and history.

## VI

While preparing displays trimly and workmanlike—with professional skill and excellence—I wouldn't recoil from sacrificing a little refinement if thereby the end of drawing attention were more surely achieved. John Cotton Dana, an American librarian for whom I had an abounding admiration, designed placards of great beauty. No lettering met with his approval unless it was harmonious, finely shaped, well proportioned, and comely in spacing. The Dana or a like model should be followed in any display, except when clearly it fails to attract. A too delicate design is flat and inanimate. Uniformity does not stimulate but enervates attention. A notice should be *noticeable*, and so many of them aren't!

Without being uniform, display to advertise the fine art department ought to be of a kind and quality to appeal to artists and to people of artistic tastes; variety, beauty, legibility, salience are essential qualities. (*See illus. facing p.* 112.) Far better to refrain from advertisement which fails to hit the mark. Lettering, for example, on the ordinary art room notice. Lay in a supply of postcards reproducing pictures, or illustrating objects of art in museum galleries. When a notice of moderate size is required, lay down a postcard in the upper left hand corner of the card, frame it in a single black or coloured line, and letter the notice in the remaining **L**-shaped space. If the picture

## SPECIAL LIBRARIES

is toned, colour the lettering in keeping; if dark, give the letters more body, if light rather less; if coloured (which is desirable) choose a harmonious hue for the lettering. The postcard need not have any relation to the subject of the notice; its function is to attract, to give an eye-catching point of interest.

If practicable connect display with happenings, or with art, education, work and life in the community. List the subjects taught in the schools and shown in the gallery exhibitions. Then draft a programme. But it must not be forgotten that many art lovers have no connection with schools or academies, and that the main business is to expound the whole contents of the department. We must follow art masters and curators to their limit, and go beyond it. Why are manufacturers not invited to send to galleries and museums photographs of artistic modern furniture, from which a "hanging committee" might draw up a "short leet" of specimens, provisionally approved, to be sent in for final selection? Then the public would enjoy an exhibition of contemporary art applied to halls, stairways; living, dining, bed and bath rooms; kitchens, pantries, garages; glass, silver, linen, china. Why not exhibitions of *modern* arts and crafts, the applied art of *to-day*: metalwork; electric fittings; textiles; ceramics and glass; stage production; plastics; printing and book illustration; packaging (biscuits, chocolates, preserves, chemicals and other articles) and other industrial arts. Can we promote education in art, appreciation of beautiful things, and prosperity among artists unless exhibitions of modern craftsmanship are held in every town, regularly and frequently? Would not the hanging committees, in arranging the exhibitions, offer valuable guidance to manufacturers who are producing for us *to-day*? There may be good reasons for not holding exhibitions of this modern kind, I admit: rich and influential manufacturers might attempt corruption, and competition would no doubt be bitterly jealous; yet for the sake of progress risks must be accepted.

There can be little prosperity for artists and designers unless more and more people are taught to value things of beauty, and unless art is applied to the common things which nearly everybody must have. An art library under the control of a librarian who realizes that it is his duty not only to help artists, collectors and connoisseurs, but to promote art education, has power for good. He isn't trammelled as curators are. Let him apply to manufacturers for photographs and catalogues; let him also cut up and mount on cartridge sheets of uniform size the illustrations from each issue of *The Studio Year Book of Decorative Art, Creative Design, Arts and Decoration* and other like periodicals and works published here and abroad. So all the material required for exhibitions is quickly gathered, and is worth displaying, though far less attractive than the actual goods. I want to be emphatic on one point. We don't doubt for a moment that in science and technology we must be modern. Why then should we go all antiquarian in the local collection or the art library? Why overlook the fact that our town is occupied by living people?—that art must flower to-day as in the past, or be a "joy for ever" only to the collector and the connoisseur.

I have laboured this suggestion of a modern side for art department display (and by "modern" I don't mean only the output of the colour dollopers and splodgers who monopolize criticism in these days) because a real effort is necessary to collect the material for it. On the other hand the photographs and reproductions of older works of art are plentiful and are collected easily. They are sold, at low prices, by nearly all the greater museums and galleries, by firms which have a reputation for making good photographs, and by societies, such as the Dürer, the Vasari and the Medici, famous for the quality of their reproductions. Pictures without text, for example Lippmann, *Kupferstiche und Holzschnitte alter Meister*, are more useful if abstracted from the volumes and mounted; so too are the many fine examples published loose in portfolios. In short, the best material for our purpose isn't lacking.

Practical difficulties I know only too well. In bygone years libraries were not planned to accommodate display. Nor to-day. Even where space is provided in great libraries it is often of the wrong kind, and quite inadequate, particularly for exhibiting the overflowing material in the art collection. Then again an exhibition in a general gallery fails to introduce people to books, which is our main object. Where display accommodation is provided in a special library, or in an adjoining room, the exhibits and the books are connected without a chance of failure.

## SPECIAL LIBRARIES

The furniture and fittings of an art library should include bookcases, screens, slopes, table showcases, illuminated wall or island showcases, and frames of several standard sizes. A bookcase and a screen may be combined economically. Make a bookcase double-sided up to 4 ft. from the base, and single-sided, for quarto and folio books, above that height. The back of the single-side part, if built properly, forms a picture screen which takes up no room and virtually costs nothing. This screen, neutral in colour, has fixed picture rails 8 in. apart, upon which standard frames, with rigid hooks at the back, are hung quickly in perfect alignment. The method is economical because the maximum number of volumes may be stored in spaces calculated to take the proportionate volume of stock in each size. The intermixture of books and pictures gives the room a homely look which is pleasing.

## VII

This chapter is far from being an adequate treatment of a subject which, in fact, requires a volume. Read in conjunction with the other chapters, however, it may suffice until a writer with ample practical experience of display in special libraries comes forward. At present few special libraries are open to the public, and display is neglected in most of them. Indeed, few libraries of any kind, general or special, are thoroughly expounded to the public; in that we all fail lamentably —oh, most lamentably. In this country librarianship hasn't been forward-looking, energetic and dynamic; in ideas we have been singularly barren, and we have left so many things undone, not always for want of money, but often for want of vision and enterprise.

> "Why not, then, have earlier spoken,
> Written, bustled? Who's to blame
> If your silence kept unbroken?
> 'True, but there were sundry jottings,
> 'Stray-leaves, fragments, blurrs and blottings,
> 'Certain first steps were achieved
> 'Already which'—(is that your meaning?)
> 'Had well borne out whoe'er believed
> 'In more to come!'"
> *Browning: Waring.*

CHAPTER VII

## 4. ENTRANCE, CORRIDOR AND EXTERNAL WINDOW DISPLAYS

### I

A RULE to begin with. *No book of any kind, rare or not, should be exhibited unless a copy of it can be produced for reading either in the library or at home.* As far back as I remember the bookseller, when the occasion warranted it, has set apart a whole window for copies of a book of the week or the season, and for publicity matter about it. The first massed array I saw was of *In Darkest Africa* by Stanley, the greatest, of the *Life of Gladstone* by Morley. Such shows are profitable to the bookseller, with many copies to sell, but not to the librarian, with few to lend. Will a prudent bookseller display a book not in stock, unless he can get copies by return of post? Is it then prudent for a librarian to show a book when all the copies are out? No. Therefore (1) displays *within libraries* are of a changing miscellany of books, all issuable on demand, the showcases for them being near the assistants who change books; while (2) displays *in entrance, corridor or outside windows* are of placard (in which term I include posters and showcards) and other exhibits (rarely books) advertising the library service as a whole, or by departments, subjects and specialities. The outer shows are intended to lure in the passer to look at the books; the inner to reveal the contents of the library to him. This chapter therefore will contain few references to book displays, which indeed have already been described.

### II

Two elevations of the Baltimore Public Library have been designed on the lines of a big department store. Thirteen great windows, beautiful in shape, are for displays illustrating the work and contents of the library. When I saw them a number of questions jumped to my mind. But as the library had not been long opened, and as the

## WINDOW DISPLAY

U.S.A. was deep in an economic pit, apparently bottomless, and the conditions therefore abnormal, I did not ask them. It was doubly significant however that the Carnegie Corporation of New York had made a three-year grant-in-aid of the window displays, first because a subsidy was justifiable only if the experiment was new, important, or on a large scale, and then because it implied that the upkeep of so many windows looked like eating into money. And so I tacitly questioned. Are not thirteen windows too many to fulfil the simple function of luring the onlooker in to inspect books? Can Baltimore afford to maintain so many? Has it enough material to supply a continuous, varied series of displays, thirteen at a time? Over a long period will there be an equivalent return in *extra* use for the annual outlay? Would not two windows be enough? Cleveland has only two, though they might be larger. Remember that, besides the thirteen windows, Baltimore has twenty-seven showcases within.[1] Cleveland has an even larger number in its corridors. Though I cannot answer these questions for American librarians, I aver that no British library can afford the money and the labour to organize displays in thirteen front windows, or would earn enough additional use to recoup the outlay and the trouble. The prospect of planning the changes in thirteen windows every three weeks (as in Baltimore) for two or three years would daunt me, keen displayer though I am. However, Mr. Joseph Wheeler has courage and enterprise in ample measure, and is to be admired.

My ambition halts at two, or at most three, roomy front windows in a central library: and at four corridor or entrance shows, the latter preferably where they can be seen from outdoors.

A commercial library, if apart from the main building, should have its own window, with book displays within, near the open shelves; a corridor exhibit is hardly necessary.

At a large branch a window facing the street, and book displays inside, are enough, without entrance or corridor shows. (*See illus. facing p.* 48.)

Every approach or front window should be big enough to attract the attention of people on the other side of the road. Peepholes in

[1] *Reorganization of a Large Public Library: Ten Years' Report of the Enoch Pratt Free Library*, 1926–35, p. 138.

the façade, one on either hand of the main door, are playthings. It is an economical plan to design the entrance of a central or branch library as a piazza, loggia or foyer. Protect the street front with metal doors and windows glazed from top to bottom with transparent glass. Recess the windows into the sides and back of the loggia, where, visible from outside, they draw people in to gaze at them under cover from the weather. Or try this plan at a branch in a large system, or at the central library of a small or middle town, if you can move the committee to withstand the urge toward a public building. Erect the library over shops. Between them run an arcade to a stair, leading to the library, at the far end of it. In the arcade and on the stair recess show windows. People will use the arcade as the approach to the library and as a shelter. The plan has these advantages: a site may be got right in the heart of the local business quarter; the rents of the shops add to the library's income; the library above will get better air and more natural light; and the arcade will advertise it. But the shops must be deep, with cellars, so that the tenants have storage, and the site must be in the central or local business quarter, or the shops won't let. A vulgar plan? That's the beauty of it.

Excepting the last the libraries in mind hitherto are of the public building type. But I prefer (and the loggia idea reminds me of the fact) a library resembling a department store even more than Baltimore does. Away with dead-wall libraries. Let people look into them. Have big low windows, through which passers see the bookcases and the readers moving among them in the home reading and junior libraries. The reference room may be more secluded. The new Fountainbridge branch at Edinburgh is an attempt at this visible-interior library. A large part of the well-lighted interior is open to the view of citizens passing. So the building advertises its function. The turreted corner, bounding the main stair, is floodlit after dark: a pillar of flame. No building in the neighbourhood is brighter; the cinemas are more garish, not more thrusting.[1] (*See illus. facing p.* 145.)

---

[1] Many books on shop windows have been published. One most fertile in ideas is the well-illustrated *Smaller Retail Shops*, by Bryan and Norman Westwood (Architectural Press, 1937). See also *The Architecture of Shops*, by A. Trystan Edwards (Chapman and Hall, 1933) and *Shop Fronts*, by Frederick Chatterton (Architectural Press, 1927).

WINDOW DISPLAY

### III

The artificial lighting of approach and external windows calls for careful study by architect and librarian. Most windows are too high ceiled and too deep. The top of the glazed opening need not be more than about 8 ft. from the pavement or floor, and the deck of the window not more than 4 ft. deep if the front is of plane glass, or 5 ft. if of curved, non-reflecting glass. Thus a clear window 2 ft. 6 in. from the ground, 5 ft. 6 in. above the deck, and 10 ft. long, before a recess 4 ft. deep, is about right for a good show.

The lamps should be hidden from any onlooker, no matter how near he stands to the pane. Therefore they should be snugged against the inner front of a well, which reaches some feet above the glass, and reflected down on to the display. If the well cannot be deep enough, conceal the lamps by hanging them as high as possible above a frosted glass ceiling. In a window of this area ten or twelve moderate lamps are better than two or three of high power. Bright, well-diffused, almost shadowless illumination, without glare, spottiness, or reflecting surfaces, is the standard to be achieved, and with care and thought it may be. The material exhibited under so revealing a light must be faultless in workmanship, and everything about and within the window perfectly clean, because any blemish will be conspicuous.

For all the windows curved non-reflecting glass is better than any other. I don't mean the K-Ray glass, noted on p. 117; that has its convex surface to the onlooker, and is intended to protect notices, paintings or other articles in shallow, upright cases. The window glass now referred to has its concave surface to the onlooker, and behind it colours look brighter and purer, and the display is not broken up by reflections from stationary and moving objects in the street. Properly fitted with this glass a window appears *unglazed*. Some traders object to the curvature because the contents of the window are too far back to be seen until the passer is nearly in front. Another objection is the greater depth of the window. All the same the values of any well-lighted display behind non-reflecting glass are so heightened that these objections should be ignored. Diagrams of non-reflecting windows may be examined in *Glass in Architecture and*

*Decoration* by Raymond McGrath and A. C. Frost (Architectural Press, 1937, p. 553)—a valuable book.

Approach windows, in entrances and corridors, should be lighted as radiantly as front windows, and the lamps, except where the daylight is ample, should burn all the time the library is open. (*See illus. facing p.* 160.) In addition to the general scheme have windows in the dull parts of the approach. Hitherto I have assumed that the windows are recessed in the wall, this method of fitting being economical in first cost, and in space. But a lighted showcase will stand against a wall in which a window cannot be cut, or, double-sided, as an island in a corridor or recess.

While the approach windows should be well and continually lighted, the entrance and corridors, even after dark, need only dim lights, if any. At Cleveland the gay and brilliant windows in the twilight corridors look snug and sociable and friendly; good for business, too, because the windows draw people to them, as I observed myself.

In this country the illuminated stair window at the Scarborough Public Library is a model. (*See illus. facing p.* 160.) That at the Golders Green branch of the Hendon Public Libraries is a showcase for books, so are those in the hall of the Leith Public Library, which the enemy has put out of action.

Coloured lights? No; I don't like them. The colour should be in the display. Far too many coloured lights burn wastefully, though they add to the gaiety of the streets. Among all this garishness a flood of white light is a beckoning relief. At all events coloured light is out of place unless the exhibits are in black and white.

## IV

For every window we require not fewer than twenty-six displays a year, the assumption being that each will be on view a fortnight; an average period. An exhibit on reference work may remain in the window for a month without becoming stale, one on an unpopular subject for three weeks, while the interest of another on a topic of the day (a kind I don't recommend) might end in a week. The dura-

## WINDOW DISPLAY

tion of a show also depends upon the strength of the bookstock behind it. Remove it when its work is done, when all or nearly all the books on the subject are out. What d'ye lack? Well, don't advertise that you can lend it.

This figure of twenty-six shows for each window every year is a unit enabling us to determine whether our non-fiction stock in its extent, variety and quality, requires one, two or more windows to advertise it; or none at all! With an average of one show a fortnight Baltimore's thirteen front windows call for 338 shows annually; or one show every three weeks, 221 (see p. 151). In Edinburgh our non-fiction stock, before the war plentiful and of good quality (for we buy comparatively few novels and ought to buy fewer) would not sustain more than two 10 ft. windows at the central library, or fifty-two fresh and attractive shows a year I am referring now to windows advertising the library's functions, administration, and contents, not to internal showcases of issuable books.

We not only have to relate the number of displays to the stock, which, if inadequate, ruins our advertising, but the cost of them to the results. If a display fails to win more use for books on its subject, or to persuade the public that the library is well-managed by wide-awake and vigorous custodians, money is more or less wasted. Therefore all displays should be costed not only to check results, but to discover the most economical way of achieving them. Some displays cost too much because little thought has been given to organizing them. Are we to employ assistants on lettering and placard making? Preferably not. Anyway we ought to keep an account of the value of the time they spend upon this work, as well as watch its quality. Often they are engaged upon tasks which outsiders can do better and cheaper; and showcard writing is one of them.

Let me explain how we may decide whether the cost of a show is justified or not.

During an Edinburgh Education Week a stall of considerable size was taken in the Exhibition Hall for a much commended display. Yet during the week and for a month afterwards fewer readers enrolled than in the corresponding period of the year before The show brought no rag or tatter of business. Did the library get enough general publicity from the week to warrant the outlay? I doubted, and made up my mind never to co-operate again.

Return to our windows. The additional use of books on any subject displayed is calculable. But when weighing the profit we ask several questions: (1) Was the subject popular or unpopular, wide or limited in appeal? (2) Was the worth of the general advertising justified by the number of people who stayed to look at it? (3) Was the subject well- or ill-represented in the library?

Let me try to answer the questions.

(1) If I had three shows, (*a*) on the British Navy, (*b*) on American History and (*c*) on Gaelic Language and Literature (diligently collected at Edinburgh) I should expect the consequent *extra* use to be in these *proportions* (*a*) 20, (*b*) 4, (*c*) 1—twenty books on the British Navy, or four books on American History, for every one of the books on or in Gaelic. Note: *extra* use. With these proportions I should be content. We must allow for relative popularity. If none of the shows earned any issues above normal, from the point of view of *return in use* they failed. When costing a window show make a credit allowance for material usable again.

(2) How are we to estimate general advertising value? A difficult question. When we display reference books or a whole window of periodicals, we don't look for calculable results. Probably the results are not calculable. But let me take a grand subject for a display—BOOKS OF GREAT INFLUENCE—on which we might arrange one comprehensive window, or several windows by selecting the books of one or two classes at a time. Thus, Fichte's *Der geschlossene Handelsstaat* (*The Closed Commercial State*) an early, if not the earliest harangue on autarky, the same philosopher's *herrenvolk* doctrine in *Reden an die deutsche Nation* (*Addresses to the German Nation*), *Capital* by Karl Marx, *Mein Kampf* by Hitler, the seed-thought of which is all in Fichte,[1] *Der Mythus* by Rosenberg, the works of Lenin, and the speeches and writings of Mussolini, might be shown, with illustrative material and terse extracts on picture placards, as examples of books which had Atlantean power in modern politics. *Utopia* by More,

[1] For some time before the U.S.A. entered the war in 1941 a Fichte (pro-German) society had been in existence in that country.

## WINDOW DISPLAY

*Contrat Social* by Rousseau, *Population* by Malthus, *The Wealth of Nations* by Adam Smith, *Liberty* by Mill, the *Grundlinien der Philosophie des Rechts* by Hegel, *Uncle Tom's Cabin* by Stowe, *The Origin of Species* by Darwin, *Looking Backward* by Bellamy are other detonating works. Such books, and others about them, would not be read much oftener for these shows, which however are general advertising of originality and drive if planned to demonstrate the power of the book.[1]

If many people stopped to take a good look at a window show I should believe it to be worth while as general advertising. Direct and calculable results are more satisfactory, but the incalculable, the imponderable, isn't to be dismissed lightly as of unknown hitting power, and therefore worthless. The difference between a library which develops, and another which neglects display, is that between one concern awaiting, and another intent on business, between a cool "how d'ye do" and a warm handclasp with a cheery word of welcome.

(3) Any display inadequately supported by bookstock within the library is not only worthless, but thoroughly harmful to business, because readers are disappointed. Therefore the question whether the bookstock behind the display is sufficient must be honestly answered. The relation between bookstock and display is considered in Chapter IX; here I need only remember the duty of revising selection. Choose the subject of a display six weeks or two months beforehand. Review the bookstock, select requisite additions, and get them into the library before arranging the window. Display compels us to tackle the job, often postponed, of revising stock habitually. Inadequate

---

[1] *Uncle Tom's Cabin* and *Looking Backward* may seem out of place in this list. Of the former more copies were sold than of any other novel in the nineteenth century: it was a book, Professor Trent tells us, that stirred the world and was instrumental in bringing on a civil war and freeing an enslaved race. *Looking Backward* was a picture of a machine-made Utopia. It had an enormous sale all all over the English-speaking world, and was freely translated. Its influence upon politics was fleeting, for equality and socialism made little more progress after than before it. Upon economics its power was great and perhaps disastrous, for it finally reconciled the labouring classes to machinery by forecasting that in a mechanic age their lives would be richer and easier. Bellamy did not foresee that the outcome might be great unemployment and the accumulation of overwhelming military power in the hands of a few. Still, the book, though its aim went wrong, is an example of one that had great power.

stock defeats the displayer. With plenty of books he augments the number and variety of window shows. More shows, more subject reading, and therefore a richer library.

## V

It is autumn, the time to frame our programme of windows for next year.

Note a difference. Though the shows (being as it were dissolving) for internal cases should be planned ahead to attain a coherent variety in the series, they call for little preparation, as only books (presumably already in stock) and a few placards are wanted. The displays in front windows, on the contrary, must be organized well ahead of the dates of showing because provocative and titillating placards designed in the turn of a hand are likely to be ineffective, and poor in execution, and properties and exhibits, hurriedly collected after a few days' notice, will not make every window a first-rate instalment of an integrated but ever-varying series.

As an exercise let us make a two-year calendar for double front windows; that is to say, four shows a month or ninety-six in as many weeks. Thereafter, with additions and variations, the material, or most of it, may be used again. Though the calendar is framed for a large central library, nearly all the subjects are purposely ordinary and even commonplace, so that most are quite suitable for the lesser windows of smaller libraries, assuming them to have their proper subject bookstocks, instead of the love stories of Rosa Dartle, the bloodstained marionette romances of Two-gun Roughrider, and the trigger-tales of Bobby Automatic—

> "Crime, that breaks all bounds,
>    Bigamy and arson,
> Poison, blood, and wounds,
>    Will carry well the farce on
> Now it's just in shape;
>    Yet, with fire and murder
> Treason, too, and rape
>    Might help it all the further."
>
> *Lord Neaves.*

# WINDOW DISPLAY

| *First Window* | *Second Window* |
|---|---|

### January
1 Kitchen gardening     3 The Age of Elizabeth
2 Floriculture     4 Economic geography

### February
1 Economic geology     3 U.S.A. history and travel
2 Sea adventure. Voyages     4 American literature

### March
1 Cookery     3 Domestic arts
2 Botany     4 Great biographies

### April
1 Works of great painters     3 Country cottages and bungalows
2 Geology     4 Travel at home and abroad. Holidays

### May
1 Field and farm     3 Photography
2 Nature study. Flowers of the countryside     4 Sports and pastimes (outdoor). Camping

### June
1 British animal life     3 Angling
2 Great novelists     4 English cathedrals and abbeys

### July
1 Travel and adventure in many lands     3 Mountaineering
2 Art of the film     4 Wales and the Welsh

### August
1 The Branch libraries     3 Careers
2 Greece and Rome     4 Scottish literature

### September
1 Aids to reading and study     3 Reference work
2 Schools and education     4 Fleets of the World

# MANUAL OF BOOK CLASSIFICATION

*First Window*      *Second Window*

### October

1 Engineering and engineers    3 Chemistry in the service of man
2 Local government    4 Drawing. Design

### November

1 Oriental art    3 Age of Dr. Johnson
2 Astronomy    4 Art in everyday life

### December

1 India    3 The Tropics
2 Great musicians    4 British Navy, past and present

### January

1 Child welfare    3 Office management
2 English poetry    4 Advertising

### February

1 Bible. Christian history    3 Health and nursing
2 Broadcasting. Wireless    4 Ballet and the dance

### March

1 The Building arts    3 The Electric age
2 Modern European history    4 Engraving

### April

1 The Near East: Egypt, Palestine    3 Annual report of the Library
2 Anthropology. Natural history of man    4 Domestic architecture

### May

1 Labour history and biography    3 Needlework, Dressmaking
2 Shop architecture, fittings    4 Citizenship

### June

1 Water colour art    3 Switzerland. Alps
2 Maps, old and new    4 Devon and Cornwall

### July

1 Edinburgh, past and present    3 Popular science
2 Scotland    4 Australasia

ILLUMINATED SHOW WINDOW ON STAIR
Scarborough Public Library

*Facing p.* 160 *(see p.* 154*)*

## WINDOW DISPLAY

*First Window*                     *Second Window*

### August

1 Handicrafts
2 Amateur theatre. Community drama

3 Co-operation
4 Age of Dickens

### September

1 Music
2 Italian art

3 Concert season
4 Accounting. Auditing

### October

1 Machines, Tools
2 Economics. Statistics

3 Art of the book. Fine printing
4 Woodworking

### November

1 Housing and town planning
2 Arts and crafts

3 Heat engines
4 The Children's library. Books for the young

### December

1 Industrial psychology
2 The Ancient world

3 The Canadian scene
4 Mechanical drawing

The reader, running his eye over these ninety-six subjects, will note how many more there might be: the Weather; Authorship and literary aids; Big game hunting; Physical culture; Ballads; The Nation's larder; Indoor games; Aeronautics; Science of life; Journalism; English history; Mythology; Bench and bar of England; Ships and shipping; Christmas books; The Seasons in nature; South Africa; South America; Caricature; Bakery and confectionery; Plant geography; Etching—I write them down as they come to mind.

Repeat seasonal subjects—Kitchen gardening, Floriculture, Sports and pastimes, Indoor games—every year, the old display material being refreshed with new items; and all the subjects at the end of two years. The calendar may be extended by introducing displays on topics of the day, though for my part I avoid them as needing no advertising at that time. Many subjects suggest others: Fleets of the world—Armies; Local government—Parliament and central govern-

WINDOW DISPLAY, Designed by Mathilde Kelly
Hild Regional Branch, The Chicago Public Library

ment. When the stock is large, some of the above exhibitions may be divided: Floriculture into Rock gardens, Greenhouses, Orchids; Nature study into Wild flowers, Insects, Butterflies and Moths; Photography into Colour or Architectural or Portrait or Artistic photography; The Electric age into Lighting or Heating or Transport; Music into Beethoven or English music or modern music, or other parts; Edinburgh, past and present, into Edinburgh Castle or Holyroodhouse or what you will; The Art of the book into Book illustration or Fine printing.

In all windows include a condensed, boldly lettered indication—a brief alphabetic directory-index—of the classmarks of the subject and its allies. On the Building Arts, for example:

| | |
|---|---|
| Bricklaying | 693.2 |
| Carpentry | 694 |
| Concrete | 693.5 |
| Drawing for builders | 692.1 |
| Heating | 697 |
| Joinery | 694.6 |
| Masonry | 693.1 |
| Materials | 691 |
| Painting | 698 |
| Paperhanging | 698 |
| Plastering | 693.6 |
| Plumbing | 696 |
| Slating | 695.2 |
| Specifications | 692.3 |
| Stones, building | 691.2–3; 553.5 |
| Tiling | 695.3 |
| Ventilation | 697.9 |
| Wood | 691.1; 581.6 |

This directory—an ordinary example has been intentionally chosen—analyses the subject and its relations into all their parts, any one of which may remind a reader of some definite information he would like to have. That the Directory-Index is desirable I know because passers make notes of the classmarks. On this account the books on the subject which the window advertises should be in their places on the

## WINDOW DISPLAY

ordinary shelves in class order, where readers may find and borrow them. Later on, when the display is withdrawn, revive the declining interest in the books, which by this time will have been returned to the library, by showing them in an internal book showcase.

Don't show a book in an approach or front window, unless it be rare, or obtainable only for reference: the kind of book that is worshipped but not read, such as Burns's copy of Fergusson's poems, or that give "character to a library" and none to readers, who rarely look at it, such as the *Antichità Romane* by Piranesi or the *Reichenbachia* by Sander. Objects which rivet attention upon a show are desirable: here are some examples:

SEA ADVENTURES: Models of ships, Sea pictures

MACHINES. TOOLS: A small lathe, or other simple machine tool

ENGRAVING: Engravers' tools

NEEDLEWORK: Examples of fine needlework and embroidery

ACCOUNTING. AUDITING: A comptometer or other calculating machine

WATER COLOUR ART: Some good examples of original water colour drawings

Few are the subjects that cannot be illustrated by exhibits which focus attention.

Many of the required articles may be borrowed from museums, galleries, local departments or manufacturers. Indeed the displayer cannot do better than seek the aid of curators, and heads of local departments. If he takes care in his shows to advertise the museum as well as the library he should have no difficulty in obtaining specimens from the curator. Each of the local departments, Health, Electricity, Education, Public Works and the other services, ought to be able to collaborate in several windows, and will do so readily if the department and the library are advertised equally. Sometimes clever amateurs or enthusiastic specialists will prepare shows; recently I had a first-rate demonstration-exhibit of plant diseases.

## VI

As an exercise, let us plan one window. I say "us" because I want readers to improve upon my scheme, as no doubt they will. What subject shall it be? The United States? It is a fine example, and not too easy.

First we must review the stock on U.S. history, biography, constitution, topography, maps, commerce, literature, art, architecture and natural history. Is there enough in the home reading and reference libraries? What books should be bought?

"All very well," the critic objects; "but readers aren't interested in the United States. I'm not going to buy a lot of books nobody wants."

"Ah, ah; the old story. Do you know that they won't read 'em? Have you tried? Anyhow ought a librarian to be a led ass? Isn't it his job to try and get people to read informative books? What's his job if it isn't that? And even if people don't want to know anything about the U.S.A.—a statement I believe to be quite unfounded—oughtn't we to try to arouse their interest? Or are we simply to issue Rosa Dartle?"

Revise the stock thoroughly, and order the books in good time.

Now for the rallying exhibits. Prepare for two big maps by obtaining pieces of 8 or $9\frac{1}{2}$ mm. plyboard about 48 in. square, or 60 by 48 in. Cover them on one side with cartridge paper, which if evenly damped can be pasted down without wrinkles. On this paper trace a pencil outline of the United States. Then divide the map vertically to show the areas of Atlantic, Eastern, Central, Mountain and Pacific times. Instruct the showcard writer to paint the outline half-an-inch thick, to colour the time-areas, and to letter the names of the lakes, the great rivers, and a few cities. Also get him to write on the map the following copy: "The time is the same throughout the British Isles. But in the U.S.A., over 2,700 miles across at the widest point, there are five time-areas. The people on the Atlantic coast get up four hours earlier than those on the Pacific." (The word "copy" means the short statement, message, slogan or blurb lettered on a placard. I would prefer "brief", but copy is the accepted term.) What use is the

## WINDOW DISPLAY

map? Geographically, none. But it makes a colourful show, and it does drive home the fact that the U.S.A. is of great area. The other map, similarly made, by showing in colour the isotherms of December or January would make clear to the dullest person the range of climate in the States. But who wants to know about the climate? Does that matter? The map is really a pictorial placard to beckon people to the window. The copy for the map should be in these or like words: "Oranges and lemons ripen in California while blizzards blow in New York."

Meantime write to U.S. Government departments, to selected oil, fruit, railroad, river and lake shipping and manufacturing companies, explaining what you want to do, and asking them to send photographs, illustrations and maps. More than you want will come, but the surplus may be filed away in the commercial department, or reserved for other displays. Mount the material on cards which bear appropriate copy in letters not smaller than one inch for capitals, and ⅝ in. for lower case. Then arrange the cards, the short directory-index of the subject (see p. 162), and your own contributions in the window, before a backcloth of neutral-coloured canvas, gracefully draped.

The most significant parts of the display are your own contributions. They will comprise illustrated placards leading up to the analysis in the directory-index: portraits of great Americans, illustrations of the Grand Canyon, the Rockies, Niagara, New York, reconstructed Williamsburg (for Colonial architecture) and the like. Fine coloured brochures are obtainable from Washington's home at Mount Vernon, and from General R. E. Lee's home at Arlington; cut them up and mount the pictures in groups on cards.

In arranging the display make a group or groups of the components. Don't put the items in a straight line, or equal distances apart, as if the window deck were a draught board. (*See illus. facing p.* 161.) Don't have placards equal in size or alike in shape. Collect a few properties which can be used over and over again: cubes, plain pedestals, midget platforms of different sizes and shapes, and some circular, square and irregular boards to form middle backgrounds. These properties, the kind that a repertory company travels with, but on a smaller scale, are made of light plywood. They may be painted and repainted in any colour (but never with glossy paint) or draped with textiles which set off the other components of the show. (*See illus. facing p. 64.*)

Now look at the window as if 'twere a stage, and arrange the material in a group, with one main point of interest. If there are any subordinate points, and there ought not to be more than two, they must be designed or arranged for the sole purpose of throwing the main point into higher relief. A fine booksellers' display at Leavitt's, Manchester, resembled our inside displays rather than our front window, but it was a model example of grouping into one main and two subordinate (but not distracting) points of interest.

Some librarians put lists of books in their windows. I don't. I prefer them inside the library, where readers will find the books included in them. To show in a window more than the onlooker can absorb in a minute or two is an egregious error.

Can you improve upon this U.S.A. show? I hope you can.

## VII

All that I have written above applies as much to entrance and corridor as to front window shows. But the former are particularly convenient for liaison and general publicity, which may take many forms; a few I offer as examples.

The liaison frame in use at Edinburgh has a movable back, $29\frac{1}{2}$ by $24\frac{1}{4}$ in., the front side of which is divided by strips of black card into nine sunk areas, which take nine variously-coloured placards of equal size (9 by $7\frac{1}{4}$ in.). Each card advertises a department or speciality of the library. For example, a liaison frame in the entrance of the central library contains nine cards lettered with copy and enlivened with pictures, which advertise and indicate the whereabouts of the reference, the home reading, the special collections, the junior libraries, the newsroom; the branches; the registration office. If nine divisions are not enough we double the number by adding a companion frame. These directory and publicity cards, thus framed, attract by the

## WINDOW DISPLAY

pithiness of the information on them, and by their gay colours, their unofficial, almost theatrical look. The cage of a public lift is a first-rate place for liaison placards, which should be equal in size to those in the frames—for ease in changing—and arranged in the same way, except that the glazed panel for them is not a loose frame, but an integral part of the cage. The liaison frames may be used in any library

| | | |
|---|---|---|
| [Portrait] **EDISON SCIENTIST INVENTOR** | | French grey card<br>—Black silhouette portrait. Orange letters |
| "It was the books I borrowed from the Detroit Public Library in the days when I was a train boy and too poor to buy them that gave me the scientific information I needed for my early experiments. I cannot be too grateful for the library privileges accorded me and I hope we may speed the time when every boy in America—as well as every girl and every man and woman—may have free access to books." | | —Blue letters |
| **LIBERTOWN LIBRARIES** | | —Orange letters |

where there are no entrance and corridor windows, or in public offices, schools, colleges, and technical institutes. But similar placards of a larger size (say $12\frac{1}{2}$ by 10 in. or 25 by 20 in.) look better, and are more noticed when they are shown in windows.

Recalling to mind the number and variety of placards designed to advertise a single commercial article, we cannot set a limit to the number and variety of those illustrating the hundreds of subjects represented in a well-stocked library. Again I say, boost reading and books, and the library only as byplay. Here, for example, are other placards, which may be framed and hung wherever they are well seen, or exhibited in a show case, in central or branch libraries.

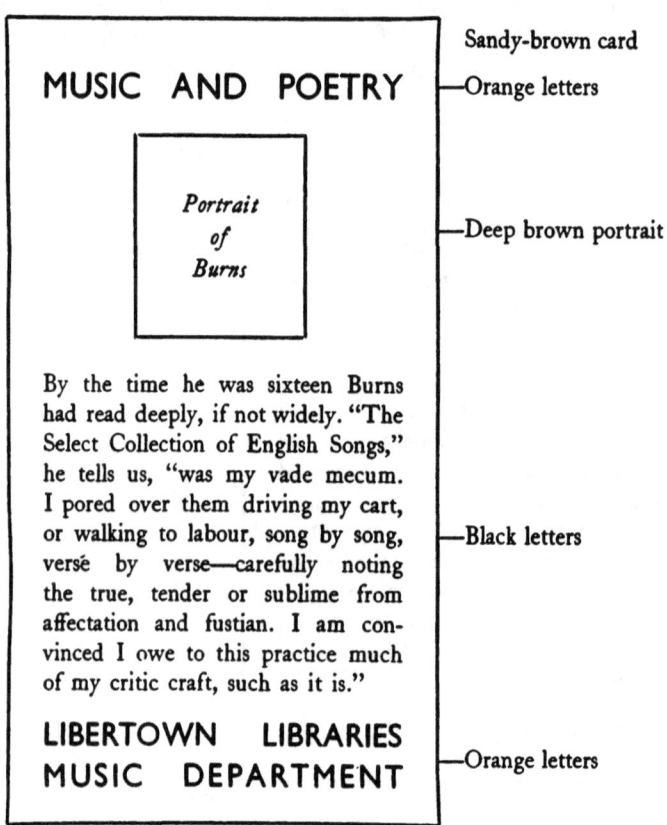

READING BIOGRAPHIES. Many autobiographies and biographies contain references to the early reading of their subjects. Extract these passages, letter them on rather large placards, and add a portrait or a picture. Then you have a range of interesting exhibits, which hundreds of people will read. One placard of the kind is described on p. 215 (*see illus. p.* 208); others are shown on p. 167 and above.

## WINDOW DISPLAY

BIOGRAPHICAL PLACARDS. A series on musicians will advertise the music biographies and scores; on artists—the art books; on scientists, inventors and technicians—the scientific and technical department.

SUBJECT PLACARDS. Posters illustrating historical events remind readers of the history class. There are more general types on: WHAT CELEBRATED MEN HAVE SAID ABOUT BOOKS AND LIBRARIES; THE HISTORY OF LIBRARIES; THE STORY OF THE BOOK; THE HISTORY OF LEARNING—or CIVILIZATION, if you still think you can persuade anybody to believe in it; THE DEVELOPMENT OF THE ENCYCLOPAEDIA; THE HISTORY OF THE ENGLISH DICTIONARY.

Finally, every placard (poster or showcard), large or small, even if there are half-a-dozen together, should have under the more prominent brief the name of the library, and, if required, the name of the department issuing it.

## LIBERTOWN LIBRARIES
## SCIENCE DEPARTMENT

Display the placards in central and branch libraries, and in technical, commercial and art colleges.

# C. DISPLAY BY SELECTIVE PROCESSES

### CHAPTER IX

## 1. CLASSIFICATION AND DISPLAY IN RELATION TO BOOKSTOCK

### I

Of the preparations for receiving readers, book selection is the most important, and therefore I begin with a brief account of the relation of classing and display to bookstock. This part of the subject has been overlooked, though the relation is clear and significant. Classification is display, and display advertising. Nothing is more futile than puffing what we haven't got at all, or in ample quantity. What is the good of trying to group books by literary warrant, and of co-ordinating groups by degree of homogeneity, when the gaps in the stock are numerous and wide enough to disintegrate order of any kind? The librarian is reluctant to class when, as a consequence, he displays the imperfections of his library. And if he does carefully group and order his books, readers, deriving little or no benefit from his effort, wonder why he did it, until he himself comes to believe that he wasted time.

Here is a plain example. Imagine two libraries of a size, about 25,000 volumes each, one for reference and the other for home reading, both classed by LC to an equally minute degree. The grouping and order are more apparent in the reference library than in the other, for two reasons: novels form from 16 to 48 per cent (pp. 176–82) of the home reading library, and many non-fiction books are in readers' homes, or in hospital. Therefore while 25,000 books are co-ordinated in the reference library, only about 12,000 are co-ordinated *and present* in the home reading library. Observing that every addition to a reference library augments its power and clarifies its ordering, we are inclined to allot to it more and more books which are therefore reserved, in fact but not by rule, for a few students among authors, journalists and other people who enjoy the ordering of their own time and leisure, while those who cannot leave their affairs or their work to pass hours in the library are deprived of books necessary to them for study at home: to a marked degree the reference library is anti-democratic. The true remedy is threefold:

(1) buy more and better books for the home reading libraries, and encourage study at home,
(2) watch the use of books attentively, and add to the most-used groups, each of which should be represented upon the shelves after readers have borrowed what they want,
(3) buy fewer novels.

## II

For years we have cried out loud for more books, if not for better books, in home reading libraries. Improvement is hardly noticeable. Selection is not yet organized everywhere to reveal good books. Very gradually but certainly books become less durable. In too many libraries the disciplining of readers who ill-treat books is far lighter than in earlier days. We are not therefore building up, with the necessary skill and care, home reading libraries of educative power.

Some time ago I collected from a number of libraries specimens of buying-lists prepared for book-committees. I noted how few products of eminent publishers were included, and how the selection followed publication ruts. Why, I can only imagine. We like to examine books before acquiring them; are we inclined partly to limit our choice to the stocks in local bookshops, the proprietors of which dare not be adventurous? Do we read methodically the reviews in specialist journals, or are the narrow columns of the popular journals wide enough for us? Are readers' suggestions taken mostly from the publishers' announcements in popular and crank periodicals, and do the staff fail to broaden the basis of selection with suggestions of good books, those which don't jump to notice because they are economically advertised? Is the liaison tight between the counter staff, who handle books, and the accession staff, who select and co-ordinate them?

Cheapness is a trap. The book-jobber was unknown half-a-century ago. No data has been collected to tell us even approximately the yearly total he and his fellows draw from municipal library funds. Far too great I know, for a good reason: the remainder and job-lot market flourishes mainly upon our custom; a book's prime attraction to a committee is its low price. Not that a remaindered book is always worthless. A few are jobbed by publishers who haven't enough capital to advertise, or to hold on to slow sellers. Others, special in kind, don't attract enough buyers to exhaust an edition. But many are by careless or incompetent authors who have been found out: test a number of their books by looking up the reviews in *specialist* journals. And most of the remainder are potboilers which have boiled nothing for authors or publishers. It is noteworthy that publishers of highest repute do not remainder. Bearing in mind how many thousands of books are jobbed, we are bound, when selecting *new* publications, to winnow with exceptional care the chaff from the corn. The clues to quality are: the standing of the author in a profession and his authority on a subject; the English of the writing; the publisher's good name; the preface, table of contents, footnotes, illustrations, appendices, bibliographies and index; the quality of manufacture, on which little is spent if the publisher is doubtful about profit; and the reviews written by authorities. No trouble is too great to find the best for our library; no trouble better repaid.

Am I exaggerating when I affirm that book production is now less durable? Examine books published in the 1860's and 1870's, to go back no further. I take from my shelf the 1872 reprint of the delightful, ever fresh *Budget of Paradoxes* by Augustus de Morgan. The cloth binding is strong and unbroken. The quite ordinary paper is white, opaque and tough; it has received the type-face sharp and clean, and it does not soil readily. Now seventy years old, the book will wear well, even if handled by the public, for a long time, and when at length the cloth binding breaks, in leather it should endure for a century, unless dictators burn it. Many books of that time are equally tough. A comparable book nowadays (to note only one point)

## RELATION TO BOOKSTOCK

is printed on paper which quickly becomes woolly and dirty at the edges, its texture being too friable. That ordinary production isn't of former quality is undeniable, though the printing art has improved. Inferior manufacture shortens the life of a book.

While production deteriorates, the education of readers in caring for books is neglected. Admittedly checking readers is more difficult when books are poorly manufactured. Yet much can be done. In earlier days exemplary fines were the rule; the money was worth collecting, the discipline salutary. Now we are as fearful of driving business away as a political wangler is of losing votes. True, some readers abandon their tickets and evade payment. Either be thankfully rid of them, or keep them in membership by compelling them to pay. More business is forfeited by lending readers soiled and broken books than by fining defaulters. Moreover librarians fall into the habit of maltreating books as they fall out of the habit of compelling readers to care for them. Not long ago when I was being taken round a fine new library building, I saw the assistants chucking (chucking is the right word) returned books *into a floor bin* under the counter. I left quickly before I exploded. Need I add that the shelves were almost empty. Such treatment is by no means uncommon. In bygone days discipline was rougher, but effective. Many years ago an irascible librarian was walking through the home reading library one Saturday evening when it was crowded with readers, and, looking up, he spotted in the gallery a midget assistant standing upon a number of folio volumes, and reaching up for a book. He sizzled with wrath.

"Noggs," he yelled, "d'ye hear me, Noggs?"

"Yes, sir."

"If I catch you standing on my books again, I'll box your ears."

Noggs would rather have been spanked in the privacy of the chief's office than suffer this cruel public reprimand, because for a week or two he was teased mercilessly by fellow-assistants and readers who remarked on the brightness of his ears  But note the phrase "*my* books": the old-time librarians always talked of the books as theirs. But we don't evade retribution. A well-to-do booklover intended to bequeath a large and valuable special collection to the library in his native town. One day however he entered a room where a large quantity of books were spread out edge-down on the uncovered floor, and over the front rows assistants sprawled their weight to arrange those at the back. The librarian himself was directing this crime. The bequest went elsewhere.

Stop the waste of books, and fill the shelves.

### III

More and better books, but also the right books for our library. To note use, to add books until some are always on the shelves.to represent the favoured groups, is one of the arts of librar nship.

At one time young librarians had the idea of a representative collection drilled into their heads. To every topic in Dewey its quota of books; if only one or two, whether readers wanted them or not. Even to-day practice isn't much changed (see pp. 196–7). Another unwritten rule ordered us to develop the "long suits" of a library, its richer parts. In Edinburgh one "long suit" is the Scottish collection, which ought to be maintained, without stint of labour and money, in a subject department. On the other hand a minor "long suit", on Egyptian archaeology, was bequeathed to us, but why develop it for the two or three students of the subject in Edinburgh?

No; watch the borrowing of books, group by group, and add to them so that readers, as far as practicable, are guaranteed adequate reading in courses, and favourite groups are always represented; then the co-ordination of stock will be as clear to readers as the colours and lines in a spectrum of the sun. "Laws, like houses, lean on one another", and books too, in both senses. Cut back the remainder of the library, the unused, the less-favoured parts, as we prune the dead wood of plants to improve the fruit on the new. Develop here and limit there; two vital operations in librarianship. About reading in courses, possible only when the range in book selection is wide, I write no more than enough to illustrate clearly its relation to classing. The variety and extent of a technical college's curriculum are determined by the number of classes that can be formed. One, two or three students of a subject must go untaught, a class not being economical; the fact is unfortunate, the result unavoidable. The librarian is not so hampered, for he can and should plan a curriculum vastly more extensive and diverse. Indeed the authors in his library, for people able to study from books, may take the places of flesh and blood teachers at the college. The scope and wide variety of his curriculum are limited only by the number of groups, each large enough to allow students to read in courses, that he can acquire from his bookfund. College teaching is limited by the number of classes, the library's teaching by the number of effective book groups; and though the groups may outnumber the classes enormously, yet the librarian of any but a universal library is bound to a curriculum. Looked at from an educational point of view every good library is constructed, group by group, and to class a library not so constructed is futile. Imagine an assemblage of gifts, of books bought for their cheapness, or for their topicality as they drop week by week from the press, or for their ephemeral utility as "something to read", or because they are on a subject, of limited appeal, not yet represented; a miscellany, ill-balanced in grouping, not only weak in books for continuous study, but giving readers none of the advantages of classification, for the good reason that the co-ordination which reveals is not itself discernible, and cannot be indicated plainly by shelf, tier or even case guides.

Too many municipal libraries are inefficient because their stocks of first-rate books are meagre and ill-constructed. Note how the librarian chases his tail. Being few in number his books cannot be classed and displayed to full advantage; as they cannot be arrayed in a revealing co-ordination and effectively displayed they are not greatly used; and the less they are borrowed the more reluctant he is to add to their number.

## IV

It isn't necessary to search for another good reason why libraries are not being built up everywhere for educational work. Far too many novels are bought. In the long run they are more expensive than other books, though on an average first cost is lower. Poorly manufactured, and treated badly by readers who respect them little, they age in one winter of life. Why not let the twopenny libraries bear the cost, and take the exiguous profit? Is it our business to enervate the mind? Here let me note a curious contradiction in policy. Book committees, often keen to prevent overlapping, decline to buy good books which may be in the university, college and society libraries of their area, though the municipal library alone is open to all comers, and though the students without the privileged circles may be more numerous than those within. On the other hand, many of them look upon twopenny libraries as competitors, and attempt to drive their owners out of business by providing great quantities of novels, generally of poor quality, for free borrowing.

It may be instructive to tell the reader how I measured the loads of fiction bought by municipal librarians, who bang the big drum of education with all the wallop of a circus drummer. I first got scriptural authority from manuals and the papers of leading writers. I arrange the figures in chronological order, the better to indicate our erratic "progress" in solving the Great Novel Question.

| | | Per cent |
|---|---|---|
| 1893 | A.L.A. *Catalog* | 16 |
| 1903 | Barrett, *L.A.R.*, V.6: 179 (*Branch stocks only*) | |
| | Croydon | 33·6 |
| | Birmingham | 47·7 |
| | Bristol | 33·9 |
| | Leeds | 42·8 |
| 1904 | A.L.A. *Catalog* | 16·3 |
| 1904 | Willcocks, *L.A.R.*, V.6: 342 | |
| | 10,000v: central library | 25 |
| | 30,000v. ,, ,, | 23·3 |
| | 60,000v. ,, ,, | 16·6 |
| 1909 | Brown, *Guide to Librarianship* (average in British libraries) | 20 |
| 1920 | Williams, *Book Selection* | 15 |
| 1931 | Doubleday, *Primer* (pp. 28–9) | 40·49 |
| 1934 | Oliph Smith, *L.A.R*, V.1: †XIX | 27 |
| 1937 | Brown-Sayers, *Manual* | 16 |

## RELATION TO BOOKSTOCK

Williams gives 25 per cent and Brown-Sayers 28 per cent for literature, which includes novels. As the A.L.A. *Catalog* allows from 28

### TABLE I

| Authority | | Novels | Total H.R.Stock | Percentage of Novels |
|---|---|---|---|---|
| Aberdeen | 1905–6 | 7,211 | 34,128 | 21·1 |
| ,, | 1935–6 | 13,277 | 70,976 | 18·7 |
| Birmingham | 1905–6 | 52,758 | 117,871 | 46·4 |
| ,, | 1935–6 | 152,664 | 536,613 | 28·4 |
| Chelsea | 1905–6 | 5,799 | 25,845 | 22·4 |
| ,, | 1935–6 | 7,510 | 41,022 | 18·3 |
| Croydon | 1905–6 | 12,381 | 41,229 | 30·02 |
| ,, | 1935–6 | 60,865 | 185,491 | 32·8 |
| Huddersfield | 1905–6 | 7,205 | 19,593 | 36·7 |
| ,, | 1935–6 | 24,524 | 62,327 | 39·3 |
| Leicester | 1905–6 | 21,540 | 53,601 | 40·1 |
| ,, | 1935–6 | 41,983 | 102,280 | 41·04 |
| Lincoln | 1905–6 | 2,290 | 9,762 | 23·4 |
| ,, | 1935–6 | 11,274 | 27,461 | 41·05 |
| Richmond | 1905–6 | 4,424 | 18,324 | 24·1 |
| ,, | 1935–6 | 8,301 | 37,267 | 22·2 |
| Rochdale | 1905–6 | 17,089 | 45,270 | 37·7 |
| ,, | 1935–6 | 34,324 | 61,641 | 55·6 |

to 30 for literature and novels together, the proportions of Williams and Brown-Sayers would be about the same; I therefore put 15 against Williams and 16 against Brown-Sayers. Mr. Oliph Smith, calculating differently, would spend 20 per cent of the bookfund on novels, which, at present prices (1940), works out at 27 per cent of stock.

Varying methods of reckoning produce this bewildering range. Strike percentages on the whole stock, reference and home reading, and comparison is misleading, as the authorities which immure great quantities of books in reference departments will return lower percentages than those who favour a liberal home reading policy. Unfortunately our teachers propagate these discrepant figures in lectures and textbooks. Well, well! "It is the nature of all greatness not to be exact."

Where could I get true figures?

The Statistics in Table I are for 1905–6 and 1935–6, these being the earliest and the latest, at the time of writing, that I could abstract from annual reports. Table II is compiled from *London Statistics*, published by the L.C.C., the year 1904–5 being the earliest and 1936–7 the latest at my disposal. The years 1904–5–6 are well-chosen, albeit by accident, because by that time library practice had become established, and 1935–6–7 are years long after the first great war and not yet disturbed by the premonitions and events of the second. The percentages are struck on the proportion of novels to total home reading stock, the latter including juvenile books of all kinds; no other comparison would be fair.

This diversity in practice explains why the writers of manuals offer conflicting testimony. In Table I lowest figure for 1935–6 is 18·3, the highest 55·6. Decreases at Aberdeen are from 21·1 to 18·7, at Birmingham from 46·4 to 28·4 (fine progress!), at Chelsea from 22·4 to 18·3, and at Richmond from 24·1 to 22·2. Increases at Croydon are from 30·02 to 32·8, at Huddersfield from 36·7 to 39·3, at Leicester from 40·1 to 41·04, at Lincoln from 23·4 to 41·05 (an increase of over 17), and at Rochdale from 37·7 to 55·6 (another increase of over 17).

Rather than extend the above table I prefer to take figures for all the municipal libraries in one area, and here the admirable statistical department of the L.C.C. comes to my aid. The following figures are for the whole administrative county of London, the centre of literature, art, science, commerce and industry of the British Commonwealth.

## RELATION TO BOOKSTOCK

### TABLE II

| Authority | | Novels | Total H.R.Stock | Percentage of Novels |
|---|---|---|---|---|
| Battersea | 1904–5 | 13,946 | 38,602 | 36·12 |
| ,, | 1936–7 | 19,450 | 68,279 | 28·48 |
| Bermondsey | 1904–5 | 9,478 | 32,551 | 29·11 |
| ,, | 1936–7 | 15,525 | 61,263 | 25.34 |
| Bethnal Green | 1904–5 | — | — | — |
| ,, | 1936–7 | 22,715 | 71,666 | 31·69 |
| Camberwell | 1904–5 | 16,073 | 49,582 | 32·41 |
| ,, | 1936–7 | 23,005 | 86,310 | 26·65 |
| Chelsea | 1904–5 | 5,691 | 25,087 | 22·68 |
| ,, | 1936–7 | 7,424 | 44,703 | 16·6 |
| Deptford | 1904–5 | — | — | — |
| ,, | 1936–7 | 16,973 | 59,688 | 28·43 |
| Finsbury | 1904–5 | — | 19,352 | — |
| ,, | 1936–7 | 13,871 | 43,153 | 32·14 |
| Fulham | 1904–5 | — | 22,460 | — |
| ,, | 1936–7 | 14,593 | 57,659 | 25·30 |
| Greenwich | 1904–5 | — | — | — |
| ,, | 1936–7 | 35,993 | 85,804 | 41·94 |
| Hackney | 1904–5 | — | — | — |
| ,, | 1936–7 | 59,033 | 122,780 | 48·08 |
| Hammersmith | 1904–5 | 6,789 | 25,076 | 27·07 |
| ,, | 1936–7 | 28,337 | 71,973 | 39·37 |

MANUAL OF BOOK CLASSIFICATION

TABLE II—*Continued*

| Authority | | Novels | Total H.R.Stock | Percentage of Novels |
|---|---|---|---|---|
| Hampstead | 1904–5 | 10,721 | 32,666 | 32·82 |
| ,, | 1936–7 | 29,293 | 79,600 | 36·80 |
| Holborn | 1904–5 | 7,775 | 20,434 | 38·04 |
| ,, | 1936–7 | 10,564 | 27,108 | 38·97 |
| Islington | 1904–5 | — | — | — |
| ,, | 1936–7 | 27,328 | 89,912 | 30·39 |
| Kensington | 1904–5 | 11,620 | 37,152 | 31·27 |
| ,, | 1936–7 | 15,401 | 61,648 | 24·98 |
| Lambeth | 1904–5 | 27,004 | 77,829 | 34·69 |
| ,, | 1936–7 | 45,959 | 136,311 | 33·71 |
| Lambeth and Camberwell | 1904–5 | 5,974 | 12,899 | 46·31 |
| ,, ,, | 1936–7 | 8,078 | 20,036 | 40·31 |
| Lambeth and Croydon | 1904–5 | 2,906 | 7,613 | 38·17 |
| ,, ,, | 1936–7 | 5,735 | 21,527 | 26·64 |
| Lewisham | 1904–5 | 13,403 | 36,378 | 36·84 |
| ,, | 1936–7 | 53,655 | 117,808 | 45·54 |
| Paddington | 1904–5 | 2,275 | 8,907 | 25·54 |
| ,, | 1936–7 | 13,678 | 45,216 | 30·25 |
| Poplar | 1904–5 | 9,647 | 30,075 | 32·07 |
| ,, | 1936–7 | 34,683 | 110,328 | 31·43 |
| St. Marylebone | 1904–5 | — | — | — |
| ,, | 1936–7 | 12,271 | 58,372 | 21·02 |

## RELATION TO BOOKSTOCK

### TABLE II—*Continued*

| Authority | | Novels | Total H.R.Stock | Percentage of Novels |
|---|---|---|---|---|
| St. Pancras | 1904–5 | — | — | — |
| ,, | 1936–7 | 15,435 | 49,874 | 30·94 |
| Shoreditch | 1904–5 | 11,683 | 27,144 | 43·04 |
| ,, | 1936–7 | 16,057 | 46,527 | 34·51 |
| Southwark | 1904–5 | 15,096 | 44,689 | 33·78 |
| ,, | 1936–7 | 24,680 | 72,048 | 34·25 |
| Stepney | 1904–5 | 12,776 | 48,848 | 26·15 |
| ,, | 1936–7 | 34,567 | 135,176 | 25·59 |
| Stoke-Newington | 1904–5 | 4,784 | 15,948 | 29·99 |
| ,, | 1936–7 | 10,840 | 37,049 | 29·25 |
| Wandsworth | 1904–5 | 19,309 | 62,383 | 30·95 |
| ,, | 1936–7 | 62,520 | 227,598 | 27·46 |
| Westminster | 1904–5 | 24,082 | 74,325 | 32·4 |
| ,, | 1936–7 | 40,691 | 153,202 | 26·56 |
| Woolwich | 1904–5 | 6,927 | 22,552 | 30·71 |
| ,, | 1936–7 | 40,904 | 105,541 | 38·75 |

The lowest percentage for 1936–7 is 16·6, the highest 48·08, these figures being rather better than those in Table I. The libraries showing decreases are: Battersea, 36·12 to 28·48; Bermondsey, 29·11 to 25·34; Camberwell, 32·41 to 26·65; Chelsea, 22·68 to 16·6; Kensington, 31·27 to 24·98; Lambeth, 34·69 to 33·71; Lambeth and Camberwell, 46·31 to 40·31; Lambeth and Croydon, 38·17 to 26·64; Poplar, 32·07 to 31·43; Shoreditch, 43·04 to 34·51;

Stepney, 26·15 to 25·5; Wandsworth, 30·95 to 27·46; Westminster, 32·4 to 26·56. The increases are: Hammersmith, 27·07 to 39·37 (a jump of over 12 per cent); Hampstead, 32·82 to 36·8 (why here, of all places?); Lewisham, 36·84 to 45·54 (an increase of eight); Paddington, 25·54 to 30·25; and Woolwich, 30·71 to 38·75 (another increase of eight). When we remember how few novels are of cultural or literary value it is impossible to believe that the standard for selecting novels in many public libraries is higher than that of the twopenny libraries. A shameful confession to make, but true; and the ratepayer ought not to contribute to this waste.

From municipal libraries in the Administrative County 18,689,554 volumes were issued for home reading in 1936–7. Of these 3,827,102 were from non-novel stock (excepting juveniles) and 11,699,811 were novels. The population in that year was 4,397,003, so that the issues a head of the population were: non-novels, 0·87 and novels 2·66.

The experience of officials in charge of libraries where the non-novel stock has been built up proves that 15 per cent of novels is ample, though I would prefer not more than 7 per cent, which is my estimate of the number of novels fit to be included in the Literature class, the separate Novel class being abandoned, as it ought to be. In the long run larger issues may be obtained more easily for the same expenditure if the non-novel side of the business is soundly constructed.

## V

In this chapter I raise the following questions:

(1) The *quality* of non-novel stock: is it good enough?—is too much money spent on remainders, jobbers' junk and ephemeral books?

(2) The *quantity* of non-novel stock: is there enough, in each group of subjects, to retain readers?—is book selection constructive and based upon observed use?—if not, what benefit can readers derive from the classing of ill-co-ordinated stock?

(3) Are the members of the staff vigilant in observing reading?—

## RELATION TO BOOKSTOCK

is the liaison tight between the counter staff which handles books, and the accession staff which selects and classes them?—if not, how can a curriculum of book-groups be formed, and how is unused or little-used stock to be "pruned"?

(4) Are the members of the staff able to receive serious readers and to satisfy them?—if personal service isn't just right how can we avoid failure in measuring demand for good books?

(5) University, college and special libraries draw some serious readers away from us: is enough weight given to the fact that the readers and students entitled to borrow from them are far fewer in number than those who are?—is the existence of these libraries an excuse for keeping unprivileged readers short of good books?

(6) Is any estimate drawn up of the number of books issued from popular circulating and shop libraries?—of the extent to which they relieve municipal libraries of non-educational work?—or are they looked upon as competitors, to be fought even at the sacrifice of good books?

(7) Is the purchase of novels chosen on twopenny library standards a justifiable charge upon public funds?—at any rate ought we to buy them while we are short of books of the better sort?

These questions are important. In sum they amount to this: Can we expect to do better work when our non-novel stock is too meagre for co-ordination and display. "The mill stands that wants water."

CHAPTER X

2. HOME READING BOOKS IN RETIREMENT

I

THE aim of physical display (classing and exhibition) as compared with literary display (cataloguing and indexing) is to thrust books, particularly the matter of them, into conspicuity. That the whole contents of a library were in the beginning, and remain, picked books is an unwarranted assumption, for, however well-chosen, some books are better than others by all criteria or, if not in the front row, better for specific ends and particular readers. Therefore the exhibitor's aim is to throw the hand-picked books, the *best* matter, into conspicuity. In the greater art galleries, where curators have spacious rooms and varied material to exhibit, a wall is sometimes regarded as a background for a beautiful ensemble—pictures, sculpture, tapestry, china, and furniture being hung or arranged against it so that no object is dominated by another, no colour here kills colour there, no propinquity is inharmonious, and no flatness, incongruity or want of symmetry prevents the wall from being an integral demonstration, in which everything is a separate and distinct but irremovable element in the pattern of the whole. That is the art of display by selection, harmony, differentiation, distinction and imagination.

"Isn't it rather odd," I am asked, "to compare a celebrated art gallery with an ordinary home reading library?"

"No," I reply; "the principles of exhibiting are everywhere alike. Think of a library as an exhibition and in a flash we see that many of the curator's arts may be applied in our display, although our material is different in kind. We select, distinguish, harmonize. Develop or rather continue the process of throwing the best into prominence by removing the worst. Take out books which, by their general appearance, lower the attractive value of the whole. You know what I

## DISPLAY BY SELECTION

mean. Books which repel because they're shabby, partly obsolete, no longer topical. Books which gather dust for months in the year because they're seasonal reading. As the liquor is the clearer when the sediment is deposited, so the remaining books stand out and invite more careful attention when the surplusage is away."

"But when you recommend the removal of this surplusage," objects my critic, "do you mean that only a few books should be left on the shelves in the formal classing?"

"No, no. Only a barren pantry is more lowering to the spirits than empty shelves. No, let all books on display be the best of their kind, colourful in binding, clear in lettering, and fresh in appearance, and distinguished by their arrangement."

"Easy to advise that; not so easy to get all that. Bright display, eh? Much depends on circumstances. Tell me, how can a librarian fight against the slow never-ending deposit of soot which falls from our smoke-polluted air on to everything?"

"That's true, though you're wandering from the point, and you wouldn't be a librarian if you didn't. But, look here, have you made a really good show of your books, pamphlets and pictures on smoke-pollution?"

"No, I haven't," was the retort. "Have you, and what was the result?"

"Well, you bowl me clean," I admit. "I haven't made a show. But your comment reminds me that I *didn't* put on a show, and ought to have done. After all our business is to educate. Education embraces everything from Roman history to caring for a baby, from astronomy which reveals the stars to smoke-pollution which hides them. How we fail."

This chapter is on books in retirement or reserve, and not on those fit only for pulp. Works allotted to reserve contain matter which isn't obsolete; any of them may be wanted again, if only once or twice a year; and some belong to travelling collections which are lent temporarily to branch libraries where, if permanently immured, they would become deadheads.

Reserve works fall into one or other of two categories.

(1) The LOCAL RESERVE stored in or quite near a public bookroom

either at the central or at any branch library. It contains immediate reinforcements.

(2) The Depôt Reserve in a central repository. It is the base for the second reserve line, a backing to the whole service. Apart from the collections which belong to the travelling library service, this central Reserve is necessary because branch libraries are too numerous and too ill-provided with books, and because their storage for Local Reserves is inadequate.

## II

The Local Reserve is intended for books of the following kinds, which I put forward only as examples.

(1) Duplicates. Every library needs more than one copy of some of the books it provides: textbooks, for example, if the policy of the library does not forbid them; scientific and technical manuals which should be at call in industrial areas; general histories of our own country; classic works which ought always to be obtainable in a good edition on demand, such as separate books of the Bible, separate plays by Shakspere, the poems of Burns, great novels (*Don Quixote, Mr. Midshipman Easy, David Copperfield, Vanity Fair, Framley Parsonage*) and any book of high quality which is frequently borrowed. Keep these duplicates in Reserve, but be vigilant to transfer them to the open shelves when the copies displayed there go out.

(2) Seasonal Books on gardening, sports, play production, debating, holidays and other subjects. The librarian who works among readers will be able to pick them out at once, and he will know when to reserve and when to display them. Every Scottish library ought to hold not less than a bay full of Burns and Burnsiana, not all of them however for display continuously, for he is read perfervidly only for about half a month before his nichts in January, and much more temperately in cooler parts of the year.

(3) Pocket Editions such as the *Caravan, Gateway, Home University, New Adelphi, New Readers', Phoenix* and *Windmill Libraries, Constable's Miscellany, English Heritage,* and the *World's Classics,* are excellent for Local Reserve because readers like their

## DISPLAY BY SELECTION

attractive and handy format, and when the type is legible prefer them. In Edinburgh, during the four holiday months, a reader may borrow two books on each ticket, and may retain them, without being fined, for five weeks. Pocket editions add little to the weight of luggage; brought out and displayed, either before the holiday or the winter reading they give life and freshness to the shelves and offer readers just what they want when they want it.

(4) BOOKS TEMPORARILY WITHDRAWN DURING THE SUMMER SEASON. When the shelves are well-filled at the top of the reading season (a happy state of affairs) they will not accommodate all the books in the summer, as reading declines. Then transfer to reserve the surplus, especially those books usually read more in the winter. At Edinburgh we relieve the overflow at this season, and gratify readers by issuing two books on each ticket.

(5) LARGE BOOKS AND PAMPHLETS. What to do with large and ungainly books in a home reading library is one of those little biting problems, so numerous in our housekeeping, which irritate us into pernicketiness. Oblong volumes which project from the ordinary shelves, and thin folios, such as some of those on mechanical drawing, are examples of the books I refer to. Though I have never been and am not now quite sure what to do, I incline to allot books over ten inches in height to Local Reserve in libraries where it is commodious and where display is well organized, and in other libraries to a special "oversize" division in the public rooms. I should not be self-critical, therefore, if I had an "oversize" group in an old branch and none in a modern branch, for practice depends upon whether Reserve accommodation is adequate and near at hand. The bureaucratic mind (What a mind!) burkes the problem by allotting all large books to the reference department, and in this grave, without the fame of John Brown's body, they will moulder, but if a portable book is undoubtedly a book for home reading, then it should go to home reading, where, ordinarily in Reserve, at a proper season it will be displayed in showcases or on slopes properly designed for large volumes.

Treat PAMPHLETS in the same way. Plays, essays and other material in pamphlet form are conveniently stored in vertical files and specially indexed. From time to time display examples.

(6) CONTROLLED BOOKS. Some kinds of books ought not to be acquired if their use cannot be rigorously controlled. Marriage, motherhood, prostitution, venereal diseases and other like afflictions of the human race are subjects which ought to be represented, even in general libraries, by the works of authoritative writers, who must be distinguished from quack editors of pseudo-scientific, prurient books written wholly for monetary gain. Much as I dislike any curb, which must be applied equally to the careful and to the delinquent, I cannot afford to replace again and again books which are mutilated by snoopers who extract leaves and diagrams for preservation in their own tiny collections of bawdry. Local Reserve is the proper lodging of these books, which however should be often exhibited in a showcase. Let them be issued only to the right kind of people as far as you can judge; examine them carefully on return, and use folding bookcards, recording on the inside the names and addresses of successive borrowers. Books containing illustrations of the nude are often mutilated, and are better in Reserve, unless there is an independent art library from which snoopers may be excluded altogether.

Having given examples of the books in Local Reserve I now describe methods of storage. In some libraries a room adjoining the home reading library, or a stack on a mezzanine over a part of it, is used. These stores may be private, or open only to readers accompanied by a librarian. A park of rolling bookcases in the library itself is a more convenient and economical store. I have referred to these cases on p. 109, where I recommend them for exhibiting distributed relatives, and selected books. For Local Reserve they are parked like books on a shelf, and no barrier is required between them and the public other than a church rope. In the illustration facing p. 193 the reader will note, at the bottom left-hand corner, the floor rails between which the "rollers" (as I call them to distinguish them from carrier trolleys) run. The side wheels being on fixed brackets, and the end wheels swivelling on ball bearings, the rollers may be pulled out quietly and with ease, and, mechanically perfect when of the right dimensions, they are quite stable, and turn in their own length. The wheels, which are manufactured by H. C. Slingsby and Co., spin freely in 5 in., so that the rollers are that height above the floor. The rollers

## DISPLAY BY SELECTION

are double-sided, with 18in. haffits, and without the wheels they are 5 ft. 11 in. high; with them 6 ft. 4 in. over all. The side elevation is 3 ft. 2½ in. wide. The top and four shelves are 10 in. apart, the lowest shelf is 12 in. from the top of the plinth to the underside of the shelf above it. A ridge ¼ in. thick and ¾ in. broad on the fore-edge of each shelf keeps the books from "dancing off". Light iron tubes, not solid bars, ⅝ in. diameter, stretch from haffit to haffit midway between the shelves; they prevent rack and rattle, and serve instead of a middle lateral division. The label holder, 6¼ in. by 3¼ in., and the handle, 10 in. by 1 in., are chromium-plated. All the rollers may be fitted with double-sided titleboards. Hardwood is the best material for rollers intended for public rooms, Oregon pine for those intended for private stores; a steel roller is a heavy and rattlebang contraption, nearly as noisy as a *Waltzing Matilda* tank.

The park is advantageous because (1) storage is economical, for the rollers, parked close together, take up little space and accommodate many books, (2) access is immediate, a light pull bringing a roller out for the inspection of the books and (3) no time is frittered away by assistants who must attend readers in an adjoining stack.

### III

The DEPÔT RESERVE is stored in a central repository. It may be accommodated conveniently in the same building with the travelling service. This Reserve contains

(1) LITTLE-USED BOOKS WITHDRAWN FROM CENTRAL AND BRANCHES. Failing display by rotation of stock (see pp. 196-209) some books allotted to branches more or less quickly become stale to readers. If in good condition they may be transferred to a branch where they will be fresh to readers, or sent to Depôt Reserve where they are at call by any library, central, branch or station. Here are two examples of such books, H. G. Wells, *The Future in America*, is being taken out only now and again. Discard it? No; it is in fresh condition, it deals with a great and important subject by a celebrated English writer. Dean Stanley, *Life and Letters of Dr. Arnold of*

*Rugby*, was borrowed twice in a year; it is the most ill-digested stodge I ever attempted to read, yet educators will need it sometime or other, and it must go to Depôt. Having made many errors in discarding I prefer, when in doubt, to send books to Reserve. Even dingy, shabby books, valuable for the matter in them, or on account of their authors, are better in Reserve than in the dustbin.

(2) WORKS IN A NUMBER OF VOLUMES, which take up more room than their aggregate issues warrant, belong to the same category as those in (1) above. For example Burke, *Collected Works*, in twelve volumes, is indispensable not only for its contents but for its general index, but if, in the aggregate, the issues are few, and room is lacking, turn it over to Depôt Reserve, whence it may be obtained if needed. Buy good annotated editions of *Reflections on the French Revolution*, *Thoughts on the Causes of the Present Discontents*, and *Letter on a Regicide Peace*, to take the place of the dozen volumes.

(3) DUPLICATES OF CENTRAL STOCK, not worth allotting to any branch, properly belong to Depôt Reserve. Every library receives as gifts copies of books already in central or some branches. If of the right editions, substitute them for copies in worse condition, and relegate the evicted to Depôt. Substitute a gift for a stock copy, unless that is in better condition, because books with gift labels in them attract other gifts.

(4) NEW BOOKS OF LIMITED APPEAL are best in Depôt Reserve, if the interchange is efficient; on that subject more later. It isn't easy to name books in this category because the examples would not be the same in all communities.

The critic pounces upon me. "Oh no, but I can't let you slip away with that excuse. Suppose the town is industrial?—what books there?"

"If there's no autonomous scientific and technical department for home reading and reference at central, the leading books should be in all branches above Grade Three (see p. 205). The same books for other branches should be in Reserve."

"Very well," is the reply; "but if the district isn't industrial—dormitory suburb, for example—aren't technical books wanted there?"

"Yes. But for that suburb perhaps all the books we're thinking of

## DISPLAY BY SELECTION

should be in Reserve. Perhaps, I say, because we can be sure only after watching use in a library where all the methods of advertising books by display have been well tried."

"If interchange is good, no doubt you're right," admits the critic. "But what other kinds of books would you reserve in this dormitory?"

"Music. Put the greater number of music scores in Reserve. Unless there's a central department."

"None in branches?"

"Oh, yes. Collections just large enough to indicate that music is provided, and to advertise Reserve. Let me recall an incident. A conscientious librarian—you know, one of those cheery fellows with dry mathematical minds—got a musician to make a list of scores 'no library should be without'. He bought sets for each branch. He couldn't have done a sillier thing. Standardization means stagnation. Instead of moribund model groups he should have lent the branches varied collections from the travelling service, and formed at Depôt Reserve a master collection from which to draft reinforcements."

"Music, however, is quite special," returns the critic. "There can't be many other kinds of books."

"Oh, plenty. But leaving out the numerous minor groups, what about books on local affairs, and in foreign languages? The obstacles we throw in the path of readers wishing to acquire a knowledge of foreign languages and literatures! Well, well. Didn't your newspaper the other day tell you that the B.B.C. had to employ 364 foreigners, including sixty-one Germans, to reinforce their foreign speaking staff and this—mark you!—in the midst of our most terrible war.[1] If every considerable library service had a properly-staffed department, in tight liaison with Reserve, ten times the number of foreign books would be read. And I don't exaggerate. I've made the calculation for Edinburgh, where the organization of the foreign library is simply deplorable."

"Well, but in smaller towns———"

"In smaller towns the foreign books should be in Depôt Reserve. That's the proper place for them."

"But can this Depôt Reserve be got to work?" asks my critic.

[1] *Parl. Debates*, 19 November, 1941.

"Ah, there's the rub," I admit. "The success of Reserve depends upon three factors. First, the methods of advertising its existence. Then, quickness and accuracy of communication. Finally, economy and speed of transport."

But I had better explain these points in more detail. It is unavailing to lure a buyer into a shop until you have a wide range of goods for him to choose from, or to advertise a Depôt Reserve ill-provided, and ineffectively staffed. Therefore the librarian holds his peace about the new department until, after patient development, its resources are plentiful. Depôt Reserves, hopefully inaugurated, have been found wanting and condemned as unwanted because they were prematurely advertised. They are large branch libraries, got together quickly, with some expenditure, and developed with unending patience for the service of whole towns; not fortuitous accumulations of junk, but well-built collections. That they are partly formed of withdrawn books, of gifts, and of collections preferably mustered at a centre should not be an excuse for making old curiosity shops of them; indeed, when they are inaugurated, and thereafter annually, they should benefit as do other branches, from the bookfund. One point must not be overlooked in forming them: they are counterparts of branches, the opposite to the apposite.

Having founded Depôt Reserve as a going concern, the next duty, no easy one, is to advertise it. With the rank growth of advertising, people have developed blinkers to ward off its vehemence and punch. For this reason I shall invariably recommend that display be interesting in itself, and that it advertise by its independent pictorial and narrative character rather than by the directness of its appeal.

The difficulty of making Depôt Reserve known is the main cause of its failure. Where personal guidance is liberal and continuous the problem is trifling, because the librarians won't neglect to draw upon Reserve. But where guidance is impracticable, or where it cannot fulfil all requirements (and that is well nigh in every town) other means must be found. Perhaps the ideal way is to lodge at each branch a manuscript catalogue of Reserve; sheaves being preferable because readers never hesitate to consult anything in book shape. Put the catalogue in a case plainly and boldly marked to indicate the nature

*Photo: F. B. Savage*

BOOK CRADLE AND ILLUMINATED SHOWCASE FOR SERIES
Leith, Edinburgh

*Facing p.* 192 *(see pp.* 103, 186)

## DISPLAY BY SELECTION

and value of its contents; and illuminate the sign above it with a few hidden lamps of changing hue, the expenditure on the clockwork fitting and on current being quite justifiable on the ground that an unadvertised Reserve is a wasted Reserve. Another way of drawing attention to both Reserves is to hang framed notices here and there in the bookrooms:

> ### BOOKS IN RESERVE
>
> Readers are asked to note that, in addition to the books now exhibited in the cases, the Public Libraries contain many books which are held in reserve, some in the Local Reserve at this Branch, obtainable immediately on demand, and others, in central Depôt Reserve, obtainable within twenty-four hours. *A reader who cannot find a book that he wants should apply at the counter.*

Depôt Reserve cannot be of the greatest utility unless transport is quick. A branch librarian telephones to Depôt while the reader waits. "Hullo! Is the first volume of Masson, *Life of Milton*, in? Yes? Good. Let me have it to-morrow." Then he turns to the reader saying: "The book will be here for you after five to-morrow." Any slower procedure isn't the best that can be done.

### IV

The problem of transport cannot be thoroughly examined here, partly for want of space, and partly because prices are so fluid now that I can only try to draft a formula which will enable us to decide without them. Daily carrying isn't economical unless an average of about forty volumes are wanted at each branch every day. A Venesta box will take about sixty octavo volumes. A larger box isn't conveniently handled, a smaller adds to the total weight, unless cartons are used. Carriers under contract transport the Venesta for sixpence or a shilling both ways, or for £15 a year, counting three hundred

*Photo: C. S. Minto*

ROLLING BOOKCASES, FOUNTAINBRIDGE, EDINBURGH

*Facing p.* 193 (*see pp.* 107, 109, 113)

working days a year.[1] This calculation is basic because it enables us to determine whether transport by a library-owned van is economical or not. A van costs £500 a year for depreciation, labour, running repairs, replacements, petrol and oil. With commercial transport at £15 a year, one box going out and in from each branch for three hundred days a year, thirty-three branches may be fed for £495 a year. With more branches or more boxes a library van is an advantage; with fewer it is not. As the comparison is unaffected by any changes in costs, which would fluctuate in the same degree both for private and commercial transport, or by the carriage in the boxes, at the same time, of other portables, it may be accepted as a guiding rule. For example, if fewer than forty books are wanted by a branch, the carrier will call every other day, or even more infrequently, particularly in the off-reading season, unless the aim is to supply the books, however few in number, no matter the cost.

"No matter the cost?" The question merits an answer. Ought we to measure the *volume* of transport in relation to the *quality* of the stock transported? Yes; I think so. When I took a ticket at the British Museum I had to name the subjects I proposed to study. Why not? The object of the inquiry is to limit the privileges to people who are reading for a purpose. *Aut disce, aut discede.* A like check, even more firmly applied, would reduce the cost of interchange without any disadvantage to students. We are too incurious and nonchalant. Many applications are lodged for books which ought to be in stock at branch, let alone at central libraries; others for books unlikely to be wanted for any serious purpose. Were a committee of research librarians to scrutinize many lists of borrowings through local, regional and national exchanges, they would chafe at the dearth of good books in our municipal libraries, and they would, I think, be inclined to limit interchange to special and abstruse books, if only to compel local authorities to buy more books, and to depend less upon eleemosynary aid from their neighbours.

Another point. A van at £500 means a sacrifice, at pre-war prices,

---

[1] I have averaged prices. At Edinburgh before the war the carrier charged fivepence for transporting a full Venesta, threepence for a carton 16 × 16 × 12 in. Empty Venestas, on return, were carried without charge.

## DISPLAY BY SELECTION

of 2,000 new books a year, or 10,000 in five years; that is to say, 292,000 issues in five years, assuming that books go out on an average ten times annually. Will the van earn a greater issue?—without compensation for its cost in terms of new books? No expenditure on administration and equipment should be incurred unless it is amply justified by the greater use of books.

The solution of this problem of transport will be reached only if better selection is founded on a wider survey of book production and upon closer watch of use; if the multiplication of trivial and ephemeral stock is avoided by building fewer and larger libraries in urban areas; and if display is well-planned to bring the best books to the notice of the people most likely to profit from them—this last above all, because we have no measure of the full utility of a library until its contents are thoroughly known both to actual and potential readers and students.

CHAPTER XI

## 3. ROTATION OF STOCK

### I

In America the phrase "chain stores" denotes what are commonly known here as "multiple shops". The word "chain" implies clearly linked groups of libraries nearly equal in bulk, but with varying contents. Such groups seem to me a practical and imperative reform in municipal library organization. What, you will say, has the chain idea to do with book grouping and display? The reply is simple: libraries in chains must contain books specially grouped to aid people who take up course reading, and to retard staleness. Why class books? To reveal knowledge in them, to thrust subject books into prominence. Why display them? Again to reveal books, thrust them into prominence, and freshen the library. Why rotate stock? To bring more books into notice, and to retard staleness. Three aims essentially one.

### II

Three branches, opened in Coventry not long before I went there, were almost identical not only in size, appearance and layout of buildings, but in volume and quality of bookstock. My predecessor had followed the common practice (for we all did it) of making a list of books "no public library should be without", and had bought all of them for each of the branches, which were so much alike that it always seemed to me time-wasting to visit more than one. The buildings in and out, were from the same packet. Shakspere, Macaulay, Carlyle and all the other books on the model list, in the identical bindings (for not even the editions differed) occupied the same relative positions on metal bookcases finished in green to match the plants, which were aspidistras of uniform growth. The assistants, cantanker-

## ROTATION OF STOCK

ously human, were not all of equal height, and they had nonconforming (but attractive) faces, while they had bought overalls to harmonize with their complexions, and were quite happy without official uniforms, which probably would also have been in reseda green. Otherwise the regimenting, common thirty years ago, was perfect, and when I took my regular jaunt to see whether the branches were yet standing, I could not help thinking and speaking of them as the Triplets.

About the time of my arrival the Triplets, though but a year old, were becoming stale to readers. Then I hardened my opinion, before held without much confidence, that libraries ought to be organized in chains, as librarians are organized, much less intelligently, by the L.A. Education Committee. However, little could be done at that time. The first world war was raging: any radical change was a dream of the peaceful future; indeed then and long after the want of money was so hobbling that neither bookstock nor labour sufficed. Change was more difficult because each library's stock had been clamped to it by separate accession registers, by book labels independent in print and colour, and by other bureaucratic tape and sealing-wax I have now forgotten. As books were published, the stocks at the Triplets were varied, but the additions were not difficult to count, and the range of them was too confined (war driving books into fewer channels of interest) to leaven the lump of Lubbocky books which formed the tough core of each collection. A preparatory change was made: each accession number, by adding a digit before it, was turned into one which had no duplicate anywhere in the service: thus

    at Earlsdon 7642 became 77642
    at Stoke   3821   „   83821
    at Foleshill 4193   „   94193

while numbers up to 69,999 were reserved for Central. These figures, being from memory, may not be accurate, but no matter: I am explaining the method.

To retard staleness the organization should have been utterly different. Leaving out of account reference books, not three, but seven collections of books were required, even if the aggregate did not exceed that of the three.

|  | Volumes |
|---|---|
| A depôt reserve | 3,000 |
| Identical branch collections of 600 vols. each (A, B, C) | 1,800 |
| Chain collections of 4,400 vols. each (1, 2, 3) | 13,200 |

The Triplets, as I found them, contained 18,000 volumes, a quite inadequate number; however, my seven collections, for true comparison, are about equal to that aggregate.

What was Depôt Reserve to contain? Many of the books on my predecessor's model list, with any good gifts, or duplicates, or new books for which demand was limited. A branch librarian would have drawn upon it as necessary. Though desirable from the first, it could have been brought together at any later time, and I would have preferred to add 1,000 additional volumes to each branch. Meantime Central would have been drawn upon as a reserve, even though an energetic branch librarian creditably but inconveniently borrowed too freely to help his readers.

The "identical collections" (A, B, C) made up of those books which all would-be readers among adolescents are attracted to read, and try to read, when they are ripe for them, ought not to have exceeded 600 volumes for each of the Triplets. Here are examples roughly in chronological order:

| *Before* 1850 | *After* 1850 |
|---|---|
| PLATO, Republic | MELVILLE, Moby Dick |
| PLUTARCH, Lives | GONCHAROV, Oblomov |
| MORE, Utopia | TROLLOPE, Barsetshire Novels |
| CELLINI, Autobiography | BORROW, Lavengro |
| CERVANTES, Don Quixote | MILL, Liberty |
| SHAKSPERE, Works | MEREDITH, Richard Feverel; Sandra Belloni; Vittoria; Harry Richmond; Beauchamp's Career; Egoist |
| MILTON, Poems | |
| PEPYS, Diary | |
| BUNYAN, Pilgrim's Progress | |

## ROTATION OF STOCK

### Before 1850

DEFOE, Robinson Crusoe
SWIFT, Gulliver's Travels
FIELDING, Tom Jones
STERNE, Tristram Shandy
ROUSSEAU, Social Contract
GOLDSMITH, Vicar of Wakefield
SMITH, Wealth of Nations
BOSWELL, Johnson
BYRON, Poems
SHELLEY, Poems
LAMB, Essays
AUSTEN, Pride and Prejudice; Mansfield Park; Emma
SCOTT, Waverley; Guy Mannering; Antiquary; Old Mortality; Rob Roy; Heart of Midlothian; Fortunes of Nigel; Quentin Durward
KEATS, Poems
GALT, Annals of the Parish
DE QUINCEY, English Opium-Eater
MITFORD, Our Village
BALZAC, Eugénie Grandet; Old Goriot; César Birotteau; Cousin Betty; Cousin Pons
MARRYAT, Peter Simple; Midshipman Easy
DICKENS, Pickwick; Twist; Nickleby; Old Curiosity Shop; Chuzzlewit; Christmas Books; and Stories; Dombey; Copperfield; Great Expectations
LOCKHART, Life of Scott
GOGOL, Dead Souls

### After 1850

READE, Cloister and the Hearth
TURGENEV, Fathers and Sons; Virgin Soil
TOLSTOI, War and Peace; Anna Karenina
DOSTOEVSKY, Crime and Punishment; Idiot; Brothers Karamazov.
HARDY, Far from the Madding Crowd; Ethelberta; Return of the Native; Trumpet Major; Mayor of Casterbridge; Woodlanders; Tess; Jude; Wessex Poems; Dynasts
TWAIN, Tom Sawyer; Huckleberry Finn
STEVENSON, Treasure Island; Kidnapped; Catriona
YEATS, Poems
DOUGHTY, Arabia Deserta
KIPLING, Plain Tales; Soldiers Three; Jungle Books; Puck; Kim
HOUSMAN, Shropshire Lad
CONRAD, Nigger of the Narcissus; Lord Jim; Typhoon
GRAHAM, R. B. C., Tales
SHAW, Earlier Plays
MACHEN, Hieroglyphics
BUTLER, Way of All Flesh
WELLS, Kipps; Tono-Bungay; Mr. Polly
GALSWORTHY, Forsyte Saga, Plays

## MANUAL OF BOOK CLASSIFICATION

*Before* 1850

DUMAS, Three Musketeers; Monte Cristo; Vicomte.
THACKERAY, Vanity Fair; Pendennis
BRONTË, C., Jane Eyre; Shirley; Villette
BRONTË, E., Wuthering Heights
ARNOLD, M., Poems

*After* 1850

BENNETT, Old Wives' Tale; Clayhanger
MOORE, Mummer's Wife; Hail and Farewell; Héloïse and Abelard
MASEFIELD, Gallipoli; Collected Poems; Bird of Dawning
CATHER, My Antonia
HUDSON, Far Away and Long Ago
BROOKE, Collected Poems
MEYNELL, A., Poems
FORSTER, Passage to India
O'CASEY, Plays
SACKVILLE-WEST, The Land
LAWRENCE, Seven Pillars of Wisdom
MORGAN, Portrait in a Mirror; The Fountain
BRIDGES, Testament of Beauty
COPPARD, Fares Please

This list includes only examples, mostly nineteenth-century books of established reputation. Some should be duplicated even in the libraries of the grade I am now considering, for they are long-life books which ought always to be ready for any reader, up to demand. Another point: let them be in good editions; it is a grievous fault to buy cheap copies of books with everlasting contents, and to keep them when they are dirty, faded and dilapidated. Old decayed friends are not well received by booklovers.

Include in the identical libraries modern non-fiction works which are popular and likely to be wanted for a number of years. Examples are:

BRYANT, Samuel Pepys
MUNTHE, San Michele

BUCHAN, Memory-Hold-the-Door

ROTATION OF STOCK

FLEMING, Brazilian Adventure
Oxford Book of English Verse
HOGBEN, Mathematics for the Million
VAN LOON, The Arts
CURIE, Madame Curie
HITLER, Mein Kampf
Oxford Book of Ballads
LIN YUTANG, Importance of Living
VAN DOREN, Benjamin Franklin

## III

The chain collections (1, 2, 3) for the branches should comprise about 4,400 volumes in each, with few books of the same kind in more than one of them. I indicate rather particularly the books eligible.

## HISTORY OF ENGLAND

### 1

CLARK, G. N., *ed.* Oxford History of England. 14v.
WILLIAMSON, J. A. Evolution of England.
RANSOME, CYRIL. Short History of England from the earliest times to the present day.
FISHER, MRS. H. A. L. Introductory History of England and Europe from the earliest times to the present day.

### 2

OMAN, SIR C. W. C., *ed.* History of England. 7v.
GREEN, J. R. Short History of the English People; rev. and enl. with epilogue by A. S. Green.
TOUT, T. F. Advanced History of Great Britain.
CARTER, E. H., and MEARS, R. A. F. History of Britain.

### 3

HUNT, WILLIAM, and POOLE, R. L., *ed.* Political History of England. 12v.
TREVELYAN, G. M. History of England.
MUIR, RAMSAY. British History.
HEARNSHAW, F. J. C. Outlines of the History of the British Isles.

## MANUAL OF BOOK CLASSIFICATION

Though these lists include twelve general histories to be divided among the three collections, they are to be regarded as *hors-d'œuvre*, and not as an adequate meal on this subject. It may be urged that Green and Trevelyan ought to be in all three libraries, and, though doubtful about Green, I would not disagree; the main point is that each chain differs almost wholly from its fellows.

## VEGETABLE GARDENING

### 1

THOMAS, H. H., and CASTLE, F. R.  Vegetable Growing for Amateurs.
MONMOUTH, TREVOR.  Vegetable Culture for Amateurs.
KNOTT, J. E.  Vegetable Growing.
SANDERS, T. W.  Kitchen Garden and Allotment.

### 2

SMITH, THOMAS.  Profitable Culture for Vegetables.
SHEWELL-COOPER, W. E.  Vegetable Garden.
SANDERS, T. W.  Vegetables and their Cultivation.
DAVIDSON, H. C.  Vegetable Culture.

### 3

WHITEHEAD, G. E.  Plain Vegetable Growing.
MACSELF, A. J.  Vegetable Grower's Treasury.
BRISTOW, ALEC.  How to Run an Allotment.
BRETT, WALTER.  Vegetable Growing for Home Use and Sale.

## ARABIA

### 1

PHILBY, H. ST. J. B.  Sheba's Daughters.
STARK, FREYA.  Seen in the Hadhramaut.
KIERNAN, R. H.  Unveiling of Arabia.

## ROTATION OF STOCK

### 2

THOMAS, BERTRAM. Arabia Felix.
STARK, FREYA. Southern Gates of Arabia.
RIHANI, AMEEN. Arabian Peak and Desert.

### 3

CHEESMAN, R. E. In Unknown Arabia.
PHILBY, H. ST. J. B. The Empty Quarter.
SEABROOK, W. B. Adventures in Arabia.

## BOOKS OF ADVENTURE

### 1

WHYMPER, EDWARD. Scrambles among the Alps.
SCOTT, Sir R. F. Last Expedition.
REITZ, DENYS. Commando.
BUCHAN, JOHN. Book of Escapes and Hurried Journeys.

### 2

SHACKLETON, Sir ERNEST. Heart of the Antarctic.
SMYTHE, F. S. Kangchenjunga Adventure.
SLOCUM, Capt. JOSHUA. Sailing Alone Around the World.
BUCHAN, John. The Last Secrets.

### 3

SHACKLETON, Sir ERNEST. South: Last Expedition, 1914–17.
NEWBOLT, Sir HENRY. Book of Good Hunting.
TAMBS, ERLING. Cruise of the Teddy.
TSCHIFFELY, A. F. Tschiffely's Ride.

In most subjects the material is ample from which to choose variations for a chain of four or five libraries of 4,400 volumes each.

In a longer chain the collections would be repeated, or they would include books too special for minor branch libraries.

When planning a chain the books should be chosen as for one library, and then divided into as many parts as there are libraries, each therefore being differently constituted, excepting for a few books. "Excepting for a few books", I say, because it isn't prudent to neglect the demand for best-sellers of high quality. Such books, being few, are better in the identical collections until their popularity declines, when surplus copies may be transferred to Depôt Reserve, or distributed in the chain. The great, the everlasting novels, belong properly to the identical collections, and other good novels to the chain. That ruck of fiction which helps to create a lazy and unthinking democracy, if demanded by readers, and granted by a pusillanimous committee, should be regarded as unavoidable dregs and dottle, and not as a calculable and profitable part of the library.

To begin with, the stock at Earlsdon would be formed of identical collection A and chain collection 1; that at Stoke of B and 2; and at Foleshill of C and 3. These libraries are moved on a stage at the end of two years, when it is manifest, as it will be if they contain no more than 6,000 volumes, that they are becoming stale to readers: then A and 1 go to Stoke, B and 2 to Foleshill, and C and 3 to Earlsdon; and later they tour again. If new publications are added regularly to 1, 2, and 3, and if shabby, broken books of an ephemeral kind are withdrawn and not replaced, the three libraries will never become stale, as the changes cover about six years, the rotation afterwards being repeated. Thus the chain operates over a long period. The rotation must be continued, if we are to enjoy its benefits, which are real, because readers are more faithful to a service which cannot become stale. And with faithful readers the committee may adopt a higher standard in selecting books; and high time they did, too!

Note that it is simpler to move the whole of each library, and the catalogues with them, than to separate the parts; and the most convenient time is in the morning between six and ten, or on a weekly half-holiday, and spring is a good season for change and energy. Books out when the change takes place are set apart as they come in, and forwarded later.

ROTATION OF STOCK

## IV

Even greater obstacles blocked the way to reform at Edinburgh because the district libraries were "old established firms", and so unequal in size that there was no arranging them into groups for a long time. However each book got an unduplicated number. As developments took place the following classification of libraries was adopted tentatively:

|  |  |  | *Volumes* |
|---|---|---|---|
| First Grade Branches | (1) | | 35,000–40,000 |
| Second ,, ,, | (2) | | 30,000–35,000 |
| Third ,, ,, | (1) | | 25,000–30,000 |
| Fourth ,, ,, | (0) | | 20,000–25,000 |
| Fifth ,, ,, | (1) | | 15,000–20,000 |
| Sixth ,, ,, | (1) | | 10,000–15,000 |
| Seventh ,, ,, | (3) | | 5,000–10,000 |
| Eighth ,, ,, | (3) | | Below 5,000 |

The figures in brackets indicate the numbers of libraries in the grades. Only the Seventh and Eighth grades had enough libraries in them to form a chain, though one exchange could have been made between the two libraries in the Second Grade.

The purpose of the grouping was to facilitate exchanges between approximately equal libraries. For success there should be not fewer than three libraries in a group. I am persuaded that the above classification of the branches existing when it was framed must be simplified. If I had my way few branch libraries would be built. Many years ago at Croydon Mr. Jast fought against extending the branch service. Was he right? At that time I was doubtful because central accommodation was limited, and town transport inadequate. With more experience and the development of mechanical transport, that dreadful invention of idiotic humans, I came to believe firmly that the inhabitants of large towns and cities, compactly built round well-marked centres, would be better served by a great central library, organized departmentally by subject, than by a central and a sprinkling of potty branches, none of which gives competent service to readers wishing to carry on their studies at home. The ward system!—how evil have been its effects. Without it I'm sure we should not have had so many trumpery libraries. I have little hope of convincing librarians, let alone ward-ridden councillors, of the soundness of this opinion. When peace comes an altogether new policy may be dictated. If the war ends without an effective answer to the bomber we may be compelled to do what has always been desirable: break up our cities and big towns, those great, filthy, sweltering wens of pullulating humanity, and build towns of moderate size, where people may live and work, nearer the fields. Britain has plenty of living room if the people are distributed in well-planned urban areas, served by efficient transport.

However, to my business. In towns up to 50,000 people, and in rural areas, libraries cannot be large, and in them the only cure for staleness is to run the chain throughout a county or over several towns working in co-operation. In big towns I dislike small libraries because they are kept fresh only by the chain, which at best is a bond inferior to amalgamation, though often an unavoidable bond if an effective service is to be maintained. Staleness kills the appetite for reading. When people have borrowed all they want to read in a library it is to them a Mother Hubbard's cupboard. I have found it most difficult to explain clearly to laymen how small proportionately is one man's "holding" (shall I say?) in a public library. We ourselves misinterpret statistics by forgetting this limitation of interest, the few plums that any individual can yank out of the library pudding. In my time I have read perhaps more omnivorously than has been good for mental health. Not long ago, with time to kill in a good library of nearly 40,000 volumes, I tested myself as fairly as I could. I ran my eye over the books, noting what I had and what I had not read. How limited was my share in that library! Great quantities of books I hadn't read, and never shall read; never should read if I could begin life over again. The books I had read on religion would go in a small attaché case; those on science in a suitcase; and I could put what I had read on chemistry in my pipe and smoke it. So many men, so many opinions, thoughts, interests; but therefore of course so many and various limitations.

Condition of stock is but an outer mark of staleness. If books are faded, dirty and shaky-loose, people are repelled though they haven't

## ROTATION OF STOCK

read them and would like to. The causes of staleness are (*a*) selection of ephemeral books (*b*) static condition of stock (*c*) too many replacements of books already well read—a variation of (*b*)—(*d*) neglect of reserves within and without the service, and (*e*) neglect of the display necessary to expound the full resources. Many librarians have adopted the plan of filling small libraries with pastime novels, which are worn out quickly, and replaced with others of like quality. This kind of rapid change is prodigal and unsatisfying to readers who look to a public library for good books. If concentration of resources is impracticable, the only way to counter staleness is to organize chain libraries of high quality.

And the larger the chain libraries the better. In recent years policy in Edinburgh was being shaped to provide greater libraries, and fewer grades of them, and only the war hampered our advance in this direction. The grades now favoured are:

|  | Volumes | Period of Change |
|---|---|---|
| *Permanent branches* |  |  |
| First Grade | Above 35,000 | 6 years |
| Second Grade | 30,000–35,000 | 5 ,, |
| *Temporary branches* | 5,000 approx. | 2 ,, |

The classing is in fact an affirmation, which can be buttressed by facts and figures, that no branch is effective with fewer than 30,000 volumes. Yet even a library of this grade is more powerful in link with others of the same or larger grade, though we need not move them on so often as we do libraries which are too small to counter staleness for any length of time. Assume that novels form about fifteen per cent of the whole, and juvenile stories (which become stale very slowly because youngsters read them only for three or four years and then pass to the adult library) 5 per cent, then the 30,000 volume library comprises about 6,000 novels and children's tales. If the identical collection amounts to 2,000 volumes, then the library is made up:

|  | Volumes |
|---|---|
| Chain collection | 22,000 |
| Identical collection | 2,000 |
| Novels and Tales | 6,000 |
|  | 30,000 |

To get three chain collections of 22,000 volumes we form one library of 66,000 volumes, and divide it into three parts, each covering the class tables, but each different; a task of no difficulty.

In 1938, during the rebuilding of the Fountainbridge Branch (F) at Edinburgh, we decided to change its bookstock with that at Stockbridge (S) of about equal volume. The method was straightforward and thorough. The F library was revised class by class, one being completed before another was begun. Every book was examined: if dirty or too old it was thrown out; if faded and a little poor in health but yet valuable for its matter, it went to reserve; if likely to serve more turns at a branch it was cleaned, repaired, or rebound. Newer or better books were chosen for each part of the main class. Philosophy at F, having been renovated, was put in place of S's Philosophy, which was removed, examined, reinforced and packed until the new building for F was ready. So class replaced class until both libraries were overhauled. By reviewing one and the same class in the two stocks before tackling another class, the labour was hardly greater than for one. The choosing of books, too, is a far lighter, and more engrossing job, more thoroughly performed, when the selector has the class tables before him as a guide.

The result of this exchange was that two thoroughly fresh libraries took the place of two stale libraries. The cost of the work was but little more than that for one. The issues at both libraries were greatly augmented. In part success followed the revision, but in greater part it followed the exchange, the larger benefits of which, however, could not be obtained because the two collections were not to a high degree wholly different, as they would have been had the chain system been in operation.

## V

When travelling libraries were formed in Edinburgh, collections from the Depôt Reserve were lent not only to works, schools and institutions, but to the branch libraries, where, though adding some freshness to the permanent stocks, they were never large enough, even when a thousand or more volumes, to achieve anything like the

# BAIRD INVENTOR OF TELEVISION

"For months Baird laboured patiently in this attic endeavouring to persuade his nightmarish collection of apparatus to show some results. With the patience of the true research worker he attacked the problem from every angle, and when occasionally he ran against snags in branches of science ··· he browsed over technical books in the public library".

## EDINBURGH LIBRARIES

READING-BIOGRAPHY PLACARD
By T. S. Carruthers
Card, cream. Large letters, orange. Small letters, royal blue. Portrait, brown.
Size, 22 × 16 in.

*Facing p.* 208 (*see pp.* 167, 168, 215)

success which follows a complete change. It is preferable to lend subject collections. The subjects, however, must be chosen with forethought, because those which are intended to encourage course reading must be followed by others on the same subjects, or students will be irritated and frustrated. For example, any collection on Philosophy will attract the specialist who expects to continue his line of reading without interruption, and when it is taken away, it must be followed by others of the same kind, or he is befooled. On the other hand grouped books for general readers are loans which counter staleness and develop use. Books of adventure from all parts of the classification will be relished for their flavour of action and peril: on mountaineering, travel, exploration, flying, incidents of the war and the like. Another collection worth making, particularly in ports and seaside towns, includes books on everything relating to the sea: voyages, sailors' lives, seafaring, fishing, navigation, storms and wrecks, ships, and oceanography. There are many subjects of a general kind, hundreds of books attractive to a full circle of readers. Another example: the local collection, which should always be at Central, often contains many duplicates which have come in as gifts. They may be gathered to form a travelling library without weakening Central, and will be borrowed freely at any branch.

ENSIGN POSTER
Original in Colour, Six printings, 24 × 16 in.
By Miss W. Forgan

*Facing p. 209 (see p. 226)*

# D. PRACTICAL DISPLAY

CHAPTER XII

## ORGANIZATION, METHODS AND MATERIALS

### I

THE organization of display is a manageable job in all well-stocked libraries, but commonly the smaller must depend upon outside help, while the larger may have an internal department.

A borough librarian may be fortunate enough to enrol among his assistants a young man or woman with a gift for lettering, placard design and display methods generally. A winter's training at the local art school, if the tutors there are not crazy modernists, should develop the gift into a craft. But caution is necessary. I have seen examples of amateur "art" which reminded me of the crooked efforts of general shopkeepers in English villages. Unless the amateur has talent, engage a commercial placard writer, who will do the work more quickly and cheaply than the sign-painter; every town with a shopping centre provides a living for one or more of them. As a rule their art is rather uncouth and homely: they have not forgotten the old Christmas cards: but they can be led gently into the long path.

Select the tint of the placard, and the colours of the lettering. Point out to a writer approved lettering in a book of examples (see p. 217). Tell him how you want the lettering set out, either by outlining a plan, or by indicating an example. Then he will know that you are a fusspot; even his first attempt won't lift a hair of your head; and in no long time he will be turning out placards of middling and occasionally of good quality. Indeed a card writer in my employ has done severe Roman lettering nearly to perfection.

Suppose we have to instruct him to make a placard. Select a coloured picture on an appropriate subject from a magazine, an almanac, an

## DISPLAY: ORGANIZATION METHODS

advertisement or elsewhere. Draft the copy (the slogan or message), and sketch the layout of the picture and the lettering. Tell the writer what colours to apply: the card should tone with the high lights of the picture, the lettering with the dominant shade or shades in it, the whole being in harmony when completed. He will often surprise you by the vigour of his treatment and the deftness of his touch. His taste may not always be pleasing to the hanging committee of an esoteric art academy, but his work will convey a plain message, which is what you are after. Delicate refinement, as I have said (p. 146), isn't always salient enough.

A few words on colour, which bothers many people who are afraid of the jeering aesthete. One rule is safe: Copy nature. Nature's colours always harmonize. Kant used to remark that we might take a lesson in the proper harmony of colours from the common auricula. The pale yellow of the primrose has its perfect counterpart in the fresh green of the leaf. The dark bronzy-green foliage of the *lobelia fulgens* is the fit setting for the deep scarlet blossoms. A green field with broad splashes of burnt-red sorrel and yellow trefoil is always right whether the day be clouded or sunny, for colours really in harmony are so under all degrees of daylight. I am not suggesting that these harmonies, numerous as they are, should never be broken, but unless sure, after long study of good placards, that more radical treatment won't be incongruous, it is better to stick to a rule which can never be wrong. The best book for flower colours is *The Wilson Colour Chart: Horticultural*, published by the British Colour Council in 1938.

Here are a few notes of colours which look well together; the names are those on the Petragloss colour card issued by Messrs. John Line & Son:

| *Colour of lettering* | *Colour of card* |
|---|---|
| Orange chrome | French grey |
| Cambridge red | Biscuit |
| Lemon chrome | Light leaf green |
| Brown | Light stone |
| Light blue | Lemon chrome |
| Light leaf green | Biscuit |

MANUAL OF BOOK CLASSIFICATION

| *Colour of lettering* | *Colour of card* |
|---|---|
| Primrose | Iceland poppy red |
| Jade | French grey |
| Dark stone | Light stone |

As all poster colours have body or opacity, the displayer will find the sample books of commercial paint makers more useful than those of artist's colourmen. Some firms send out adjustable harmony guides, and with one of them at his elbow a writer *cannot* go wrong *if he has any skill in matching colour or mixing pigment*. Such a guide will combine these colours:

        Pale yellow—Ruby—Light blue
        Deep yellow—Mauve—Dark green
        Violet—Bright green—Orange
        Dark green—Deep yellow—Purple

and many others. The various Ostwald Harmony Selectors and Colour charts (Dryad Press) are thoroughly reliable; refer also to *Handbook of Colour* by J. A. Judson (Dryad Press) and *Colour in Display* by Quentin Crisp (Blandford Press, 1938). *Colour Science* by Wilhelm Ostwald (2v., Winsor and Newton) is too advanced for our purpose, but excellent for those people who want to study the subject deeply.

II

In larger services it is a good plan to appoint a man with experience in placard art, who can be trained, without much difficulty, to undertake the kind of work we require in writing or painting letters, and in picture-making. Generally a man or woman from a school of commercial and publicity design is better for our job than one from a public art school where the post impressionist, the surrealist, the cubist and other wild men play around: our publicity must beckon people of intelligence and common sense, not only extroverts with long hair and sandalled tootsies.

Can even the larger services afford to engage a displayer? To answer clearly I must refer in a few words to the propriety of recruit-

## DISPLAY: ORGANIZATION METHODS

ing librarians for bibliographical rather than for administrative functions. One effect of our obstinacy in pushing forward the library mechanic as a paragon, capable of doing anything with books and readers, is that, having no real approbation for ourselves as specialists, except in the routine of classing and cataloguing, we neglect to recognize the duty of recruiting specialists in their trades. Is it an assistant's job to label and repair books? Certainly not. A girl trained in a binder's shop does the work twice as well at lower cost. Ought a librarian to run the business offices of a library? Many of us think so, but secretaries, typists, book and storekeepers can do it better Should an assistant act as debt collector? Only if you can't get somebody better. And one alert dun who does nothing else will collect more overdue books and more unpaid fines than assistants, and he will soon acquire a wide knowledge of the defaulter population of a large town. And is it economic for librarians to organize the practical and mechanical side of display, exhibition and publicity? Yes, if a displayer cannot be afforded, but otherwise, No: a man or woman trained for the work is far superior.

Room on the staff can be found for a displayer by getting rid of that perambulating functionary the superintendent, or inspector of branches. What are Mr. Super's duties? He selects and buys books. But heads of branch libraries, if other than mechanic librarians, can select with greater knowledge of readers' wants, while the accession department co-ordinates. All the business, secretarial and accounting, for branches filters through his hands, when it would be managed better in the general office by people skilled in these crafts. What is left for Super?—only a certain amount of overlooking, but the art of poking a nose up in the air, gaping round aimlessly, and seeing nothing in particular, has been acquired to perfection by the librarian and his deputy, who have plenty of time to give to it. What is a hierarchy anyway? It is a fine system of passing orders down through four or five well-paid intermediaries to the man who does the work. The librarian and the deputy should deal directly with this man and his brethren. And one of the men with whom they ought personally to shake hands is the displayer, who has the sole responsibility to them for a specialist job of fructifying value. Therefore I argue that the larger service can afford to employ him, and will employ him, when library management is taken seriously.

What are his duties? Here a word of caution. We must not expect to find a man who can overlook advertising and printing, design, paint and write placards, as well as select and group books for displays. We require a man who has the art of making known, by exhibition and publicity, the books chosen by branch and departmental librarians; he co-operates with them as an advertising manager does with the proprietor of a store. He should be able therefore—

(1) To prepare window, bookcase, shelf and display guides, and to arrange exhibitions and window displays of books, prints and other material, throughout the service.
(2) To letter boldly, attractively and with good taste.
(3) To make up placards with pictures, copy, and simple designs in poster colour.
(4) To advise, on the few occasions when necessary, in obtaining designers of printed placard, placard blanks and poster stamps; and to instruct card or sign-writers not regularly employed.
(5) To train people to help him in these duties.

On some of these points I have more to write.

### III

The copy for a placard is the message, legend, slogan, brief or blurb; the content of the lettering. When writing copy—

(1) State one thing at a time; be simple, epigrammatic, persuasive, exemplary; avoid the imperative.
(2) Be sure of facts, tell the truth; don't exaggerate or hold out extravagant hopes; promise nothing you cannot perform. In short avoid "gammon and spinnage", or ballyhoo.
(3) Draw attention to particular rather than to general features; have groups of readers in mind.

## DISPLAY: ORGANIZATION METHODS

(4) Don't suggest lazy reading and love of ease; profitable reading is hard work.

(5) Don't try to be humorous or witty: if you fail you will be misunderstood or laughed at; if you succeed you must continue to play the fool, until people don't attend to what you say, but only to your way of saying it.

Here are some examples of copy-writing. I begin with a few which are too long.

(1) YOUR [OWN] STOCK IN THE PUBLIC LIBRARY: [WHY NOT] CALL [THERE] AND DRAW A DIVIDEND[?] Cut out the words in square brackets. American copy, and probably effective where so many people speculate; here, No.

(2) BRAIN FOOD A SPECIALITY[. FOOD FOR THOUGHT SERVED REGULARLY] AT THE PUBLIC LIBRARY [CAFÉ]. This copy, with a picture of a waitress carrying books on a tray has more appeal than (1) but eight words tell the story better than thirteen. American. In England there's no great market for brain food.

In the following examples I have referred, when necessary, to the picture which gives point to the copy.

(3) READ ABOUT YOUR JOB. Dictatorial, if not impertinent.

(4) READING ABOUT HIS JOB. With a picture of a young man reading. Far better than (3) because exemplary, not dictatorial. Don't clothe the young man in jeans: all workers don't wear 'em: I don't myself.

(5) TAKING HOME BOOKS ABOUT THEIR JOBS. With a picture of readers streaming out of a library, books under their arms.

(6) READING ABOUT THEIR JOBS. With a picture of students reading in a reference library.

(7) BAIRD, INVENTOR OF TELEVISION. (*See illus facing p.* 208.) Simple and persuasive; true and unexaggerated. Suggests the value of reading and study, and gives but the barest mention of the library's function as an agent. Read what is said about "reading-biography" placards on pp. 168–9.

(8) THE FOLKS WHO READ ARE THE FOLKS WHO SUCCEED. Not true. Many people succeed who seldom read anything but a newspaper or a stock exchange list. What is success anyway? Making money? I've known a happy tramp. And a rich man who couldn't eat a sausage and digest it.

(9) YOUR PUBLIC LIBRARY WILL LEND YOU BOOKS ON ANY SUBJECT. May be used fairly only at large, well-stocked central libraries.

(10) BOOKS FOR ALL READERS. Like (9) for large libraries.

(11) KNOWLEDGE WINS ON PAY DAY. Sometimes! This reminds me of an uptown pastor in New York who put upon his church notice board this copy: "Come to church. Christian worship increases your efficiency." And quite true: watch a Quaker! The appeal to self-interest is effective at first, but risky in the long run. Those who heed the slogan, and don't soon get more pay are disinclined to think well of the library, or to continue study. "You can't fool all the people all the time." (11) smacks of publicity for cram colleges and peppers-up of memory.

(12) MEN OF LETTERS IN EDINBURGH. With an uncoloured plan of Edinburgh, the literary landmarks being indicated in coloured lettering. The map, if big, is good advertising for towns with literary associations.

(13) TO GET THE BEST OUT OF A BOOK CHOOSE AN AUTHOR WHO KNOWS HIS SUBJECT, READ ATTENTIVELY AND REFLECT. A stimulus to careful reading. All men and some women are naturally lazy and don't need urging into slothful habits, and the armchair, fire, toddy and book business is overdone by chairmakers, distillers and booksellers.

(14) CHOOSE FOOD FOR THE MIND AS CAREFULLY AS FOOD FOR THE BODY. Not much good in Britain, where cooks are never born and can't be made, so that we eat because we must, not because we would. But worth trying in Chelsea and Cheltenham.

One bit of copy used to boom the reference library got me unexpected diversion. It was quoted from *Tales of a Grandfather:* "Do you leave such a matter in doubt? I will make sicker." Critical Scots, staff and readers, came down on me like birds of prey on a carcass. "Your spelling's wrong. It should be 'mak siccar.'" Playing my natural part of a genial dunce, I sent for the *Tales.* To my critics'

## DISPLAY: ORGANIZATION METHODS

bewilderment the great Scott had written "make sicker". So incredulous was one that he demanded the first edition. There too, "make sicker". This happening was another indication that posters are read, notwithstanding the grunts of what's-the-good-of-anything hole-pickers; but the copy wasn't well chosen, because probably hundreds of citizens noted the "error", sniffed and went on their way thinking the worst of our upbringing. The common form to-day is "mak siccar", particularly among the wilder natives, now usually to be found in London and the environs of Tyndrum. Your copy must not only be, but look right. In the old days artists taught that a freak apple depicted faithfully was bad art: an apple should look like an apple: now the more it resembles a lump of putty or a ball of wool the greater the art. But advertisement of a general service should be catholic and not esoteric in its appeal; while a special service requires peculiar and distinctive persuasion.

As a rule I dislike copy advertising the library generally. I think it misses the mark simply because it is general. Copy on particular classes or groups of books is more direct. However, the above examples exemplify method.

The style of the lettering must be chosen carefully for each placard. Roman lettering—the Trajan alphabet, named after the inscription on the Trajan column at Rome—is beautiful, refined, clear, dignified. For monumental inscriptions, permanent designations of public buildings in the classical style, and art department notices, none is better; but the displayer ought not to keep to one style, because uniformity is tiring to the onlooker. There are plenty of good letters illustrated in these books: **The Art of Lettering*: report of a special committee of the British Institute of Industrial Art; *Manuscript and Inscription Letters* by Johnston (Pitman, 1909); *Plain and Ornamental Lettering* by Fooks (Pitman, 1927); *Elements of Lettering* by Goudy (Lane, 1922); *Lettering of To-day* published by *The Studio* (1937); *Pen Lettering and Practical Alphabets*, published by the Blandford Press (1936); *Practical Lay-out and Lettering* by Mitchell (Black, 1935); *Making a Poster* by Cooper (Studio, 1938) and *Poster Design* by Graffé (Chapman & Hall, 1932). The books marked with an asterisk illustrate only the purer types of lettering;

the others are more irreverent. Choose lettering which is bold, firm, plain and round, but which suggests ease of pen and brush; avoid a condensed, ornamental, rococo style. A mixture of lower case and capital letters in the right places is more legible than a layout wholly in one or the other. In my opinion (but I am not an artist) the following example is a bit of silly affectation:

libertown dramatic society<br>
present<br>
the mikado<br>
in the<br>
town hall<br>
on friday, march eight

In short, write English.

Some firms manufacture sets of wooden or metal stamp-letters which are inked on a pad, and impressed on the paper or card to make up notices or copy. Have nothing to do with them. The ink never gives enough body to the lettering, and the general effect is horribly mechanical. I would rather letter a notice with a stick of firewood dipped in ink.

All letters on a placard should be in one style, though the sizes of them may vary.

For front windows big letters are often required. Copy from a lettering book on to fibrous wallboard a good example of plain block letters. Cut them out with a fretsaw. Any letter, once cut, may be used as a template for another copy. Arrange them in the order required, bore two or three tiny holes in each, and pin them with light headless sprigs to the background (*see illus. facing p.* 97). These cut-out letters must be painted, the edges darker than the face to give them a deeper shadow. Letters eight inches tall, and cut out of half-inch Bituminous Board manifest a saliency and acuity of definition which letters painted in the flat, even with shading, cannot have. Any deft boy or girl will quickly learn how to handle the saw. There are many kinds of fibrous board. The best known to me (but I have only used a few kinds) is Fyburstone, made by The Patent Impermeable Millboard Co., Ltd., Sunbury-on-Thames, Middlesex, in

## DISPLAY: ORGANIZATION METHODS

half-inch and three-eighths thicknesses: it is tough, cuts sweet and clean, requires no smoothing of the edges, and takes paint as readily as a pretty girl's cheek. I prefer the thicker material. Half-inch Bituminous Board, made by Edward Lloyd Wallboards, Ltd., London, is nearly if not quite as good: it is tough, easily cut and paintable; and for larger letters I prefer it because its face and the cut edges are not so smooth as Fyburstone.

Add that the "cut-outs" are cheaper, and usable again and again, if fixed with thin headless sprigs, and the displayer will jump at the chance of getting such emphatic letters. And by the way they look particularly commanding with no background near them.

### IV

Home-made placards must be very good indeed if they are to be attractive. While hardly distinguishable in precision and strength from the coloured examples of a high-class firm of printers, they are the more attractive for that pliancy and ductility of lettering, and uniqueness of pictorial effect, which enable us to tell hand from machine work.

Before attempting to make them, collect a large assortment of unmounted pictures, plain and coloured, big and little, if good of their kind, and likely to be useful. Many illustrations published by galleries —the British Museum for example—are cheap but good, and the displayer will welcome them. Back numbers of periodicals, discarded books, publishers' announcements, old trade catalogues, calendars, advertisements, posters, theatre souvenirs, travel brochures, propaganda like that once issued by the Empire Marketing Board, and by the G.P.O. (especially the fine school placards) will provide a multitude of varied pictures. Please don't run away with the idea that pictures so gathered are trashy. I have got calendars with large and fine pictures, carefully reproduced, of water-colours of Alpine and Highland scenery, and periodicals, such as the *National Geographic Magazine* and the *Connoisseur*, which provided colourful reliefs on placards. True, I prefer illustrations of middlebrow standard because they are more general in their appeal than the exotic, the bizarre, and the high-arty.

Remember that a picture may be used to illustrate more than one subject. A series of coloured pictures such as those of Ludovici, published at Dickens House, will make effective placards on Dickens, or London, or Coaching (Travel in all ages); a view of Wastdale will do for Mountaineering, the Lake District or Physiography.

Roughly class the pictures and store them unmounted in broadside folders, using plenty to analyse the material intensively, so that any subject is quickly findable. Either compile your own list of class headings, or adopt one of those in *The Picture·Collection Revised*, published by Newark Public Library (N.J.), *The Picture File* by N. O. Ireland (Boston: Faxon Co., 1935) or *The Picture Collection* by D. H. Stokes (District of Columbia Public Library, 1929). The Stokes list is much shorter than Ireland's.

A placard of lettering only may be quite effective in conveying a message, but with a good illustration it is bound to hit the mark more directly. A large colour print of John Knox's house at Edinburgh will draw eager attention to copy announcing a display of books about him. A bold, simple picture of a machine with copy about mechanical engineering books, cannot fail in attracting machinists, fitters, motor repairers, aircraft makers, and like folk. Be direct. For example, if you want to advertise books on machine design use a heavy and vigorous reproduction of a drawing of some mechanical detail, not a picture of an engine.

A placard ought to have no more than two points of interest: the picture and the copy. Keep the balance between the two parts: don't let the picture outweigh the copy, or the copy the picture. When using good prints, especially, the balance must be true. A fine reproduction of a Rembrandt engraving, with well-grouped lettering in the Trajan style, will arrest the attention of anybody interested in art.

But surely no good reproduction would be attached to a placard? Why not, if it can be done without injury? Note that I am writing about reproductions, not original prints.

A print which ought not to be cut or damaged may be attached

## DISPLAY: ORGANIZATION METHODS

to a placard in the following way. Outline on the card in faint pencil the area of the engraved surface, and cut out all within the line. Letter the copy on the sunk mount so made. Then hinge the print behind the mount, and frame the card behind the glass. No print treated in this way will be injured unless it is hung on a damp wall or, if coloured, in a sunlit position.

If the displayer has a simple reflex copying apparatus he can make nearly perfect facsimiles of almost any print. Every copy so made is the size of the original. The process isn't difficult. In a dark room lighted by a pale amber or yellow lamp the displayer lays the document paper, emulsion side down, on the print or book illustration, where it is held in place by a heavy sheet of plate-glass which is pressed down with the fingers. Sometimes a sheet of zinc covered with felt or other yielding material is placed below the print to ensure an even surface. Soft, even, reflected white light is turned on, and in half a minute or so the document paper picks up an exact negative image, the whites of the print affecting the emulsion and the blacks leaving it unchanged. Stronger direct light may be used if it is passed through a special yellow or light green filter. A positive is taken by using the negative in the same way as a plate or film negative. Unfiltered, direct light may be used in this part of the process. For good and colourful placard work it is desirable sometimes to tone or stain the copy. The "etching" on the placard in illus. facing p. 112, originally black, was toned to the right shade of brown or sepia by treatment with a sulphide toner, but hypo-alum, or a mixture of sulphide and mercury, gives an equal result. With copper toning a print becomes any colour the displayer wants between full red and warm black; with vanadium—green; with iron—blue; and so on. The *toning* process should be distinguished from *staining*. In toning, only the areas darkened by exposure are affected, the whites remaining unchanged. The aniline dyes, or stains, in red, yellow, blue or green, and in intermediate shades by mixing, colour the whole of the print, including the whites. Again, toning acts on the chemical emulsion of the paper by bleaching the image in one solution, and by re-developing it in another to the colour required. Stain colours the whole print right away, bleaching and re-development not being required. Further information on this process will be found in the *Dictionary of Photography* by Walls (latest ed., Iliffe).[1]

Booklovers are always attracted by title-pages, and nearly everybody likes quaint and old-time engravings. Obtain photostat or reflex copies of the titles of great and originative books, and mount each at the top or the left top corner of a large card. On the remaining part of the card letter, in round bold type, brief entries of books on subjects allied to the subjects of the book illustrated. If the reproduced title is of large folio size, mount it either at the left side of an oblong card, so leaving the right side for the lists of books, or at the centre to leave room for two lists, one on either hand. Here is an example: get from the British Museum a photostat of the title of Bacon's *Instauratio Magna*, 1620. The title of this book, a folio, was finely engraved by Simon V. de Passe, and it shows a ship in full sail between two large pillars. This picture makes an excellent cynosure for a list of books by and on Bacon, and of histories of the sciences. Here are some other examples, the subject headings being chosen to indicate the books the titles illustrate, not the subjects of the books whose titles are reproduced:

## AGRICULTURE AND GARDENING

GERARDE. The Herball or General, Historie of Plantes (London, 1633).

[WORLIDGE]. Systema Agriculturae (London, 1675)—view of farm, windmill, church, gardens and orchards.

VOLKAMER. Hesperides (Nuremberg, 1713–14).

## AMERICA

SMITH. Generall Historie of Virginia, New-England, and the Summer Isles (London, 1624)—a very fine engraved title.

---

[1] The above passage on the Reflex copying process is based on information supplied to me by my former assistant Mr. C. S. Minto, now deputy-librarian at Edinburgh. I know nothing about the subject. Mr. W. E. Cossons (Cadbury Bros. Ltd.) expresses the opinion that "reflex" photographic methods "give a much cleaner copy than photostat" (*Times Literary Supplement*, 10 January, 1942, p. 19).

## DISPLAY: ORGANIZATION METHODS

### ART
Vasari. Le Vite de' piu Eccellenti Pittori, Scultori, e Architettori (Florence, 1568).
Palladio. I Quattro Libri dell' Architettura (Venice, 1570).

### ASTRONOMY
Hyginus. Poetica Astronomica (1482).
Copernicus. De Revolutionibus Orbium Coelestium (Basle, 1566).

### BRITISH HISTORY AND TOPOGRAPHY
Speed. The History of Great Britaine (London, 1611).
Stow. The Annales or Generall Chronicle of England (London, 1615).
Seller. The Coasting Pilot: describing the Sea-Coasts . . . of England . . . (London, 1671)—very fine.

### HISTORY AND GEOGRAPHY
Schedel. [Nuremberg chronicle] 1493—a page with an illustration; there is no title.
Cunningham. The Cosmographical Glasse (London, 1559).
Raleigh. The History of the World (London, 1614).

### MATHEMATICS
The Earliest printed Euclid (Venice, Ratdolt, 1482).
Napier. Mirifici Logarithmorum Canonis Descriptio (Edin., 1614).
Rathborne. The Surveyor (London, 1616)—engr. title illus. globes, levels, geometry, arithmetic.
Napier. Rabdologiae (Edin., 1617).
Newton. Philosophiae Naturalis Principia Mathematica (London, 1687).

### POLITICAL SCIENCE
More. Utopia (Basle, 1518)—use both title and view of island of Utopia.
Hobbes. Leviathan (London, 1651).

## MANUAL OF BOOK CLASSIFICATION

Sometimes an illustration from an old book is better than the title, or an illustration may be used as well as the title: More's *Utopia* contains a view of the island. Prof. Wolf's grand *History of Science, Technology and Philosophy in the XVIth and XVIIth Centuries* (London, 1935) is a gallery of old-time pictures of mechanical devices, portraits and titles—see for example illus. 271, facing p. 521, for a centre-piece for an engineering poster. If the lists are long, two or more titles of books on like subjects may be copied. Engraved portraits, the fine one of Galileo Galilei, for example, to illustrate astronomy, may be added. It isn't necessary to have the originals of these books, some of which are museum pieces, while others are better in modern editions. Nor is it desirable to choose only engraved titles; any finely printed title will do. All the photostats may be filed for use on other occasions.

A few words about silhouettes may meet with approval. Here is a poor, uncoloured print of a heavy extruding press. Trace it in outline, omitting all details save those required for a silhouette. With carbon paper transfer the outline to a placard. Then paint opaque colour within the outline. A black silhouette of this kind on french grey, primrose, orange or green makes a placard which will brighten the eyes of a mechanic: it is clear and massive.

Another example. Portraits of the right size are difficult to find, but can be made. Take a print of Dickens' head in *full* profile. Rule across the traced outline a network of equal squares. Draw a like network with squares double or treble the size on the card. Then, using dividers, it is child's play to transfer to the card an outline double or treble the size of the original. (Alternatively, use the Episcope, see p. 229). Apply paint to all the area within the outline, and the result is a recognizable likeness in silhouette, forming a grand centre- or top-piece for a placard. A head in scarlet on a black-lettered buff card isn't likely to be passed unnoticed. A deep orange silhouette portrait-bust on a black medallion is a rich cynosure. Life is added to silhouette portraits if a high light is given to just one small detail: for example, if a nick or a line represents the collar in the Dickens' bust. Readers will do well to look through *Ancestors in Silhouette* by Edouart (Lane, 1921) or *The History of Silhouettes* by Jackson (Connoisseur, 1911).

## DISPLAY: ORGANIZATION METHODS

Silhouettes may be cut out of paper. Imagine that we want a placard on the architecture of cottages and country dwellings. We find a picture of a modern cottage set amid trees. Transfer an outline of it to coloured papers, apple green for the trees, and orange for the cottage. Cut out in silhouette, fit the papers together and paste them down on to cream card, and letter the copy in mauve; a gay and eye-catching placard, if you use Ostwald coloured paper, and get the colours right by the adjustable harmony card. The process is so simple that any neat-handed girl can get excellent results. *The Art of Silhouette Cutting* by Sims (Warne & Co., 1937) is well worth reading.

Unframed placards for display within the library ought to be protected, even if no great trouble has been given to making them, unless they are exhibited in showcases or windows. Frames are the best protection. Three sizes, determined by the areas of the manufactured card and of its economic divisions, are most convenient. I prefer placards *on* cards. The normal placard size of sheets of tinted and coloured card is 25 by 20 in. Cut in half it is a showcard $12\frac{1}{2}$ by 10 in. None of the card is wasted when so cut. The frames wanted then are 25 by 20, and $12\frac{1}{2}$ by 10, these being inside measurements. The backs of the frames are movable. Sizes larger than 25 by 10 in. I call posters, but for convenience, as I have said, I denote all three sizes by the word "placard". If frames must be dispensed with, transparent celluloid wrapping, commonly used for chocolate boxes, is an excellent protection. Gum strips of brown paper—the broadest packing ribbon will do—on to the back of the card, in a cross with the arms pointing to the four corners. Then the card will remain flat; at any rate it will not warp much. Cut off a sheet of the transparency (taking care not to pucker it) about 4 inches longer and broader than the card, or 2 inches overlap all round. Lay the finished placard card face down upon the sheet, weighting the back of the card to keep it flat. Then fold the margins of the transparency, drawing it tight, over the edges of the card, and gum them to its back. This envelope keeps the card clean, and is easily and quickly renewed if necessary, without injury to the display surface. It is a good plan to file placards, many of which may be used again and again, in their envelopment.

Every placard should bear the library's name lettered clearly, but not to dominate the copy or the picture.

Don't listen to people, of the "what's the good of anything" type, who tell you that placards are not read. Even when in wartime they spread like a plague, they are observed and noted, as my own eyes have shown me. They have (1) *informing* value (2) *reminding* value and (3) *ensign* value. When a placard is shown for the first time passers notice and read it; then it informs them. Later they notice without reading it; it reminds them. In the end, becoming stale, its work is done. When anybody is observed to ignore a placard we cannot tell whether they have read it, or another copy, before. In Edinburgh we collected over 27,000 books for the forces in about a year by writing a single letter to the newspapers at the beginning of the campaign, and by displaying one placard at each branch throughout the campaign. The placard, however, should be in an isolated setting, and should have force in its punch. Is more proof wanted? Here it is. Display a placard making any appeal. Take it away when the results decline, for then it is becoming stale. For a time show no placard. Then make another, quite different, and the appeal gets a fillip, though the results may not be as gratifying as at the beginning.

Of the *ensign* value of a placard I cannot write with the same certitude. The Edinburgh Libraries got Miss W. Forgan to design a placard which depicts a boy seated, not lounging, in an armchair, and reading intently. What he is reading is illustrated in a background: a flaming tropical seapiece, with the figure of Long John Silver on the yellow sands before an ancient ship. The copy reads, "Books for all readers. Edinburgh Public Libraries." *(See illus. facing p.* 209.) It is rich in colour and tells a plain tale well. I cannot remember a better library placard on this side of the Atlantic, though my opinion is no doubt biased. This Treasure Island placard, like the flaming torch outside a county library station, is an ensign; it marks the place of a public library. It also has reminding value. But in the main it is an ensign. I believe it to be worth the money spent on it.

## DISPLAY: ORGANIZATION METHODS

### V

The displayer, if worth his pay, will make a particular study of lettering and placard work, so that he becomes competent not only to train assistants and to instruct intelligibly the writer or painter, if an outside man is employed, but to advise in choosing an artist, on the few occasions when the services of one are needed.

The Edinburgh "ensign" reminds me of the difference between the printed placard and the home-made. The latter is for temporary or periodical exhibition in showcases, windows and elsewhere, when only one of a kind is required, though several kinds may be desirable. Printing is necessary when many copies are wanted to make a service widely known. Placards printed in colour eat into money. A thousand copies will cost about £160–170 for printing. Well, here's a point for debate. If we must pay so much for printing isn't it prudent to fee a good designer to the tune of £45–50? I think so. After all a thousand copies will last many years if they are posted only where they will do some work, in schools, colleges, public buildings, outside branch libraries; never on hoardings. The ordinary artist should not be commissioned, unless he is a successful poster designer. Most designers of the front rank are specialists: Leslie Carr, Fred Taylor, Frank Newbould, E. A. Cox, and F. Gregory Brown, to name only a few. When the need of economy is urged the specialist knows how to produce a design which, while effective, requires no more than three printings, but the artist not knowing any better, runs amuck: the Edinburgh "ensign" required six printings, which was a little extravagant.

Pictorial poster stamps, which have great publicity value if stuck on correspondence, leaflets or notices, should always be specially designed. They may be reduced from a placard which isn't too full of detail: the Edinburgh "ensign" was so reduced. Here is another way of using them. On the front of a printed folder describing a branch library, leave a blank space a little larger than the size of the poster stamp. Lay down one of the coloured stamps in this space on each of the folders; a job as simple as labelling books. A folder or a notice so treated attracts the eye like a warm light in a dark countryside. Don't stick the poster stamps on envelopes, but on the letters inside.

## VI

As our displayer ought to be qualified to arrange shows, he will study good books on shop window dressing, museum and art gallery arrangement, and trade catalogues of shop and museum fittings. It is his (or her) business to find ways of exhibiting that are simpler, more arresting and more beautiful than others. Many exhibitions, and more shop windows, are overcrowded, carelessly arranged and untidily labelled. On the whole, British and (more strangely) Italian shops and exhibitions are inferior in exhibition art to American and German.

Examples of good display will be found in *Museums and the Public* (Carnegie United Kingdom Trust, 1938) *Manual for Small Museums* by Coleman (Putnam, 1927) and *Museums and Art Galleries of the British Isles* by Markham (Carnegie United Kingdom Trust, 1938).

Many books on shop window display are more instructive to the displayer than those on museum display. Here are some: *Show Window Backgrounds* (a mixture of examples; Blandford Press), *contemporary art applied to the store and its display*, by frederick kiesler (pitman, 1930)—I copy the author, title and publisher as printed to suggest the ultra-modernistic style of the examples—*Store Interior Planning and Display* (offers many interesting suggestions; Blandford Press, 1930) *Window Display for the Footwear Trade*, and *Window Display for the Grocery Trade* (Blandford Press), *Art of Window Display* by Down (useful, but not very selective; Pitman, 1931) *More Sales through the Window* by Knights (Pitman, 1931), *Training in Commercial Art* by Danvers (Pitman, 1928) and *Selling through the Window* (contains many ideas; The Studio, 1935). Such books as these need not be bought only for the displayer's use. In every town, no matter how small, the collection of books on shop window display cannot well be too large. Most shopkeepers will borrow them quicker than they borrow novels, when they are known to be in stock.

## DISPLAY: ORGANIZATION METHODS

### VII

The tools and materials required by the displayer are not expensive. The tools include:

Drawing table, large size, tilting
Drawing instruments
Straight edges, steel
Squares, set and T
Guillotine, hand
Knives, stencil
Fretsaw
Paint brushes, sable and camel hair, including lettering pencil brushes. Choose brushes with nickel, not tin hairholders
Pens, lettering—various sizes
Pens, poster
Reflex copying apparatus (see pp. 221–2)
Silk screen apparatus, and accessories
A Zeiss-Ikon Adoro Episcope

The Silk Screen process is an inexpensive method of manifolding placards of which a limited number of copies is required, from 50 to 500. A good screen is manufactured by the Selectasine Silk Screens Ltd. As this apparatus is not likely to be required by any but the largest municipal libraries, it is better that its working be explained to the operator by the makers than by me in this book. Two satisfactory books are published by the Blandford Press: *Silk Screen Practice* by F. A. Baker, and *Screen Process Production* by H. L. Hiett.

The Episcope is a simple and inexpensive apparatus for enlarging. The Epidiascope serves for enlarging and for lectures. Put an illustration under the lamps, and focus the lens until a copy of the picture is projected at the required size on the placard which is to be painted. As the projection is in the colours of the original it isn't difficult to match and paint over them. In this way an enlarged copy of a black and white or coloured picture may be transferred to a placard by a displayer who has no great skill in drawing and painting, especially if only broad effects are aimed at. Copyright pictures may not be used without permission, but many illustrations, not subject to restrictions, are available; maps for example (see pp. 164–6).

The materials required include:

> Cardboard of various colours, light and dark. The Dryad Press supply a good range of attractive colours. Messrs. W. J. Saville & Co. Ltd., Eagle Wharf Road, London, N.1, supply a 6-sheet board (GM quality) with a grey board centre; it is made in a variety of shades, and does not warp.
>
> Papers, coloured: Ostwald series from Dryad Press.
>
> Bituminous board and Fyburstone for cut-out letters.
>
> Colours, poster. The best are the Ostwald series obtainable from the Dryad Press.
>
> Ink, waterproof india.
>
> Pencils, drawing.
>
> Canvas: red, blue, orange, brown, green, buff for backgrounds and draping.

## VIII

"But look here," exclaims the critic. "You're practically suggesting that we have a department for this business."

"In large services, certainly. Why not? "I reply. "We've binding shops in libraries. Cleveland and other libraries in the States have publicity departments. Advertising of the right kind's as necessary as classing and cataloguing. Haven't I been urging all along that classing, cataloguing, indexing, guiding, display are parts of the one job—making books known? Nobody objects to a cataloguing department. Why boggle at one for publicity?"

"You admit the smaller libraries can't afford one?"

"Certainly. But much simple work, as I have told you, may be done in them. Besides, if libraries were well-stocked and weren't dead-alive, supply firms might be persuaded to take up placard making as side-lines to their businesses."

"Well, well; perhaps. But I'm doubtful about these firms. Wouldn't they impose stereotyped forms of placards? Printed things and so on."

## DISPLAY: ORGANIZATION METHODS

"No; not if we insisted upon placards being specially made for our particular needs. To each library its own placards. For my part I'd prefer them to be made at the library. I've shown they can be."

"I note you harp upon the need of adequate stock," says the critic.

"Oh, yes; that's the crux of the business," I answer emphatically. "But let me explain a little more clearly that I not only mean volume, but breadth, by adequacy. Many libraries, particularly small libraries, aren't catholic enough in selecting books. Librarians are too literary, too historical."

"You mean ——"

"I mean—well, for example, take the subject we've been discussing. Every town, even the smallest, has shops. Yet how many libraries have books on shop window dressing? You know the answer. A living library should contain books on every subject the townspeople may take a legitimate interest in. Far too many libraries are celebrated for what they haven't got. Not long ago I tested a library in a residential town of moderate size. There I found Gibbon, Macaulay, Tennyson, and many other books 'no library should be without.' Right enough. But no book on furnishing a home. None on internal decoration. Nothing on arranging flowers. Two trumpery cook books, one on French dishes. A book on embroidery; nothing on plain needlework. Hardly a book on domestic handicrafts. One book on Canada; nothing on Australia or South Africa. No revised version of the Bible. Boswell in the Everyman edition! Nothing on insurance, English grammar, meteorology and many other subjects. No breadth."

"Yes, a true bill. But why so?"

"I think it's so because we—each of us—live in little worlds of our own. What the bookseller stocks, we stock. We overlook the books he gets to order. What the publisher boosts, we buy. We overlook the books he doesn't boost. We overlook the publishers who don't boost. We come under the influence of the rabble-rouser as much as anybody. We don't make friends with people. We don't win the confidence of readers. We're OFFICIALS, the whole pack of us. Mummified experts, my friend!"

# INDEX

*Note.*—The following abbreviations are used in this Index: Cn = Classification; DC = Decimal Cn: LC = Library of Congress Cn; P.L. = Public Library; SC = Subject Cn, UDC = Universal Decimal Cn.

Adoro Episcope, 229–30
*Adjustable* Cn., 14
Adventure, exhibiting books of, 107–8
Advertising, display by, 52; reserve collections, 192–3
Alphabet mark, 20, 134
America, LC cn., 69
Annotations, book, display in, 99–100
Apparatus for displays. *See* Properties
Art, classing books on, 59, 60; encouragement of, 147–8; modern, 147
Art department, display, 146–9; *illus. facing, 112*; storing of books, 149
Art gallery display, 184
Atlas-index, map collection, 125
Author mark, 20, 134

Bach, J. S., display on, 141
Baltimore P.L., display, 91; subject depts., 49, 95; window displays, 150–1
Barnard, C. C., *Cn. for Medical Libraries*, 48
Bay guides. *See* Class guides
Bench displays, 103
*Bibliographic Cn.*, by Bliss, 72
Bibliography, basis of, makes application of cn. easier, 36–7; book cn. to be based on survey of, 10, 17, 18, 19, 32, 38–40; cn. an aid to education in, 39; educational value to librarians of demonstrations, 122; guides to, 127; LC based on, 36–7, 59; philosophical v. bibliographical cn., 16, 17, 33
Binding, use of bright colours, 92
Biographies, cn. of, 106; exhibition of, 107–8, 128; in DC, 47; in SC, 71; placards on, 167, 168, 169; Scots, grouping of, 42
Birds, cn., 26
Bliss, H. E., 40, 72, 81
Book display. *See* Display; Exhibitions of books
Book jobber, 172
Book selection, 198–203; effect of demonstrations on, 122; relation of display to 53–72, 157, 170–83, 231; revision of stock, 157–8, 164, 208
Bookcases, art dept., 149; class guides for, 93–7; height of, 93, 95; rolling, 107, 109, 113, 188–9, *illus. facing, 193*; screened back, 149; shelved ends, 109–10
Books, care of, 173–4; chain collections, 196–209; cn. and display in relation to, 170–83; collectors', 115; commercial, 59; condition, 173–4, 206; controlled, 188; duplicates, 186, 190; durability, 172; large, 187; lists of, in windows, 166; little-used, 189–90; not to be shown unless issuable, 150; of great influence, display on, 156–7; on colour, 211–12; on museums, 228; on picture collections, 220; on shop-front design, 152 n., 228, 231; on silhouettes, 224–5; on silk screen practice, 229; pocket editions, 186–7; questions relating to, 182–3; recent additions displayed, 124; reference, for the classer, 66–7; reference in home reading library, 113–14; related,

# INDEX

34, 35, 45–6, 99–100, 106–9, 123, 132; remainders, 172; representative collections, 174–5, 196–7; reserve collections, 184–95; revision of, 157–8, 164, 208; rotation of stock, 196–209; seasonal, 161, 186; staleness of stock, 197–8, 204, 206, 207, 208, 209; watching use of, 174–5, 182–3

Booksellers' window displays, 150, 166
Bose, Sir Jagadis, 26
Botany, cn., 26–30
Bradford, Dr. S. C., *Cn. for Works in Pure and Applied Science*, Science Museum Library, 68
Branch libraries, Coventry, 196–8, 204; Croydon, 205; reserve collections, 184–95; superintendents unnecessary, 213; too many, 205
British Museum, 115, 118, 126, 141, 194
Broken order, 110–11
Brown, J. D., 13, 14, 30–1, 71, 176–7; *Subject Cn.*, 14, 28, 71, 75
Brussels Cn. *See* Universal Decimal Cn.
Brussels Institute of Bibliography, 36, 68
Bulletins, display by, 51
Burns, Robert, 91, 168
Business literature, cn. of, 48

Carnegie Corporation of New York, 151
Catalogues, card, in open libraries, 14; readers' dislike of, 105–6
Catalogues, printed, 106
Catalogues, trade, 133–4
Cataloguing, cn. and, 53–6; display by, 51; relation between display and, 53–6; reserve collections, 192
Chain libraries, 196–209
Charts in display, 104, 117
Chaucer, G., arrangement of literature in LC and DC, 76–7
Chemistry, Periodic system, 25
Chicago P.L., *illus. of display facing*, 64, 161
City planning, extension of LC for, 48
Clare, John, 91
Class guides, 93–102; avoiding abstruse terms, 97; directory plans and indexes, 101, 127–8, 162, 165; emphasis of book selection and co-ordination must be carried into, 131; for bays and divisions, 93–5; maps, 104; movable, 97, 100; to be specific, 95–7; trial cards for, 97
Classers. preparatory reading by, 59–67
Classical literature, treatment in LC, 69
Classification (book), aid to bibliographical education, 39; aid in mastering contents of library, 38–40; art not science, 36; associated with display, 50–2; based on survey of bibliography, 10, 17, 18, 19, 32, 38–40; bibliographical basis makes application easier, 36–7; bookstock in relation to, 170–83; broken order, 110–11; cataloguing and, 53–6; codes, 86–9; compilation by great bibliography agency necessary, 32, 36–8; consistency in, 85–9; co-ordination of headings, 22, 23; definition, 16, 17; diagnosing subject, 57, 73–8; dislocation, 43–4, 47, 81; display in relation to, 32–52, 53–6; exams. in, 57, 58, 85; experiments in re-grouping, 81, 106–9; form grouping, 73–8 *passim*; function in displaying books, 9–10, 32–52; grouping rather than cn., 33–6; headings in, 18, 19; index to, 38, 85–6; jargon, 58; Jevons on, 17, 24; logical absurdity of, 17, 36; main classes determined

233

by volume of stock, 131; medical libraries, 48; modifications, 47-8; most useful place, 33-5, 78-80; notation, 32, 40-5, 70, 132; organization of, 59-60; philosophical, 16, 17, 33; point of view in, 33-6, 46; practice of, 53-89; relation headings, 37-8, 40; Richardson on, 15, 16, 85; rules, 73-85; schedules to be fully used, 132; scientific compared with book, 26-30; uniformity of, remote, 32, 45-50; universal use unlikely, 45; value, 39. *See also* Names of classifications; Hulme, E. Wyndham

*Classification Décimale Universelle.* See Universal Decimal Cn.
Clerkenwell P.L., open shelves at, 51
Cleveland P.L., show windows, 151, 154, 230; subject depts., 49
Clifford, W. K., on scientific cn., 25
Clippings, 138
Code for classers, 86-9; why necessary, 87
Collectors' books, 115
*Colon Cn.*, by Ranganathan, 72
Colorado School of Mines, extensions of DC, 47, 48
Colour, books on, 211-12; combinations, 98, 211-12, 224; lighting of showcases, 154; Ostwald colours, 212, 225, 230; toning and staining photocopies, 221-2
Commercial books, classing, 59; display, 133-9; *illus. facing, 144*
Concordances, guides to, 128, 129
Conservatism of librarians, 48, 51, 85, 90, 149, 231
Copy-writing, 135, 137, 140, 164, 167, 168, 214-17; *illus. facing, 64, 112, 113, 144, 161, 208*
Copying apparatus, Reflex, 141, 221-2
Correlative lists, 99-100, 106
Corridor displays. *See* Window displays
Counter displays, 103
Coventry, branch libraries, 196-8, 204; changing interests, 48; technical library, 138
Cradles, book, 103
Criminal trials, cn. of evidence and point of view in, 46
Croydon, reference exhibitions, 123; branches, 205
Cut-out letters, 218-19
Cutter, C. A., *Alphabet Table*, 134; *Expansive Cn.*, 40, 72, 72 n.; *Rules for a Dictionary Catalogue*, 50, 53-4

Dana, John Cotton, 146
Date marks, 20, 42-4, 87
*Decimal Cn. and Relative Index*, 13, 67-8, 130-1; biography in, 47; dislocations in 43-4, 47; extensions of, 47-8; headings for Great War, 1914-18, 41-2; notation, 41-2; rules for classing discussed, 73-85 *passim*
Decimal Cn., Universal. *See* Universal Decimal Cn.
Demonstrations, assist in bibliographical education, 122; duties of assistants at, 122; effect upon book selection, 122; in reference libraries, 52, 118-23; subjects of, 119-123 *passim*
Depôt reserve. *See* Reserve collections
Designers. *See* Displayer; Placards, artists
Dewey, Melvil, 13, 67, 73. *See also Decimal Cn.* and *Universal Decimal Cn.*
Diagrams in display, 136, 138; *illus. facing, 144*
Dickens' illustrations, 220
Dictionaries, guides to, 128

# INDEX

*Dictum de omni et nullo*, 75
Directory indexes and plans in display, 101, 126–8, 162, 165
Dislocation in cn., 43–4, 47, 81
Display, advertisement, 52; aim of, 184; apparatus for, 101–3, 134, 163, 165–6; art dept., 146–9; art gallery, 184; book selection in relation to, 53–72, 157, 170–83, 231; calendar of, 158–61; cataloguing in relation to, 53–6; centre of interest in, 138, 140, 166, 220; classification's function in, 32–52, 53–6; commercial library, 133–9; cost of, 155–6; counter and bench, 103; cradle, 103; demonstrations in reference library, 52, 118–23; indexes and plans in, 101, 127–8, 162, 165; entrance, 150–69 *passim*; formal cn. as, 32–52; home reading libraries, 90–114; illuminated, 103, 111–13, 134; illustrating U.S.A., 164–6; liaison frames in, 166–7; local collection, 143–6; local galleries and museums to collaborate, 163; materials, 218, 229–30; mathematics, 140; methods, 210–31; museums and libraries compared, 184; music dept., 140–3; newspaper communiqués as, 51, 145; objections answered, 90–2; open shelves as beginning of, 50–1; periodicals, 138–9; personal guidance as, 51; properties in, 134, 165–6; reference libraries, 115–32; revising stock, for, 157–8, 164; rotation of stock as, 52, 196–209; science, 139–40; selective processes, 52, 170–209; lists of books in, 166; slopes, 117, 134; special libraries, 49, 133–49; subjects of, 158–61; table, 103; technical library, 133–9; tools, 229; uniformity, undesirable, 146; varieties, 51–2. *See also* Demonstrations; Exhibitions; Placards; Shop window displays; Showcases; Window displays
Displayer, 212–14
Distribution of related books. *See* Related books
Dramatic production, 140–3
Duplicate books, 186, 190

Edinburgh P.L., extension of LC for British Isles, 48; Fountainbridge branch, 152, 208; grading libraries by size, 205–8; *illus. facing 96, 145, 193*; local collection, 143–6 *passim*; map collection, 126; placard (ensign), 226, 227, *illus. facing 209*; travelling libraries, 208–9
Engineering industries, extension of DC for, 47–8
Engineering Societies Library, New York, 68
English literature, cn. of, 74–8, 79
"Ensign" placards, 226, 227; *illus. facing 209*
Entrance displays. *See* Window displays
Episcope, 229–30
Examinations in cn., 57, 58, 85
Exchange service, 193–5; check upon frivolous use, 194
Exhibitions of books, biographies, 107, 108; cases, 116–18; cradles for, 103; gallery for, 115; good positions on shelves, 80; home reading library, 90–114, 184; illustrating lecture courses, 123; labels for, 118; lists in, 166; local collection, 143–6; open shelf library, 80; recent additions, 124; related books, 106–9; rotation of stock, 52, 196–209; undesirable in external shows unless books are issuable, 150; *illus. facing, 64*. *See also* Demonstrations; Display
Exhibitions of specimens and illustrative material, 163; *illus. facing, 64*
Expansibility of schedules, 32, 40–50
*Expansive Cn.*, by Cutter, 40, 72, 72 n.
Extensions of DC, 47–8; LC, 48

Fiction, percentage in stock, 175-83, 207
Flint, Robert, 58
Foreign books in reserve, 191
Form, grouping by, 73-8 *passim*
Fossils, cn., 27
Fountainbridge branch, Edinburgh, 152, 208; *illus. facing, 145*
Frames for placards, 225
French literature, LC, 69

German literature, LC, 69
Gifts, result of demonstrations, 123
Glass, K-ray, 117, 153; non-reflecting, for displays, 153
Golders Green Branch, Hendon, show windows, 154
Grading libraries by size, 205-8
Great War, 1914-18, headings, 41-2
Greek literature, LC, 69
Grouping rather than cn., 33-6
Guides to indexes, concordances, bibliographies, 127, 128, 129. *See also* Class guides

Harvard School of Business Administration, cn. of business literature, 48
Harvard University School of Landscape, extensions of LC for city planning and landscape architecture, 48
Headings in cn., 18, 19; most specific the best, 40; relative, 37-8, 40
Hendon P.L., show window, 154
History, cn. of, 41-2
Hobbies, encouraging, 140
Home reading libraries, cn. in compared with that in reference libraries, 170-1; an exhibition of books, 90; display, 90-114; *illus. facing, 49, 65, 96, 160, 161, 192*; reference collections in, 113-14. *See also* Reserve collections
Hopwood, Henry Vaux, 21, 68
Hulme, E. Wyndham, 9, 15-23, 31, 32, 37, 38, 48-50, 73; definition of cn., 16, 17, 38-9

Identical libraries, 198-201
Illinois. *See* University of I.
Illuminated display, 103, 111-13, 117, 134, 153-4
Illustrations. *See* Pictures
Indexes, collection of, 128, 129; display by, 51, 99, 162. *See also* Subject index
Indexing. *See* Subject index
India, exhibition of related books on, 107
Information file, 137-8
Insects, cn., 26
Institut International de Bibliographie (Documentation), 36, 68
Italian literature, LC, 69

Jargon, cn., 58
Jast, L. Stanley, 13, 14, 30-1, 47, 123, 205
Jevons, W. S., on cn., 17, 24, 58
Journals in display, 138-9
Juvenile books, 207

# INDEX

K-ray glass, 117, 153
Kelley, Grace, *Cn. of Books*, 85

Labels for exhibits, 118. *See also* Lettering
Landscape architecture, extension of LC, 48
Latin literature, LC, 69
Law books, LC, 45–6
Law of Octaves, 25
Lecture courses, displays of books illustrating, 123
Leith P.L., show windows, 154
Lending libraries. *See* Home reading libraries
Lettering, 94–8, 118, 130, 146, 218; art dept., 146–7; binders', 99; books on, 217; cut-out, 218–19; examples of copy-writing, 135, 137, 140, 164, 167, 168, 214–17; *illus. facing*, 64, 97, *112, 113, 144, 161, 208, 209*; Roman, 95, 210, 217, 220; style, 95, 97. *See also* Class guides
Liaison frames, 166–7
Liaison lists, 99–100, 106
Librarians, conservatism, 48, 51, 85, 90, 149, 231; contact with readers surest guide to "most useful place" in cn., 79
Libraries, chain, 196–209; disadvantages of small, 205–6; graded by size, 205–8; special, 45–9, 94–5, 133–49; twopenny libraries, 176, 182, 183
Library Association Education Committee, 58, 85
Library of Congress cn., 9, 21, 29, 69–70; bibliographical foundation of, 36–7, 59; broken order, 45–6; extensions, 48; headings for War, 1914–18, 41; law books, 45–6; notation, 32, 40–5, 70; *Outline of the Scheme of Classes*, 69, 70; special divisions, 49; *Subject Headings used in the Dictionary Catalogue*, 70; textiles section, 45; use in U.S.A., 70
Lighting, artificial, window displays, 112, 153–4; exhibition cases, 116
Lists, correlative, 99–100, 106
Literary indexes, guiding to, 128
Literary methods, display by, 51
Literature treated as a form, 74–8
Liverpool P.L., 124
Local collections, display, 143–6; travelling library, 209
Local reserve. *See* Reserve collections
*London Bibliography of the Social Sciences*, 69 n.
London municipal libraries, novels in stock, 178–82
Los Angeles P.L., subject depts., 49

MacCarthy, Desmond, on subject indexing, 38 n.
Manchester P.L., exhibition cases, 116
Mann, Margaret, *Intro. to Cataloguing and Cn.*, 85
*Manuel du Répertoire Bibliographique Universel*, 68
Maps collection, display, 117, 124, 125; illustrating displays, 104, 117, 164–5; rolled, weights for, 125; storing, 125
Materials used in display, 218, 229–30
Mathematics, display, 140
Medicine, special cn. for, 48
Mendeléef, D., 26
Merrill, W. S., *Code for Classifiers*, 73, 86–9
Metallurgy, extension of DC for, 47

Mill, J. S., definition of cn., 16, 17
Mining, extension of DC for, 47
Minto, C. S., 222 n.
Modern display in art, 147
Motor cars, registration numbers, 70
Museums, books on, 228; display in libraries compared with that in, 184
Music cn., 43, 54, 55, 59, 79; books in reserve, 191; display of, 140–3; *illus. facing 113*

*National Geographic Magazine*, 104, 219
New York P.L., special divisions, 49
Newlands, J. A. R., 25
Newspaper paragraphs, 51, 144–5
Notation, 32, 40–5, 70, 132; telegraphic codes, 45
Notices to be noticeable, 146
Novels, percentage in stock, 175–83, 207
Numbers, adjustable, 100

Open shelf library, 50–1, 80; cn. to be intensive, 132; desirability of breaking up cn., 130–2; reference library, 122, 126–9; rules of display, 112–13, 126–30; legibility of signs, 130
Ostwald colours, 212, 225, 230

Palaeontology cn., 27
Pamphlets, 187
Patent Office Library, 15; cn., 21; cn. of textiles, 22, 45
Period (chronology) marking for, 20, 42–4, 87
Periodic system, 25
Periodicals, display, 138–9; indexes, 129
Personal guidance, 50, 51, 93, 95, 101
Peterborough P.L., classed catalogue, 14
Philology, LC, 69
Philosophical v. bibliographical cn., 16, 17, 33
Photo-copying, 141, 144, 221–2
Picture collection, books on, 220
Pictures, art, 148; for home-made placards, 219–20
Placards (posters, showcards), artists' fees, 227; artists' instructions, 227; colour harmonies, 98, 211–12; commercial library, 133–9 *passim*; copy-writing for, 135, 137, 140, 164, 167, 168, 214–17; Dana, J. C., 146; Edinburgh, 226; handmade, 210, 219; *illus. facing, 65, 112, 113, 144, 208*; materials, 210, 229–30; photo-copying, 141, 144, 221–2; pictures for, 219–20; protecting unframed, 225; shelf, 101–3; silk screen apparatus, 229; silhouettes, 224–5; technical library, 133–9 *passim*; tools, 229; value of, 226; window, 150–69 *passim*
Plans, directory, 101, 126–8
Plants, cn., 26–30
Plays, cn., 46
Pocket editions, 186–7
Point of view in cn., 33–6, 46
Pollard, Dr. A. F. C., universal bibliographical repertory of optics, light, and cognate subjects, 68

# INDEX

Porphyry, Tree of, 24
Portraits, 140, 224
Portuguese literature, LC, 69
Poster stamps, 227
Posters. *See* Placards
Properties in display, 101–3, 134, 163, 165–6

Ranganathan, S. R., *Colon Cn.*, 72
*Reader's Guide*, Wallasey, 99
Readers, care of books, 173–4; duty of teaching and guiding, 50, 51, 93, 95, 101
Reading-biographies, 167, 168, 215; *illus. facing, 208*
Reading, preparatory, by classers, 59–67
Recent additions, 124
Reference books, classing desk, 66–7; home reading library, 113–14
Reference libraries, 115–32; cn. in, compared with that for home reading libraries, 170–1; demonstration rooms, 52, 118–23; exhibition gallery, 115; open shelf collection, 122, 126–9; recent additions displayed, 124; unclassed, 39
Reflex copying apparatus, 221–2
Related books, annotations about, 99–100; distribution of, 34, 35, 45–6; exhibition of, 106–9, 123, 132
Relation headings in cn., 37–8, 40
Religious literature, demonstration of, 119, 121
Remainders, 172
Reserve collections, 184–95; depôt reserve, 186, 189–93, 198; local reserve, 185–9
Richardson, E. C., 15, 16, 85
Rochester P.L. (N.Y.), subject depts., 49
Rolling bookcases, 107, 109, 113, 188–9; *illus. facing, 193*
Roman lettering, 95, 210, 217, 220
Rotation of bookstock, 52, 196–209
Rules for classing, 73–85 *passim*

Sayers, W. C., Berwick, 68, 73, 75, 77, 78, 80, 81, 176–7
Scarborough P.L., show window, 154; *illus. facing, 160*
Science, books in reserve, 190; cn. of, 24–30; departmental display, 139–40
Science Museum Library, S. Kensington, 68
Scientific cn., 26–30
Seasonal books, 161, 186
Selective processes, display by, 52, 172–209
Shelf-placards, 101–3; *illus. facing, 65*
Shelf reference blocks, 35
Shepherd, Walter, on scientific cn., 24, 26
Shop window displays, books on 152 n., 228, 231; *illus. facing, 48*
Showcases, interior, 111–13, 116–18; *illus. facing, 96, 160, 192*; lighting, 112, 117, 154; reference libraries, 116–18
Silhouettes on placards, 224–5
Silk screen apparatus, 229
Slopes, 103, 117, 134; *illus. facing, 49, 97*
Smith, Oliph, 176–7
Spanish literature, LC, 69
Special libraries, 45–9, 133–49, 174
Staining photo-copies, 221–2

Staleness of bookstock, 197-8, 204, 206, 207, 208, 209
Stamps, poster, 227
Statistics, bookstocks in home reading libraries, 175-83; ease of practice in cn., 59
Stewart, J. D., 71, 90-2, 107
*Subject Cn.*, by Brown, 14, 28, 71, 75
Subject depts., 49, 95, 133-49
Subject, diagnosis of, 57, 73-8
*Subject Headings used in the Dictionary Catalogue*, LC, 70
Subject index, display by, 99; MacCarthy, Desmond, on, 38 n.; that to the cn. compared with that to the library, 38, 85-6
Subjects, classing books on related, 34, 35, 45-6, 75

Table displays, 103
Tags, 99
Technical libraries, 133-9; reserve books, 190
Telegraphic codes, notation, 45
Terminology, 10
Textiles, cn. in LC and Patent Office Library, 22, 45
Theatre dept., 140-3
Title-pages in display, 222-4
Toning photo-copies, 221-2
Tools, placard making, 229
Town planning. *See* City planning
Trades catalogues, 133-4
Trajan lettering, 95, 210, 217, 220
Transparency covering for placards, 225
Transport, 193-5, 205
Travelling libraries, Edinburgh, 208-9
Trolleys, bookcases, 107, 109, 113, 188-9; *illus. facing, 193*
"Twopenny" libraries, 176, 182, 183

Uniformity in cn., 32, 45-50, 81
Uniformity in display undesirable, 146
United States, display on, 164-6
*Universal Decimal Cn.*, 20, 37-8, 41, 68; dislocations in, 43; flexible and expansible, 42-3; notation, 42-4, 132
University of Illinois, extension of DC for engineering, 47-8

Vans, exchange service, 193-5

Wall slopes. *See* slopes
Wallasey P.L., 99, 111
Ward system, evil of, 205-6
Watford P.L., classed catalogue, 14
Weights for rolled maps, 125
Welton, J., *Manual of Logic*, 58
Wheeler, Joseph L., 151
Window displays, 150-69; artificial lighting, 112, 153-4; books on shop front designs, 152 n., 228, 231; booksellers', 150, 166; *illus. facing, 48, 160, 161*; local collection, 144; museum materials in, 163; non-reflecting glass, 153; number required annually, 154-5; programme, 158-61; properties in, 165-6; trade catalogues, 134
Woolman, John, 14

THE END

For Product Safety Concerns and Information please contact our EU
representative GPSR@taylorandfrancis.com
Taylor & Francis Verlag GmbH, Kaufingerstraße 24, 80331 München, Germany

www.ingramcontent.com/pod-product-compliance
Lightning Source LLC
Chambersburg PA
CBHW062134300426

44115CB00012BA/1923